This book endorses feminist critiques of gender, yet upholds the insight of traditional Christianity that sex, commitment, and parenthood are fulfilling human relations. Their unity is a positive ideal, though not an absolute norm. Women and men should enjoy equal personal respect and social power, which excludes patriarchy.

In reply to some feminist critics of oppressive gender and sex norms, as well as to some communitarian proponents of Christian morality, Cahill argues that effective intercultural criticism of injustice requires a modest defense of moral objectivity. The book thus adopts a critical realism as its moral foundation, drawing on Aristotle and Aquinas. Moral judgment should be based on reasonable, practical, prudent, and cross-culturally nuanced reflection on human experience, regarding which the body anchors many common aspects.

The approach is combined with a New Testament model of community, centered on solidarity, compassion, and inclusion of the economically or socially marginalized.

SEX, GENDER, AND CHRISTIAN ETHICS

NEW STUDIES IN CHRISTIAN ETHICS

General editor: Robin Gill

Editorial board: Stephen R. L. Clark, Antony O. Dyson,
Stanley Hauerwas and Robin W. Lovin

In recent years the study of Christian ethics has become an integral part of mainstream theological studies. The reasons for this are not hard to detect. It has become a more widely held view that Christian ethics is actually central to Christian theology as a whole. Theologians increasingly have had to ask what contemporary relevance their discipline has in a context where religious belief is on the wane, and whether Christian ethics (that is, an ethics based on the Gospel of Jesus Christ) has anything to say in a multi-faceted and complex secular society. There is now no shortage of books on most substantive moral issues, written from a wide variety of theological positions. However, what is lacking are books within Christian ethics which are taken at all seriously by those engaged in the wider secular debate. Too few are methodologically substantial; too few have an informed knowledge of parallel discussions in philosophy or the social sciences. This series attempts to remedy the situation. The aims of New Studies in Christian Ethics will therefore be twofold. First, to engage centrally with the secular moral debate at the highest possible intellectual level; second, to demonstrate that Christian ethics can make a distinctive contribution to this debate – either in moral substance, or in terms of underlying moral justifications. It is hoped that the series as a whole will make a substantial contribution to the discipline.

A list of titles in the series is provided at the end of the book

SEX, GENDER,
AND CHRISTIAN ETHICS

LISA SOWLE CAHILL

Professor of Christian Ethics,
Boston College

CAMBRIDGE
UNIVERSITY PRESS

Published by the Press Syndicate of the University of Cambridge
The Pitt Building, Trumpington Street, Cambridge CB2 1RP
40 West 20th Street, New York, NY 10011–4211, USA
10 Stamford Road, Oakleigh, Melbourne 3166, Australia

© Cambridge University Press 1996

First published 1996
Reprinted 1998

Printed in the United Kingdom at the University Press, Cambridge

A catalogue record for this book is available from the British Library

Library of Congress cataloguing in publication data
Cahill, Lisa Sowle.
Sex, gender, and Christian ethics / Lisa Sowle Cahill.
p.   cm. – (New Studies in Christian Ethics)
ISBN 0 521 44011 4 hardback; 0 521 57848 5 paperback
1. Sex – Religious aspects – Christianity.
2. Sex role – Religious aspects – Christianity.
3. Christian ethics.   4. Feminist ethics.
I. Title.   II. Series.
BT708.c283   1996
241′.66–dc20   95–48156   CIP

ISBN 0 521 44011 4 hardback
ISBN 0 521 57848 5 paperback

CE

In memory of
Theodore J. Mackin
1922–1994
and
André Guindon, O.M.I.
1933–1993

I permit no woman to teach or to have authority over men; she is to keep silent. For Adam was formed first, then Eve; and Adam was not deceived, but the woman was deceived and became a transgressor. Yet woman will be saved through bearing children, if she continues in faith and love and holiness, with modesty.

(1 Tim. 2:12–15)

[T]here is in man an inclination to things that pertain to him . . . according to that nature which he has in common with other animals: and in virtue of this inclination, those things are said to belong to the natural law, *which nature has taught to all animals*, such as sexual intercourse, education of offspring and so forth.

(Thomas Aquinas, *Summa Theologica* I–II.94.2)

An ecological–feminist theology of nature must rethink the whole Western theological tradition of the hierarchical chain of being and chain of command.

(Rosemary Radford Ruether, *Sexism and God-Talk: Toward a Feminist Theology* (Boston: Beacon Press, 1983), 85)

Sexuality must not be thought of as a kind of natural given which power tries to hold in check. . . . It is the name that can be given to a historical construct.

(Michel Foucault, *The History of Sexuality, Volume I*, trans. Robert Hurley (New York: Random House, 1978), 105).

It should be clear that when I invoke the term "sex," I am not referring to some innate or ahistorically given set of biological or instinctual predispositions, but to a set of practices, techniques, behavior, language, signs that are already, from the very outset social, i.e., they presuppose or are emergent with reference to the Other.

(Linda Singer, *Erotic Welfare: Sexual Theory and Politics in the Age of Epidemic* (New York and London: Routledge, 1993), 34).

[T]he gospel allows no rule against the following, in and of themselves: masturbation, nonvaginal heterosexual intercourse, bestiality, polygamy, homosexual acts, or erotic art and literature. The Christian is free to be repelled by any or all of these and may continue to practice her or his own purity code in relation to them. What we are not free to do is impose our codes on others.

(William Countryman, *Dirt, Greed & Sex: Sexual Ethics in the New Testament and Their Implications for Today* (Philadelphia: Fortress Press, 1988), 243–44)

Contents

General editor's preface

This is the ninth book in the series New Studies in Christian Ethics. It faces some of the most difficult areas within the discipline – those concerned with sex and gender in modern society.

The difficulties are twofold. The first is caused by the fact that post-industrial societies tend to acquire dragons but lose boundaries. The modern dragons of sex and gender have increasingly taken the form of patriarchy, sexism, homophobia, and hypocrisy. All of these are to be attacked in secular society. But the sexual and gender boundaries of post-industrial societies are harder to identify. Personal autonomy and mutual consent are almost the only criteria now commonly accepted in governing our sexual behaviour. Even sexual equality – or perhaps more accurately gender equality – may become increasingly difficult to defend intellectually once egalitarianism in other economic and social areas is no longer presumed as self-evident.

The second difficulty is created by the churches themselves. All too readily they become the dragons of post-industrial societies, exhibiting in ample measure the patriarchy, sexism, homophobia, and even hypocrisy that these societies so despise. Far from being moral beacons in a confused world, churches all too often become identified with the most despised features of moral behaviour in many societies today. Even the sexual and gender virtues that Christians apparently profess – faithfulness, altruistic love, and oneness in Christ – seem all too fragile in practice. In our better moments, those of us who identify ourselves as Christians are only too aware that we have almost as much to learn from as to teach our secular colleagues on issues of sex and gender.

The great merit of Lisa Cahill's new book is that it is fully aware of both of these difficulties. It listens patiently to the cultural, societies today. And it presents a lucid and critical account of Christian ethics which takes fully into account the frailties of the past and present chuches.

Lisa Cahill makes it clear that she is writing from a specifically Catholic context, albeit one which is responsive to feminism, postmodernism, and the claims of other Christian traditions. She claims that there is indeed no "neutral" language or vantage-point, no truly "secular" realm in which public moral discourse can take place at all. At the same time, she is concerned to investigate what common moral ground may be discovered to unite cultures and religious traditions. She is convinced that at least some fundamental moral experiences and values are shared by virtually all human communities, and hence adopts a critical realism in ethics.

There is, I believe, a real need for a sustained and serious work of Christian ethics in this area. The ethics of sexuality and gender are at present in a considerable state of disarray, both within Christianity and without. There is a real need for new and creative thought here. Further, I doubt if many non-Catholic Christian ethicists at present have the communal resources to make such a contribution. Yet, whilst she wishes to argue from firmly within the Catholic tradition – particularly in relation to what she regards as the essential connections between sex, love, and procreation – she is very aware of the criticisms that traditionalist Catholic stances have faced. She believes in combining a sensitivity to contemporary culture and to the moral dilemmas of contemporary culture – such as abortion, homosexuality, and child abuse – with a belief that an informed Christian culture should none the less be able at times to criticise secular culture. Her criticisms are all the more convincing because they are not patriarchal and do take the practical experiences of women seriously.

At the heart of her understanding of sex and gender today is a conviction that what have become the dominant secular virtues of freedom and equality need to be balanced by the Christian virtues of compassion and communality. This approach has much in common with a number of the books in this series. A balance of virtues is stressed particularly in Jean Porter's *Moral Action and Christian Ethics* and in William Schweiker's *Responsibility and Christian Ethics*. There are also important points of contact in her constructive Christian feminism with Susan Parsons' *Feminism and Christian Ethics*. Her sustained and imaginative use of the Bible also resonates well with Ian McDonald's *Biblical Interpretation and Christian Ethics*.

In short I have no doubt that Lisa Cahill has made a serious and significant contribution to Christian ethics in this fraught and confused area.

ROBIN GILL

Acknowledgments

This project is part of the Religion, Culture, and Family Project, directed by Don Browning, Alexander Campbell Professor of Ethics and the Social Sciences in the Divinity School of the University of Chicago, and funded by the Lilly Foundation and the University of Chicago. Members of the project met annually from 1990 to 1995, and are eventually to produce a dozen monographs or edited works. These occasions to come together and discuss work in progress in an atmosphere of tremendous collegiality, conviviality, and mutual criticism were extremely productive for the evolution of my own thought on sex, gender, and family. As a result of a research grant provided through the project, I was able to take a leave from teaching during the 1993–94 academic year. For that I am grateful not only to Don Browning and the project's financial supporters, but also to those persons at my own institution, Boston College, who generously smoothed the way and enabled me to make the most of the funding. They are Donald Dietrich, Chair of the Theology Department; Robert Barth, S.J., Dean of Arts and Sciences; and William Neenan, S.J., Academic Vice President and Dean of Faculties. A debt of thanks is owed as well to Ian Evison, Research Coordinator, who managed the project from the Divinity School of the University of Chicago, and who sent many articles and citations my way.

I have enjoyed immeasurable support, encouragement and perceptive criticism from other colleagues who saved me from errors great and small and gave me the great benefit of many good ideas. Edward C. Vacek, S.J., and María Pilar Aquino each read the entire manuscript and commented in detail. The anonymous reviewer for Cambridge University Press also offered extremely extensive comments about particulars of the argument, as well as judicious advice about its general direction. Anne Carr, Don Browning, Margaret Farley, James F. Keenan, S.J., Michael Lawler, Karen Lebacqz, Therese Lysaught, and Cristina Traina gave me help on sizeable chunks. Colleagues at Boston College – John Darr, David Hollenbach, S.J., Pheme Perkins, Stephen Pope, and Anthony Saldarini – supplemented written comments with many hallway conversations, photocopied essays and clippings, and loans of new books. Graduate students in my courses on "Sex and Gender" and "The Family" provided a lively atmosphere in which to probe these issues and very willingly engaged my questions in their papers and exams. I would especially like to mention the work of Elisabeth Brinkman, Francis Elvey, Amy Laura Hall, Christopher Kearns-Barrett, Anthony LoPresti, and Kevin McGovern. As editors at Cambridge Press, Robin Gill, Alex Wright, and Lindeth Vasey offered the encouragement, advice, and practical support necessary to turn a manuscript into a publication. Copy editor Gillian Maude and production controller Karl Howe were knowledgeable and efficient. Darlene Weaver, a University of Chicago Ph.D. candidate with whom I share many interests, expertly compiled the book's index.

Several of the chapters of the present book are based on earlier work I had done on sex and gender, and, although no previously published article has been included in its entirety and unrevised, portions of the following have been adapted: "Catholic Sexual Ethics and the Dignity of the Person: A Double Message?," *Theological Studies* 50/1 1989) 120–50; "Moral Traditions, Ethical Language, and Reproductive Technologies," *The Journal of Medicine and Philosophy* 14 (1989) 497–522; "Theology and Bioethics: Should Religious Traditions Have a Public Voice?", *The Journal of Medicine and Philosophy* 17 (1992) 263–72; "Feminist Ethics and the Challenge of Cultures," Presidential Address, *Proceedings of the Catholic Theological Society of America* 48 (1993) 65–83; "Sexual Ethics: A Feminist Biblical Perspective," *Interpretation* 49/1 (1995) 5–16; "Sex and Gender Ethics as NT Social Ethics," in John Rogerson, Margaret

Davies, and M. Daniel Carroll R., eds., *The Bible in Ethics* (University of Sheffield Press, 1995); "Moral Concerns About Institutionalized Gamete Donation," in Cynthia B. Cohen, ed., *New Ways of Making Babies: The Case of Egg Donation* (Bloomington, IN: University of Indiana Press, forthcoming).

It is customary in introducing one's published work to remember long-suffering family members who have supported one's endeavors and absorbed some of the stress one generates while struggling toward deadlines and out of any variety of intellectual bogs. In view of my present subject-matter, it is especially appropriate for me to thank Larry, my husband of twenty-four years, who has learned out of love and necessity, and not any particular feminist theory, what it means to organize five children whose mother is frantically writing. Special thanks also go to my eighteen-year-old daughter, Charlotte, who has been indispensable in organizing her father, especially while mom was away at those "Family" gatherings in Chicago. My sons James, Don, Will, and Ae, have taken to asking almost nightly, "Is that the book?," "Did you finish the book?," or "Did you type all that yourself?" Now, thankfully, the answer is "Yes" on all counts – although in the future, as in the past, my family will offer me many occasions to rethink my theories of parents and children, boys and girls, and men and women.

This work is dedicated in a special way to two colleagues who taught me much over the years. André Guindon, a gentle and honest soul, did some of the most creative rethinking of the meaning of sexuality in twentieth-century Catholicism. Unfortunately, at the time of his early death of a heart attack, the orthodoxy of his work was under increasingly intense investigation by the Congregation for the Doctrine of the Faith.

Ted Mackin, then a Jesuit, taught me as an undergraduate at the University of Santa Clara in the late 1960s. That was when it was not yet politically incorrect for the seniors' "Marriage" course to be the province of celibate male faculty in Roman collars. Ted taught it with gusto, inspiration, and intensity. Many years and several volumes on the history of marriage later, nearing the age of seventy and after five decades in the Society of Jesus, Ted fulfilled what must have been a life-long aspiration. He wed Constance O'Hearn, whom he had met a few years earlier at a conference on – what else? – marriage. As he faced a relatively brief but losing battle with cancer in 1994, he pronounced the last three the happiest years of his life. God bless both these gracious men.

CHAPTER I

Sex, gender, and the problem of moral argument

Sexual identity and behavior and gender roles are intimate components of the ordinary life of every human being. Thus, normative interpretations of sex and gender have a potentially enormous significance for all of us. This is particularly the case when they are backed by heavy social or psychological sanctions, as they have been in traditional Christian teaching about the proper hierarchy of gender, and about sexual sin. Sex and gender are so controverted today because the rigidity and stringency of their traditional moral presentation has collided head-on with historicized or "postmodern" interpretations of moral systems. The latter select sexual norms as an example *par excellence* of culturally relative assumptions parading as timeless absolutes. In particular, feminist critiques have suggested provocatively that the social control of women is a major motivation underlying a high proportion of traditional Christian sexual morality.

This project is sympathetic to these critiques. Yet, as I will also argue, Christian morality can fund strong criticism of sexual and reproductive behavior, gender expectations, and family forms which dominate women. But the fundamentally egalitarian inspiration of Christianity is perennially liable to perversion by powerful authorities interested in maintaining their status. This book is thus written from a feminist perspective, by which is meant simply a commitment to equal personal respect and equal social power for women and men. This does not necessarily mean that the sexes have no innate differences; it does mean such differences – whatever they may be – will not be accepted as warrants for social systems which grant men in general authority and power over women in general.

In addition to a feminist perspective in Christian ethics, I propose critical realism as an approach to moral knowledge. Radical deconstruction of moral foundations simply leads to a cultural relativism which enervates real moral communication, intercultural critique, and cooperation in defining and building just conditions of life for men and women. I will draw primarily on the Aristotelian–Thomistic ethical tradition to argue that it is possible to establish shared moral values, at least at a fundamental and general level. Distinguishing my project from neo-Kantian approaches to moral universality, I will make a case that it is possible to come to agreement about values which are substantive and not merely formal. The foundations of morality are not best understood as innate structures of consciousness or rationality which are self-evident at an abstract level, but as broad areas of agreement about human needs, goods, and fulfillments which can be reached inductively and dialogically through human experience. All humans – as embodied, self-conscious, intersubjective, and social – share common ground for moral obligation, insight, communication, and action. This is true without prejudice to the fact that immense personal and cultural differences create an equally immense variety of human ways of being.

One aim of the present study will be to show that many feminist deconstructions of moral foundations create a normative vacuum which cripples their political critique. At the same time, they allow values like autonomy and freedom, tracing to Enlightenment roots, to slide in as tacit universals, operative without intercultural nuancing or explicit defense. These modern values are important, and, I believe, implied by the basic human experience of being a self whose identity is developed dialectically among other selves who are all finally irreducible to one another. The signature Enlightenment appreciation of the interiority and inviolability of the self accounts for the high profile that self-determination and freedom have achieved in subsequent moral thought. This includes modern Christian thought about sex and gender.

However, these are neither the only, nor without question the paramount, experiences and values defining moral agency. Human embodiedness, as to some extent structuring our social relations, needs to be reintegrated with freedom. All must be elements in a Christian ethics of sex and gender which is committed to equality, to intercultural discernment of real goods and evils, and to the human and moral interdependence of sexual desire and pleasure, sexual commitment, and responsible parenthood.

THE STATE OF THE CURRENT DISCUSSION

The moral authorities traditionally most decisive for Christian self-understanding have been the Bible and some conception of human nature or a natural moral law. *Scripture* reveals God's will for human behavior, and maintains continuity with Jesus' life and ministry and with the first discipleship communities. Christian interpretations of *human "nature,"* as divinely created and as directed to certain goods recognizable by reason, have provided a realist approach to morality and promised common ground with other religious and philosophical traditions. Natural-law ethics presupposes natural and intelligible goods which orient virtuous activity in the practical realms of life that all cultures share (for example, care for physical life and well-being, marriage and family, education, politics, and religion). While Scriptural sources have been most central in Protestant theological ethics, an ethics of the natural law has been formative for Roman Catholic moral theology.

Incrementally, since the middle of this century, critical hermeneutics has shaken both these traditional moral foundations. Proliferating "postmodern" philosophies question whether objective moral assessments are possible at all; reason has lost its footing, they claim, and traditions their right to claim transcendence of history. Resounding with the energetic iconoclasm of Foucault and his followers, Jean-Francois Lyotard warns, in the final lines of *The Postmodern Condition*, against "the fantasy to seize reality" and charges, "Let us wage a war on totality"![1]

It was precisely the premises of stability, consistency, rationality, and the intelligibility of beings in themselves, that had provided the anchor for Roman Catholic natural-law thinking about sex in terms of natural capacities and purposes. The new emphasis on the historical production of knowledge has challenged both natural law and the assumption that biblical traditions and the teachings of a historical community can be reliable indicators of the will of God. It has raised the question whether biblical writings and Christian teachings favoring monogamy, prohibiting divorce, and abominating homosexuality, are anything more than artifacts of cultural bias.

Among these philosophical influences, the writings of Michel Foucault have had perhaps the most drastic and disturbing effect on Christian sexual morality, and they will be addressed in more depth in the next chapter. Although few Christian ethicists adopt Foucault's program entirely, many have imbibed his resistance to traditional sexual norms along with his refusal to endorse any new authority for sexual behaviors. Many feminist authors have developed Foucault's deconstruction of sexual identity and value, applying it more explicitly both to sexual orientation and to gender. To take just one example, Judith Butler maintains that gender identities are intelligible only within the binary oppositions of "compulsory heterosexuality." This socially constructed system links and regulates sex, gender, and desire, in stipulated constellations of "male" and "female," "masculine" and "feminine," for purposes of reproduction.[2] Butler is interested not only in achieving "the denaturalization of gender as such," but even in "confounding the very binarism of sex, and exposing its fundamental unnaturalness."[3]

Few if any theologians have gone so far as to premise their sexual ethics on the erasure of a two-sexed humanity. But many have asked whether gender is a dominative cultural elaboration of biological sex, not a natural category. Many are skeptical about the moral virtue supposedly inherent in some forms of sexual expression, and about the natural viciousness of others. John Boswell has questioned whether heterosexuality has functioned historically with the "natural" and normative status which anti-homosexual polemic now claims for it.[4] Mary Daly, a post-Christian feminist originally indebted to Aquinas, has rejected all patriarchal interpretations of female identity, and imaginatively reconstructed separate female worlds, words, and roles.[5] William Countryman finds that biblical teachings about sexual conduct, many of them directed toward control of women's activity, have their origin in social concerns about "purity" (i.e., as markers of social cohesion) or about property rights (including rights over women and children).[6]

Postmodern ideas have taken increasing theological hold in the last three decades. Various Christian authors have adopted a quasi-deconstructionist stance toward nature and biblical authority; yet few have given up the idea that there are some human values which sex ought to express. Most still insist on the essentially sexual nature of the person, and the liberation of sexuality from imposed constraints. Ironically, this is the very project Foucault dismissed as cooptation by a sex-focused discourse of control. Yet a newly positive Christian view of sex is put forth as a necessary and normative corrective to Stoic, gnostic, and Augustinian elements in the tradition which denigrated the body, condemned sexual desire, urged sexual abstinence, and tolerated sexual activity only in view of pro-creative intentions. Sexuality and sexual pleasure are now affirmed as good and as essential routes to personal fulfillment.[7]

This balancing move may, as Foucault warned, endow sex with a disproportionate centrality among human experiences and goods, unduly marking sexual orientation as a constituent of personal identity. But it is *de facto* the case that contemporary Western Christian ethics has tended to focus on the personal and intersubjective meanings of sex, both as communicative and as pleasurable; has downplayed procreation; has high-lighted equality and freedom in establishing sexual relation-ships; and has prized sexuality as foundational for personality, for social interactions, and even for religious experience.

In a widely cited book, even a landmark for the recent revisionist Christian appreciation of sex, the Protestant (United Church of Christ) theologian James Nelson claimed two decades ago that "our bodies are always sexual bodies, and our sexuality is basic to our capacity to know and to experience God."[8] He endorsed the emergent norm of fulfillment of one's own sexuality (sexual desire and pleasure) through freely chosen and affectively intimate relationships with other adults. Almost simultaneously, a Roman Catholic study group defined sex as "a force that permeates, influences, and affects every act of a person's being at every moment of existence," and drew the conclusion that it "is in the genital union that the intertwining of subjectivities, of human existences, has the potential for fullest realization."[9] The moral standard to guide such union is "creative growth toward integration – intrapersonally and interpersonally."[10] Robin Scroggs, writing of homosexuality, refers to a general sexual "ideal" of "a caring and mutual relationship between consenting adults."[11] Countryman develops six principles for Christian sexual ethics today which focus on ownership of one's own sexuality as "sexual property," individual freedom, equality, mutual respect, and permanency of commitment in marriage.[12] Disclaiming as "procreationist" the "assumption that sex is naturally oriented toward creation of human life," Christine Gudorf has recently said that "the general direction in which humanity needs to move is toward more pleasurable, spiritually fulfilling, frequent sex, coupled with a reduction in world population."[13]

Even the Roman Catholic teaching authority, as committed as ever to absolute norms, has come to see sex as essentially constitutive of personal identity, has adopted the language of the couple's intersubjectivity to express sex's moral meaning, and has dimmed the limelights once beamed on procreation. According to John Paul II, "sexuality, by means of which man and woman give themselves to one another through the acts which are proper and exclusive to spouses, is by no means something purely biological, but concerns the innermost being of the human person as such," and is a sign of "a total personal self-giving."[14]

All these authors, to an extent even the pope, write in reaction to restrictive traditions which inhibit the recognition, liberation, and enjoyments of the sexual self. All see these traditions as products of historical forces whose bias can be revealed by exposing their origins in attitudes or practices which run counter to what is regarded as the central gospel message: the dignity, freedom, and acceptance of all individuals, and of the goodness of God's creation.

Such revisions of traditional Christian sexual morality have raised challenges on several fronts, theological, pastoral, and disciplinary. Standard teachings and practices of the churches have been disrupted, often with divisive effects. The concrete shape of these consequences varies denominationally. In Roman Catholicism, the issue is largely one of the authority which continues to be invested in traditional norms, despite the shift, even in official documents, to more personalist foundations. The magisterium confronts the prospect of widespread noncompliance among church members, aided and abetted by "dissenting" theological voices (such as the authors of the Catholic Theological Society of America report cited[15]). The reaction from Rome is usually to draw the lines more tightly around orthodox positions, and to promulgate them more loudly.

For example, Pius XI reacted to the acceptance of artificial birth control by Anglicans, at the 1930 Lambeth conference, with the encyclical *Casti Connubii*, reasserting the Catholic prohibition. A furor over artificial contraception erupted in the 1960s, first with the Second Vatican Council, then with the papal commission on birth control (whose majority recommended acceptance of artificial contraception on the grounds of the interpersonal meaning of the marital relationship), and finally with the 1968 publication of *Humanae Vitae*, which overturned the commission's recommendation and insisted that the prohibitive tradition be maintained. At the twenty-fifth anniversary of the encyclical, the furor continued, barely abated, and a new papal encyclical (*Veritatis Splendor*, 1993) defending the moral authority of the church in all matters was shortly thereafter produced.[16] The church has also taken strong positions in Vatican-originated documents against reproductive technologies, homosexual practice, abortion, and women's ordination. But, as the Catholic laity inhabit increasingly secularized cultures in Europe and move from immigrant to mainstream status in North America, they are less persuaded to live by countercultural and, to most, counterexperiential ideals.[17]

It should be noted, at the same time, that the debates in Catholicism do not concern so much the traditional ideal of heterosexual, procreative monogamy, which most Catholics support, but the nature and extent of permissible exceptions to that norm. The area of agreement on traditional sexual values is much broader among Roman Catholics than the band of disagreement, however polarized the debates between Catholic "liberals" and "conservatives" may appear. Due partly to the influence of a monolithic teaching authority, even narrow issues, like whether contraception is permissible in marriage, have become "tests" of Catholic orthodoxy.

Many mainstream Protestant denominations have in this century maintained the Reformation's decentralization of authority, and assimilated liberal social and political values to their interpretation of Christian living, at least in the industrialized nations. Indeed, the membership of the Protestant churches has been a primary contributor to Western cultural ideals of tolerance, individual freedom, the responsibility of conscience, and personal fulfillment over against constraining "medieval" traditions. Not only Reformation faith, but also Enlightenment reason and existentialist decision-making, have been formative of modern Christian attitudes toward sexual morality, especially in liberal Protestant theology. Divorce and even premarital sex are becoming more or less accepted by laity and theologians.[18] The front-line issue for these churches is now homosexuality, especially the ordination of men or women openly in homosexual relationships.

According to the sub-dean of Westminster Abbey, the Church of England is suffering from a conflict between a formal traditional sexual ethic which forbids divorce and all sex outside marriage, while civil law, popular expectations, and their own pastoral sense lead many clergy to perform weddings for divorced persons whose former spouse is still alive.[19] As for a couple's right to express physically a deep homosexual love, "it is difficult to see why they should not."[20] Yet the bishops have concluded that relations approved tacitly for laity are not appropriate for the clergy, primarily because of potentially alienating and divisive effects on their parishes.[21]

In the last decade, the United Methodist Church, the Presbyterian Church (USA) and the Episcopal Church have established progressive study committees, whose recommended changes in traditional sexual teachings, among which those on homosexuality were the most provocative, were eventually turned down by the membership as a whole. The Evangelical Lutheran Church in America produced a draft statement in late 1994, and circulated it for comment in preparation for a June 1995 second draft. The document, controversial in the church immediately upon publication, defined marriage as a "loving binding commitment between two people," with or without ceremony, and not limited to heterosexuals.

Tensions in Protestant sexual ethics often arise from a combination of liberal leadership, an unfocused mediation of theological and moral traditions, and a membership both committed to liberal democratic values and invested in the middle-class "nuclear" family. An unresolved issue in Protestant sex and gender ethics is whether traditional Christian moral teachings, modified by Luther and Calvin in favor of the importance of spousal companionship beside procreation, can and should reshape the sexual ethos of a liberal Christianity gone too far toward individualism and subjectivism.

Sexual ethics debates in both Protestantism and Catholicism generally arise in relation to contested practical *norms* about activities which once were condemned and now are gaining acceptance. This is symptomatic of a forest-and-trees problem, which, as Michel Foucault once observed,[22] has been better overcome in relation to gender critique than to sexual ethics *per se*. Feminists have long refused to accept that sexual activity can be assessed morally without re-examining the wider social significance of sex within male and female gender assignment. They have also refused to concede that sex should be central in defining women's roles or identity. But both the revisers and defenders of traditional sexual morality tend to agree that sex and sexual identity are of central moral importance. In the contemporary setting, they also agree that the primary test which approved behaviors or choices should meet is interpersonal relationship and fulfillment. These assumptions should be subjected to more careful scrutiny. I will argue that they have considerable validity (especially the second), but that they need to be placed in a deeper and more nuanced social context, with better attention both to the familial ramifications of sexual partnerships, and to differences and similarities in cross-cultural experiences of sex, gender, and family.

Christian sexual ethics today, in its characteristic themes and emphases (the sexual body as pleasure-giving, the interpersonal meanings of sex, the priority of equality and freedom in defining sexual morality), has been quite effective in addressing the human suffering caused by legacies of negativity and even oppression concerning sex. Yet I am concerned these themes will not be adequate to the task of shaping a positive ethic of sex and gender for the future. I perceive two major problems. *First,* this renewed and more person-centered sexual ethics tends to focus on sex as a pleasurable and intimate activity of individuals and couples, and to neglect the social meanings of the body realized through parenthood and kinship. But it is the reproductive, economic, and kin-oriented contributions of sexual partnerships, as well as social control over them, which are the major practical dimensions of the human sexual experience cross-culturally and historically. Christian sexual ethics needs an analysis of the social ramifications of sex which is both critical and constructive.

Second, Western Christian sexual ethics today engages its own procreation-focused past with a hermeneutic of suspicion, but fails to deal with the fact that cultural attitudes may be at the opposite end of the spectrum from any procreative ethos, or any requirement that sex be limited to lifelong marriage. The traditional Christian assumption that sex belongs with procreation and in marriage has given Christians a tacit fund of shared values, even while it has also given them a highly visible target. But a new generation of sexual attitudes and practices in liberal democratic societies presents mutual consent as practically the sole behavior-guiding norm, and hardly encourages ongoing responsibility either for one's sexual partner, or for the procrea-

tive potentials of sex. And when an autonomous and decontex-
tualized freedom is the only sexual guide, control of sexual
"choice" by unexamined gender and reproductive roles can
still be operative. "Freedom from" traditional repressions needs
to be translated into an ethic of meaning, purpose, and even
discipline which can meet cultural trivializations and distortions
of sex. For Christian sexual ethics to have a future as more than
a sectarian relic, it must ground sexual freedom and fulfillment
in some account of the human goods at stake in sex and in the
relationships built upon it.

Contemporary Christian ethicists debating sex and gender
rightly hold up equality, intimacy, and fulfillment as moral
criteria. But they often fail to ask whether these values are any
less relative or more objective than the sexual systems they are
eager to dismantle. The practical *meanings* of equality and
inclusion may be debated by adversaries in the sex wars, but
their acceptability as moral concepts is usually taken for
granted. When we place these typically Western, even liberal,
criteria in the moral perspective of cultures, subcultures, and
continents in which hierarchy and inequality are quite explicitly
invoked as moral norms, the vulnerability of "our" own
presuppositions becomes evident. Even seemingly obvious
values like equal respect and personal fulfillment require a self-
conscious defense carried out within a serious and appreciative
intercultural dialogue. Any ethical perspective which simply
interprets cultures foreign to it in terms of "difference," or
which can bring to them only the fruits of its own particular
cultural struggle, without showing how and why that struggle
and theirs may be relevant and revelatory for one another, will
not have the right to describe itself as "seeking justice."

An ability to speak in a meaningful way about sex as a shared
human reality, and not merely the product either of individual
choice or of cultural shaping, is an especially important precondition of social and cultural criticism. Although Western
Christian sexual ethics needs to finish cleaning its own house, it
also needs to develop a discourse of sex and gender justice
which can speak to and hear multiple moral traditions in its
own culture and in other cultures. This will require meeting the

postmodern critiques of rationality and of moral value, and reconstructing some recognizable foundations for sex and gender ethics.

I believe that a cautious but essentially realist ethics is *necessary* to avoid the social ineffectiveness of moral relativism. I also believe it is *warranted* by the way practical moral debate and negotiation actually take place. A practice-based approach to moral discernment, which generalizes to objective though revisable evaluative judgments, can offer common ground for ethical critique across traditions. It also can escape the pitfalls of rigidity and abstraction to which both Kantian minimalist universalism (often in Protestant theological forms) and neo-scholastic deductive casuistry (a Catholic development) have been liable, and which have contributed to the retreat of many Christian ethicists into communitarianism.

The contributions and shortcomings of Roman Catholic moral theology will be a special concern of this study. First of all, since Catholicism is my own tradition, I continue to live and think in an inescapably dialectical relation to it. More importantly, however, its characteristic confidence in moral objectivity and universal values opens onto the sort of inductive and communal model of reasoned moral insight needed to re-establish public discourse after the postmodern critique. This confidence is not exclusive to Roman Catholic authors, but it is essential both to Thomas Aquinas' natural law ethics and to the modern papal social encyclicals. It differs from Kantian foundationalism in that it is less abstract and formal. A merely tradition-based warrant for universality in ethics would undermine itself. Instead of simply showing that an interest in the universal appeal of certain moral values and virtues typifies Roman Catholic tradition, I will propose that discourse about shared moral values is a credible project in its own right.

Chapter 2 will address the pitfalls of deconstructionism as a feminist ethical method and begin to address alternatives. It will explore the call of Habermasian discourse ethics for open, reciprocal, and critical conversation, ultimately grounded in consensus-seeking communities of practice. Still looking for an ethic which can promise substantive moral analysis, and can warrant reliable intercultural communication at the substantive level, I will move in chapter 3 to an Aristotelian–Thomistic account of human "flourishing." Such an approach begins from particular experience, uses an inductive rather than a deductive method, and offers cross-cultural moral analysis which is substantive but revisable. In chapter 4, the body will be considered as an anchor of intercultural dialogue about human needs, goods, and the ways of life that best fulfill them.

After an "Interlude" in which I draw together insights about the goods associated with embodied personhood in the spheres of sex, gender, marriage, parenthood, and family, I will turn to specifically Christian ethical resources. Chapter 5 suggests a biblical perspective on sex and gender, in which the sexual body is a symbol of solidarity and inclusion, resisting dominant Greco-Roman models of family, reproduction, and women's roles. Chapter 6 treats the mediation of this symbolization through Christian teachings on celibacy and the indissolubility of marriage. Twentieth-century debates about contraception, especially as they continue in Roman Catholicism, will illustrate the need for further reflection on reproductive embodiment. An especially important unfinished task is the integration of modern values of affection and personal fulfillment in sex and marriage with a social interpretation of parenthood and family which is responsive to injustice toward women worldwide. A key issue will be the association in Catholic tradition of sex, commitment, and parenthood, and the reformulation and viability of the unity of these values as an ideal today.

Chapter 7 will return to policy debate in wealthy nations about reproductive technologies, a social innovation which represents a split of the parental and interpersonal meanings of sex, and which, in the name of "liberty," depends upon and reinforces residual patriarchal assumptions about biological reproduction and identity. A few "Concluding reflections" will emphasize the impact that Christian moral transformation should have on human practices of sex and gender.

CHAPTER 2

Feminism and foundations

Sex and gender are "foundational" questions for contemporary Christian ethics. In accusing Christian authority of perpetrating the illegitimate hegemony of negative, distorted, repressive, or truncated views of human sexuality and of women, critics today often imply a wider deconstruction of Christian ethics, and indeed a distrust of any ethics which assumes its own objectivity or universal relevance. Thus, sex and gender controversy exposes the cracks in Christian morality's epistemological foundations.

Too many thinkers have replied to the anti-foundationalist challenge with a communitarian, even relativist, depiction of morality that abdicates the case for any broad intelligibility of Christian views of right and wrong. Most such critics aim primarily at Kantian theories insofar as they are formal and abstract, and are oriented toward universal absolute principles. In this chapter, I shall develop examples of intentional non-foundationalism in ethics, including its influence on Christian thought, and shall suggest that it is ethically inadequate. It defines the "foundations" it rejects too narrowly, and therefore can rebut only some understandings of moral objectivity and universality. In the following chapter, I shall move to an alternative – a critical realism more akin to Aristotle and Thomas Aquinas than to Kant.

The epistemological flaws in traditional Christian ideas about sex and gender have come to light because of broad shifts in philosophical paradigms of reality, truth, and knowledge. The communitarian and hierarchically ordered worldview of the medieval period gave way to Enlightenment rationalism

and humanism; and counteractions to Enlightenment rationality and capitalism – especially Marxism, critical theory, and
postmodernism – have been formative of feminist and other
socially transformative movements.

"Modernity" is a term sometimes used to refer to the phase
of Western civilization which followed the eighteenth-century
American and French Revolutions and the development of
industrial capitalism.[1] Yet it is possible to see roots of modernity
in the fifteenth-century "discovery" and colonization of the
Americas,[2] in the empiricism of Francis Bacon (1561–1626) and
Galileo (1564–1642); in Descartes' introspective rationalism
(1596–1650); and in the seventeenth century social contract
theorists, Locke, Hobbes, and Rousseau. An especially important modern influence is Newtonian science's paradigm of
objectivity and rationality, as dependent on empirical investigation or on strict deductive logic (Newton, 1642–1727).

The Enlightenment philosopher with the greatest impact on
modern ethics is Immanuel Kant.[3] Kantian ideals of knowledge
have been important in Protestant Christianity and have also
influenced the neo-scholastic moral theology of the nineteenth-
and early twentieth-century "manuals" used in Catholic semin-
aries. Imbibing Hume's skepticism about whether any moral
"ought" could be derived from the factual "is" of experience,
Kant was convinced that sense perception can tell us nothing
about either faith or morality. Faith had to depend on revelation. Morality, on the other hand, could be derived from the a
priori and universal categories which structure the understanding of all rational individuals. Central to Kant's "categorical imperative" of morality were the correlated ideas that an
action is good only if the agent could will the principle behind it
to become a universal law for everyone; and that we should
always treat others as ends in themselves. Kant's attempt to
ground ethics in universal, rational foundations is reflected
today in the many important theories which focus on the
intention of the agent as the final arbiter of morality, and on
"equal respect" as the formal criterion of action.[4]

The central and lasting contribution of modernity is its
philosophical and political recognition of the worth, freedom,

and rights of individuals, even though in practice individual liberty was secured socially and politically only for some groups and at the expense of others (colonized indigenous peoples, slaves, and women in general). Modernity distrusts traditional institutions and established authorities, whether political or religious, and encourages the critical exercise of liberty. In so doing, it accentuates older Enlightenment values, such as trust in human reason (especially scientific reason), confidence in the responsible exercise of freedom, and progress toward greater political and social equality. Yet modernization has also meant bureaucratization, secularization, and individualism, as well as the hegemony in politics and morality of science's "instrumental reason." Max Weber predicted that the narrowing of rationality to means–ends calculations would turn modern society into an "iron cage," holding us captive to market values whose ultimate worth we have forgotten how to question.

In elevating reason's epistemological status over authority, modernity has tended to conceive rationality on a scientific model, with its criteria of clarity, precision, empirical demonstration, and preference for practical results. Philosophers of science have increasingly disclosed the interpretive nature of the knowledge accumulated by even the "hard" sciences.[5] Yet a naive trust in the "objectivity" of science persists at the cultural level, at least in the industrialized nations. Charles Taylor has noted that the unquestionable accomplishment of the natural sciences, in allowing us to control our environment and improve "ordinary life," has helped put other forms of knowledge under an "epistemological cloud."[6]

Scientific methods hold a simple and pragmatic appeal, especially when we are perplexed by a pluralism of value orientations. Even moralists like data and statistics; practical decision-makers are concerned with prediction of immediate good and bad effects. "Maximum efficiency, the best cost-output ratio" is how we tend to measure the success of our decisions, in morality as in science.[7] When a scientist view of knowledge and argument is combined with a liberal commitment to personal freedom, the result for public policy, and often for ethical theory, is a "hands off" attitude to moral judgment except when individual autonomy is infringed or measurable bad consequences proven.[8]

The fundamental inconsistency in this mindset is the credence given to freedom as an overriding value – whether or not its indispensability to human well-being can be empirically upheld – while virtually all other values are subjected to a test of pragmatic utility. Thus the immorality of any sort of behavior is widely thought to depend either on substantial concrete evidence of its harmful consequences, or on its infringement of the autonomy of affected parties who have not given "consent." Remaining unexamined is the self-evident importance of autonomy over other moral values, such as commitment, honesty, fidelity, friendship, family, sense of community, intellectual achievement; as well as of the criteria by which even concrete "risks" and "harms" and "benefits" are identified and balanced off against one another.

Modern liberalism has provoked a number of critical responses, all of which can be seen as self-corrections within the modern frame. All focus on the nature of reason, and all are confident that critical thinking can unmask ideology and move society toward more humane forms. The conservative response defends traditional values precisely through a critical analysis of society and the institutions which are threatened. Like Enlightenment thinkers, conservatives challenge what they think are dominant but illegitimate sources of cultural power, for example, the reigning liberal ethos of modernity. Marxist radicals or socialist critics want to extend democratization from the political order to the economic one; contemporary thinkers indebted to Marx insist that political participation is meaningless without economic well-being. Critical theorists of the 1930s (centered around Max Horkheimer and the Frankfurt Institute of Social Research), agreed with Weber's critique of instrumental reason and with Marx's critique of class-based domination. But they struggled for a new understanding of reason as *practical*, in a context of human solidarity. Their heirs are thinkers who, interpreting Gadamer and Habermas, set out ideals of communicative action.[9]

Postmodern thinkers (and artists) appeared on the horizon in the decades after the Second World War. As one author captures it, the "characteristic images for the postmodern world are historical, relational, and personal"; "dynamic temporality rather than static substantiality is the central factor in all existence."[10] Historicity and flux take on a more sinister character in a good many postmodern thinkers, who mount an assault, not only on all "totalizing" interpretations of reality, but even on reason itself. In their eyes, modern "progress" amounts only to a series of successive dominations with no ultimate or unifying rationale. The leaders here are Derrida and Lyotard, building on Nietzsche and Heidegger. The emergent postmodern sensibility is marked by randomness, fragmentation, distrust of all "meta-narratives," self-irony and irreverence, and countercultural politics. It is abetted by philosophical pragmatics (Rorty), the debunking of scientific objectivity (Kuhn and Feyerabend), and philosophical delegitimation of historical continuity as well as of objective knowledge (Foucault).[11]

Yet postmoderns, eminently Foucault, retain the ethical and transformative interest of the Enlightenment, turning their critical edge against the deadening effects of bureaucratic, technological, late-capitalist Western culture.[12] In so doing, they rely on a modern ideal of respect for the autonomous individual (even while deconstructing the modern "self"), as well as on the viability of appeals to human solidarity in resisting oppressive or repressive regimes. For this reason, postmodernity may well be viewed as another evolution of modernity, in which reason is given a more historical and pluralistic twist, but not abandoned. It may fairly be said that all of these "anti-liberal" strands within modernity carry on modernity's key concerns. For all, reason is deployed against authority, and authority is understood as establishing and preserving social institutions and practices which illegitimately constrain choice and behavior. A special target for postmodern thought has been religious authority.

Many feminists, both philosophical and theological, have taken up the postmodern celebration of pluralism and "difference" in a critique of ideology and tradition. The modern and even liberal element continues to be present, both in the "unmasking" of illegitimate authority, and in the centrality of individual autonomy and choice. Many feminists adopt an essentially liberal framework of rights, equality, autonomy, freedom, and tolerance, when they address specific questions of gender and sexual practice. Liberalism in feminist theory is tempered by historical critique of gender bias in definitions of "equality" and by the concern that equality for women make allowances for the special reproductive demands on them.[13]

The interplay of the postmodern renunciation of moral foundations and the liberal endorsement of reason and freedom have produced an odd mix for feminist theory. The result, I shall argue, is inadequate to the task of forceful moral critique, especially in an intercultural context, where dominant cultures and "subcultures," or cultures differing by ethnic or geographical origin, need to resolve practical problems in which the needs and fates of human beings are at stake. This cannot be done without some defensible criteria of judgment. Although theological feminists, even when rejecting the authority of hierarchical traditions, ordinarily retain some normative use of the Bible, of "women's" experience as stable enough to serve as a critical norm, or of a definition of what it is to be "authentically" human in general, they often envision cultural "differences" primarily in terms of mutual recognition and appreciation. As a move in the postmodern mode of resistance to exclusion, this is valid. But the refusal of normative foundations is a liability for any proposals about social justice, feminist or otherwise.[14]

As far as the ethics of sex and gender is concerned, the broad effects of postmodernism are first seen in a radical rejection of Western "bourgeois" norms of sexual behavior. Pluralism, freedom from restraint, and the unavailability of any masterplan for sexual experiences and purposes, have become the watchwords. The radical sexual program has been exercised, however (to the extent that it is exercised practically at all), against the backdrop of cultures where certain social assumptions prevail: individual self-determination, democratic government and civil rights of citizens, access to minimal material well-being, the rights and approximate equality of women, and the responsibility of society to provide sustenance and education for children. Sexual iconoclasm attacks aggressive male heterosexuality and the more stifling aspects of the middle-class family; but it trades on the humanistic premises about autonomy and equal rights which it ostensibly rejects along with moral foundations. As we shall see below, this is true of feminist postmodernism which renounces traditional views of sexual nature in order to pursue access for women to the channels of power open to men in modern Western societies.

When sexual pluralism, rejection of authority, and the *de facto* practical priority of liberal values are linked to the question of gender the international scenario rushes rapidly into view. The struggle for women's "rights" worldwide cannot presuppose that women's equality or even full humanity will be recognized. Nor can it assume general access to democratic processes of government, nor the material security of the family, nor adequate care for all children, as anything like social priorities. Absent these assumptions, pluralism and antinomianism will not be able to combat the direct and indirect sexual coercion of women, in which the stakes are women's access to their only acceptable social roles (wife and mother), and even their survival. Therefore it is crucial to bring postmodern social critique back into connection with some understanding of reason which can surmount moral agnosticism even while appreciating cultural difference. Furthermore, the "different" social experiences of sexuality, family, motherhood, and female power around the world may have much both to teach and to learn from one another in a positive way. While the rights of individuals is a rallying cry for North Atlantic politics, Asian, African, and Latin American societies have greater respect for the importance of community and family. But the contribution of the "different" or the "plural" will be no more readily heard on the assumption that cultures have no common language than it has been on the assumption of a dominant culture's superiority.

FOUCAULT

The writing of Michel Foucault, the centerpiece of the post-modern repudiation of enshrined norms of sex and gender, is an example both of "First World" academic deconstruction, and of the ethical agenda postmodern thought preserves from modernity. Foucault's radical dismantling of objectivity in thought and morals yields an ethic of resistance which is intelligible from a personal and political point of view, yet highly paradoxical from a philosophical one. Personally, Foucault struggled to define the meaning of sexuality in relation to his own homosexuality, with which he apparently was never at ease.[15] The precepts and prohibitions of Catholic Christianity and of Freudian psychoanalysis constituted his identity in definitions whose authority he was determined to undercut. In his activism for French prison reform, Foucault saw at first hand how institutions of social control can incorporate limited critique in the form of internal self-review, escaping thorough-going challenges to the system's existence as such. By co-opting the mechanisms of adjustment, modern institutions insulate themselves from external critics who attack their essential power base.

Politically, Foucault was concerned to cultivate more critical thought patterns in which nothing is taken for granted. He wanted to awaken individuals in modern cultures to the fact that even their most "revolutionary" struggles (for example, against sexual "repression") are in reality designed by controlling systems of knowledge which select what is "problematized" and demand for it our concern and devotion. In his work on madness, Foucault explores the exclusionary and silencing functions of power. In his books on prisons and on sexuality, he shows how power acts productively to construct certain relations as problematic, and to tame or domesticate our critical sense.[16] Foucault saw modern medicalized discourses of sex as the entry point for the "surveillance" and regulation of individual bodies (particularly of women – the "hysterization of women's bodies") and of populations. Foucault blamed both Christian confessional practice and the modern sciences of sex and of sexual psychology for eliciting our obsession with sex, by the very process of requiring "confession" of sex's secrets to powerful authorities. The production and normalization of bodily experience as "sexuality" procures our complicity in our own subjugation, convincing us that the most important project of the self is to discover the "truth" of its sex. We capitulate when we seek the meaning of our lives in sexual identity, talk more and more about sex under the illusion that we must escape the "repression" of sex, and conceive fulfillment in terms of sexual liberation. But, in fact, "sexuality" itself is a social construction whose ultimate effect is control.

Foucault's entire philosophy is inspired by the body as a site of power. No wonder that feminists find his work amenable, though he does not deal at any length with gender roles. In Foucault's interpretation, sexuality and sex come into being as social power-plays; they are not biological givens which pre-exist the significance we give them.[17] According to Foucault the very notion of "sexuality" (as opposed to the body and its pleasures) is a historical construct, deployed in the service of bourgeois power.[18]

Foucault takes apart the "reality" of "sexual" experience by a historical study in which he argues, for instance, that the ancient Greeks saw the body and sexual passions much differently.[19] He shows that the "nature" of sexual desire is variable with culture, and even suggests in a few more extravagant passages that the human body itself is not a cultural constant. In straightforward, if limited, ways this is certainly true; the pliability of the human face and form have underlain cultural mediations from foot-binding and war paint to cosmetic surgery and anorexia. Some feminists carry the social constructionist trajectory to the utmost and envision commensurate pliability of the reproductive functions. Socialist feminist Alison Jaggar claims it may be possible soon to overcome the prenatal division of labor, by redesigning supposedly natural physical capacities. "This transformation might even include the capacities for insemination, for lactation and for gestation so that, for instance, one woman could inseminate another, so that men and nonparturitive women could lactate, and so that fertilized ova could be transplanted into women's or even into men's bodies. These developments may seem farfetched, but in fact they are already on the technological horizon."[20]

Foucault himself declines to define clearly any subject of hegemonic power relations, any unitary intention behind them, or any group, institution, or event whose interests they serve.[21] (In the case of sexuality, one has the impression that the interests promoted are those of the bourgeois family and of modern scientific systems of knowledge.[22]) He also offers no alternative knowledge/power discourse to replace those he wishes to disrupt. Rather than posing a "true" interpretation of sex, or establishing "valid" or "invalid" sets of interests or uses of power, Foucault promotes resistance to any and all so-called truths. If Foucault can be said to have a positive and normative moral program, it is to champion and increase resistance at all the available pressure points in the totalizing interpretations which establish "reality" for us.

James Bernauer, S.J., sympathetic to Foucault's iconoclasm, wants nonetheless to avoid some of its nihilistic implications. Bernauer sees ethics – even social justice – as Foucault's most important agenda.[23] Underlying and motivating Foucault's anti-epistemological suspicion is his interest in establishing a self-critical practice of intellectual inquiry. Foucault is ultimately concerned to foster "ethical and political solidarity in the cause of human rights," and to expand our "embrace of otherness" toward a "community of moral action."[24] Above all, we must challenge the regimes of truth which lock our experience onto their grid, inevitably excluding some persons from the realm of the acceptable and tolerated, and submitting them, even in their own self-understanding, to manipulative determinations of their identity.[25] A moving example is Foucault's portrayal of a hermaphrodite who in the last century committed suicide when forced to trade her/his rather unorthodox female gender identity for a conventional male one.[26]

In his dual commitment to the radical deconstruction of knowledge and to relentless resistance at the moral level lies the philosophical paradox of Foucault's program (and of feminist interpreters). One has the sense that, without quite acknowl-

edging it, Foucault assumes that some power configurations are
recognizably bad, and some displacements of power clearly an
improvement on the alternatives. "Resistance" assumes that
what is to be resisted can be identified, and that neither power
nor resistance is morally equal in any and every form. As
Charles Taylor has put it, "Foucault's analyses seem to bring
evils to light; and yet he wants to distance himself from the
suggestion which would seem inescapably to follow, that the
negation or overcoming of these evils promotes a good."[27]
Foucault clearly aims to demolish all ahistorical or humanist
views of human nature, whether indebted to overconfident
Enlightenment reason, or to the idealization of freedom in an
existentialist mode. Since there is no subject, will, or intellect
which is grounded outside or beyond historical conditions,
there also can be no moral sense which transcends power
relations. Or so Foucault wants to claim.

This ambiguity about the foundations and the agenda of
social critique continues in feminist thought, as well as in
Christian theology. In *Remembering Esperanza*, a book which
eloquently stresses the elusiveness of any "universal" perspective, Mark Kline Taylor lists three postmodern traits of
theology whose appeal lies precisely in their ability to shatter
the arrogance of false universals. Postmodern theology, according to Taylor, values a sense of tradition, celebrates
plurality, and resists "the systemic exercise of authority and
power and in burdensome, cruel, and unjust manner."[28] The
delegitimation of authority's claim to freedom from location or
context sponsors resistance to domination, a task which Taylor
finds crucial to biblical Christian identity. Postmodernism's
pluralist consciousness is especially obvious in feminist critiques
of gender difference, and implies that "theologians must now,
like their colleagues in other fields, work without foundations,
i.e., without a touchstone located outside the play of relativizing
forces."[29]

One might well ask, if there are no foundations, by what
criteria domination, cruelty, and injustice are to be identified,
especially as Western postmodern theologians interact with
others who may not share their liberal ethos. Nonetheless, the

foundationless mission of theology has been accepted – even embraced – by many feminists. Although postmodernism has taken a deeper hold in feminist philosophy,[30] feminist theological approaches are also chartered by Foucault's ethics of disclosure and resistance. Sheila Greave Devaney, in a remarkably strong statement, notes that movements which take historicity as a central concern reject the very idea of "objective, universally valid experience or knowledge." She urges that feminists confront fully "this progressive loss of norms for evaluating claims to truth that we face in the twentieth century."[31] She also takes three Catholic feminists to task – Rosemary Radford Ruether, Elisabeth Schüssler Fiorenza, and even Mary Daly – for not having faced up to this loss. Instead, she accuses, they each propose some kind of feminist vision whose worth is misguidedly premised on a correspondence to "ultimate reality."[32] Greave Devaney counters with her own view that acknowledging "radical historicity" requires us to move away from any "ontological" grounds and to get rid of "referential models of knowledge."[33]

RECOGNIZING DIFFERENCES

Western academic feminists are increasingly aware that the critique of totalizing interpretations serves in several senses as a warning for feminists themselves. We must be careful not to reify either women's experience or patriarchy as essential and invariant; nor to absolutize men's or women's sexuality as aggressive or receptive, dominant or nurturing. Above all, we must not impose culturally, racially, and class-biased interpretations of women's needs, values, and "liberation" on women who do not share the historical setting, privileges, and assumptions of white, middle-class, educated, North American and European feminists. Jana Sawicki puts this point in Foucauldian terms: "our discourses can extend relations of domination at the same time that they are critical of them," and "any emancipatory theory bears the traces of its origins in specific historical relations of power/knowledge."[34] One sees the truth of these assertions reflected in the racism of the nineteenth-

century women's suffrage movements;[35] in different meanings
and value given to motherhood and family in the perspective of
women worldwide; or in the differential significance of the
word "equality" in the liberal feminism of professional women
and the struggles for survival of other women who exist in
economically marginal conditions in the same societies.

Many feminists who do not share the so-called "mainstream"
cultural background insist that the difference of their own
experience and discourse, in contrast to this background, be
noticed and affirmed as equally or more valid. These women
usually work in an immediate context of resistance to assimilation to a culture and moral paradigm which threatens to
suffocate their moral cries and credos. The "universal" they
reject is described by Maria Lugones as any account of
"women's" experience which remakes others in one's own
cultural image. It is a concept of "women as women" which has
not in fact been developed out of dialogue with women who are
culturally different, or out of any other investigation of cultural
differences, but which has simply presupposed similarity.[36]

The affirmation of difference is not just an assertion of
identity and independence; it also represents faith in the
worth and socially transformative potential of particular cultural, ethnic, and racial versions of being a woman. In what
she calls a *mujerista* theology, Ada María Isasi-Díaz accentuates
the pluralism even among Latina women, using pluralism
both to resist the dominant culture and to define *mestizaje*
(being of mixed race) as a resource for identification with the
poor and oppressed.[37] Kwok Pui-Lan, originally of Hong
Kong, questions "universal" languages used by white women
to represent women of color. "The lifting up of every voice,
the celebration of diversity, the affirmation of plurality, help
us to see glimpses of the amazing grace of God in all cultures
and all peoples."[38]

But, while feminist theorists, from both "dominant" and
"marginal" cultures, encourage greater sensitivity to cultural
differences in women's experiences, the context, audience, or
intended target of this mandate can make a difference in its
meaning and effects. The "difference" talk of Third World

feminists and feminists from minority traditions in North Atlantic cultures resists assimilation to white women's experience, and is especially sensitive to the long-lasting effects of colonization.[39] However, these women generally would still commit themselves, at least in practice, to some functional understanding of humanity and human rights which includes women, especially those who do not share the privileges of dominant classes. For white academic feminists, "difference" often takes on a more epistemologically revolutionary character, in which the very possibility of shared understandings of experience among cultures, and therefore also judgment of justice and injustice, are explicitly relativized, at least at the theoretical level. Yet many who adopt a deconstructionist epistemological program do in fact presuppose modern/postmodern Western models of rationality, politics, and personal freedom in negotiating the moral uncertainty unrestricted pluralism introduces.

For instance, one practical condition of women's political struggle for liberation is some preliminary recognition of gender equality. Western feminist theoreticians typically are assertive, articulate advocates who have a toehold and voice in the academic, professional, and political spheres in which the equality and liberty of persons is at least a shared set of ideals or rhetoric of justification. Their deconstruction of an essence or nature of sex and sexual behavior is at home in this context. Practically, deconstruction serves an agenda of sexual autonomy derivative from liberal values, even though the self and the political order are seen as less stable and more subject to unarticulated power relationships than they would be in classical liberalism. Postmodern academics work on the assumption that equality and freedom are human values which should characterize sexual relationships. They are able to deconstruct all grounding of moral value, and all normative interpretations of gender or sexual behavior, because they can count on their culture's consensus about the status of liberty and equality as moral ideals.[40]

For instance, Judith Butler follows Foucault in renouncing any "search for the origins of gender, the inner truth of female

desire, a genuine or authentic sexual identity that repression
has kept from view," and instead plans to "decenter" such
"defining institutions" as "phallogocentrism and compulsory
heterosexuality."[41] The radical legal theorist Catharine Mac-
Kinnon also talks about "complusory heterosexuality" and the
artificiality of gender and even sex. "Dominance and submission made into sex, made into the gender difference, constitute
the suppressed social content of the gender definitions of men
and women."[42] MacKinnon, of course, addresses herself to a
culture (US) in which a rhetoric of individualism, free speech,
and equal rights is formative for the national myth. Presumably
both she and Butler would agree with Jana Sawicki, who uses
Foucault's discourse "to support specific liberatory political
struggles, namely struggles for sexual and reproductive
freedom."[43] Yet these feminists refuse to underwrite the kind of
explicit attempts at broader justification of the Western values
of equality and freedom which would warrant using them as
stable critical principles in intercultural discussion of gender
justice.

MacKinnon specifically holds that there can be no concept of
universal "human rights,"[44] questions the use of any "essentialist notions of sexual identity" in the "struggle" for political
change, and instead refers us back to the elaboration of
"differences" which can diversify and renegotiate the arena of
radical political struggle. In brief, we must liberate without
saying what counts as liberation.[45] If the adjudication of
"different" forms of power and suffering remains at the level of
renegotiation by struggle, it is unclear how feminism can
advance beyond the paradox of Foucault. Moreover, the
rhetoric of difference, when elevated to the level of a philosophical principle, can devitalize the cause of justice on behalf of
those whom it was initially aimed to serve. It threatens to place
the "different" beyond the scope of one's own moral compre-
hension, concern and responsibility.

It cannot be emphasized too strongly that, despite the
immediate practical importance of recovering the differences
(whether racial, ethnic, economic, or religious) of women who
have too quickly been assimilated to a white, middle-class

paradigm of "women's experience," the eradication of all unity worldwide among women or, for that matter among men and women, would have monstrous moral consequences. As an Asian feminist has written, "the very theme of difference, whatever the differences are represented to be, is useful to the oppressing group ... To demand the right to Difference without analysing its social character is to give back the enemy an effective weapon.[46]

Postmodern ethics is not at bottom nihilistic, but positive and prophetic, for it identifies and seeks to overturn real injustices in the world as "dominations." A Foucauldian approach to sex and gender persuades us to consider whether historical traditions which regulate sexual behavior have any legitimation other than the stake one group or "regime of knowledge" may have in the social control of another. However, Foucault's explicit disavowal of any normative foundation for such a critique or for the proposal of an alternative ordering has resulted in two quite obvious problems which bear on feminist theory. First is the weakness (or inconsistency) at the practical level: most postmodern thinkers count on a consensus about liberal values which they do not theoretically defend. They work out their practical programs in a context of cultural commitment to liberal equality. Second, and implied by the first problem, is the fact that cross-cultural "resistance" will be disabled if the equality of women, or even equality as a critical social principle in general, is not firmly enough implanted culturally and politically to survive its philosophical discreditation.

We cannot avoid the question whether deconstructionist sexual politics, exemplified in one of its more extreme and surely elitist forms by debates over lesbian sado-masochism,[47] really serves gender equality for women who are more marginal by race, class, ethnicity, or nationality. If one is outside the realm where one has any access to practical, political power to improve one's daily existence, or even to manage survival for oneself and one's children, a celebration of the "difference" of one's outlook and prospects is of diminished value, and may be destructive insofar as it provides no principled way not to celebrate the very fact of marginalization.

If postmodern philosophy models its discourse on Lyotard's "war" – an endless series of usurpations in which winners are established by violence and become losers in their turn – then this philosophy and its theological variants may be inadequate to their own practical program. That program implies both an ethical imperative (Resist domination!) and a basis for truth claims (You can recognize both domination and resistance when you see them).

Some feminist philosophers are beginning to respond to the methodological and political incoherence of a social criticism which denies the possibility of warranted judgment. Jane Roland Martin senses that a "chilly research climate" results when all generalization is disallowed in the name of diversity.[48] She reminds us that difference was always the starting-point from which philosophers sought common "essences" in the first place. And women's movements have taken hold and gathered momentum as women come together and realize that other women share the same difficulties and aspirations. While some generalization is undoubtedly false, "no trap is more dangerous for women than the self-made trap of false difference," which "encourages us to construct, not just other times and other places but also other women as utterly Other."[49] Susan Bordo, to whom Martin refers, makes a similar point: "attending too vigilantly to difference can just as problematically construct an 'other' who is an exotic alien, a breed apart."[50]

REASONABLENESS AND SOCIAL CHANGE

Martha Nussbaum is a white, North American, neo-Aristotelian philosopher, a professor at the University of Chicago, and indubitably a member of the intellectual elite. Yet she has great interest and considerable personal experience in economic development in India, and shows how self-congratulatory relativism functions both as a tool of one-up-(wo)manship in the academy and as a front for disregard of the plight of less privileged human beings. In a description of a UN conference she attended in Helsinki, Nussbaum treats closet essentialists to a withering description of an "elegant French anthropologist" who, with her collaborator, an economist, defended the restriction of movement of menstruating women in India as intrinsic to the "embedded way of life" in rural villages, where sexual and reproductive roles determine public and workplace proprieties. (Nussbaum's aside: the anthropologist would no doubt herself "object violently to a purity check at the seminar room door.")[51]

The anthropologist also bemoaned the decline of the cult of the Hindu goddess Sittala Devi, whose protection against smallpox is no longer as necessary in India as it was in the past. To the objection that the gain in human life surely outweighs the threatened reduction of cultural variety, the anthropologist rejoined with a rebuke to "Western essentialist medicine" and its "binary oppositions," and called upon "radical otherness" to put down any contrast between the value of life and the evil of death. Nussbaum, who certainly had women's fate in view, insisted frankly that the difference between life and death was "of the most binary kind imaginable."

The frightening aspect of this exchange is that the academic game of theoretical relativism has escaped ivory tower competitions, and ensconced itself in policy seminars where it has potential to affect practical action on international economic development (diminishing the survival and education of little girls and women). One cannot but note that the rhetoric of incommensurable worldviews occurs much more frequently in the theories of First World feminists than of Third World women scholars and activists. Commonality is essential to the fight against cruelty at the *concrete* level. Examples are not difficult to find in the realm of focused action for specific social changes. For instance, an intercontinental conference of Third World women theologians which met in Mexico in 1986 issued a final document which noted women's different situations, as well as the centrality of Third World Women's faith perspective, before it concluded with the aim to "deepen our commitment and solidarity work toward *full humanity for all*."[52]

On June 16, 1992, the *New York Times* reported another example: the Global Campaign for Women's Human Rights, backed by 950 women's organizations worldwide, seized the center of attention at a United Nations World Conference on Human Rights, held in Vienna, by showcasing the personal testimony of women about Second World War sexual slavery in Japan, the terrorism of the Shining Path in Peru, and the violence against Palestinians under Israeli occupation. Women told of particular experiences of suffering, then joined together in their demand for international recognition of women's human rights. It is true that the vocabulary of "equality," "rights," and even "justice" is a product of modern liberal culture, and should not be absolutized as the necessary framework of all social transformation. Yet human rights or some analogous concept, as including both women and men, is essential to advance women's full moral status in virtually every cultural model of the family and in all societies.[53]

The mandate to take unequivocal stands on principle when human suffering confronts us face to face is concretized again in "No Longer Silent,"[54] a film about the status of women in India. This film views women's situation, not through the theories of European social scientists, but through the eyes of women themselves. As a visual and spoken medium, rich with the sensible texture of Indian women's lives, it is effective in moving the Western viewer for a few moments closer to the inside of their worldview. More importantly, perhaps, the film is produced by Indian women and portrays Indian women and men, both educated and rural, working together to re-create their own cultural traditions.

"No Longer Silent" follows the struggles of the women of New Delhi to gain better treatment in a culture which subordinates their interests in virtually every sphere to those of men. One figure the film follows is a mother persistently hammering at a bureaucratic and sexist legal system to prosecute a son-in-law who burned her pregnant daughter and left her body in his courtyard – because the mother and her husband could not afford to up the dowry ante with the purchase of a motorscooter.

The narrator of "No Longer Silent" is an Indian feminist and organizer of rural women. She notes that among the poor, women are the most poor; among the exploited, the most exploited. Women in the audience of a feminist street play smile or titter cautiously as the male character exhorts women, in the name of tradition and religion, to be silently faithful to their duties to cook, clean, carry wood, raise children, always within "the lines men have drawn for women." Comments the narrator, "We can laugh at our pain. We can reflect on our own situation and maybe some women who see it will start to work together to change things." And, as she says toward the end of the documentary, "We see ourselves linked to women in other parts of the world in our struggle to go forward." This vision of unity does not wait for a "theoretical" rationale, but comes straight out of a practical agenda to address basic human needs.

The feminist critique is not complete, of course, until it is reciprocal among cultures. *Inside the Haveli*, a novel by Indian sociologist Rama Mehta, provides an Indian perspective on Western individualism, often so formative of the Western feminist platform. Mehta draws attention to the way in which the secluded women's world of the haveli, while constraining the freedom of adult women, also offers them social relations of support and security, and provides an extremely positive environment for nurturing children.[55]

The point of this series of examples is to show that, at the level of experientially recognized and practically important needs, social ethics proceeds on the assumption of a shared humanity and at least a fundamentally shared moral vision, whether or not the philosophical warrants for that assumption are clearly in place. Without some essential unity of human moral experience and common recognition of values, virtues, and vices, social criticism in the name of justice would be impossible.

In an obvious way, cultural variety challenges us to respect and learn from cultural differences. But imperialisms of class, race, or continent are not the only dead-end for feminist ethics. Another is the self-silencing of social protest by announcement of plurality as ultimate. Only if a revolutionary critique can be validated as something more than a power shift, can it fend off cynicism and inspire practical work toward a new social consensus. The premise that agreement can be accomplished, and that an objectively better state of affairs can and should be sought, is actually operative within intercultural debate aimed at specific goals, for instance by international relief agencies or the UN, undertaking famine relief, agricultural development, reduction of infant and child mortality, or the limitation of armed hostilities around the globe. When we come together to address practical needs, we can and do assume a fund of common values. These values may be general and subject to a great variety of cultural specifications, but they are nonetheless crucial to mutual moral recognition and communication. Granting that significant differences will characterize the institutions which in a given culture will *support* and implement these common values, we may most readily reach agreement in identifying specific matters of practice which *damage* human well-being.

It will be the aim of the next chapter to examine the nature of these assumptions, to clarify in what way they are justified, and to set the affirmation and clarification of common moral ground within a theological perspective. This project goes forward on the premise that while abstract universalism is arid or oppressive, and scientific rationality is too narrow for the discernment of many values and virtues, to abandon any ideal of reasonableness and shared values would be morally disastrous.

The task before us is to redevelop a concept of rationality which is more flexible and fruitful, more comprehensive both in terms of paths humans take to knowledge, and of the intercultural dialectic out of which knowledge comes. Truly reasonable and sustainable convictions need not be the products of linear propositional reasoning, and are usually guided and supported by imagination, feelings, and in Hilary Putnam's phrase "our full sensibility."[56] Putnam criticizes the narrowness of philosophies (like logical positivism) which have bought into scientific definitions of argument, evidence, and verification, thus discrediting "reason" as morally serviceable at all. Not very many philosophers actually behave as though worldviews could be simply incommensurable, or that, short of a purely logical, linear argument, no objective case can be made for one's worldview, goods, or values. The identification and balancing of a number of human goods, as well as a proportional estimate of the place of freedom among them, will require a broader account of what Aristotle called human "flourishing," an account built inductively and incrementally on the dialectic of practical moral experiences across traditions, cultures, and times.[57]

GROUNDING MORAL COMMUNICATION

I have argued that many feminist approaches to sex and gender, in advancing the cause of women's equality, have resorted to postmodern deconstructions of moral knowledge. Feminist deconstruction resists patriarchal traditions which turn bias into domination by pronouncing it "reality" (and enforcing it as such). Yet many feminisms of Western, democratic politics and academia rely, even as they celebrate difference and take apart moral "objectivity," on a liberal cultural ethos which idealizes a basic set of human rights centered on civil liberties and freedom of personal conduct, especially among "consenting adults."

Not only does this consensus about equal rights, the political precedence of freedom, the determining role of concrete harms in limiting it, and the right to legal protection, not exist worldwide.[58] It also is not adequate to the full range of moral values deriving from broadly human experiences such as maleness and femaleness, sex, intimacy, marriage, parenthood, and family. Societies in Latin America, Asia, and Africa can offer perspectives on sex, gender, and family which are important complements to the liberal "human rights" tradition. Thus the question of how to sponsor value discernment, judgment, and agreement *across* traditions and cultures must be raised at a fundamental level.

Because of their growing dissatisfaction with philosophical styles which claim to be truly foundationless, or which concede equal validity to an indeterminate plurality of mutually incompatible moral foundations and agendas, feminists have turned increasingly to two philosophical revisions of "universalist" thinking, with a third added from a religious or theological standpoint. The first is Habermasian discourse ethics; the second is an Aristotelian–Thomistic ethics of human nature or basic moral experiences; the third is liberation theology, which begins from specific communities of experience but appeals to broad standards of justice.

The emphasis in my development will be on the second approach. It implies a stronger claim about intercultural communication than does discourse ethics, and it moves much more decisively toward substantive moral debate. And, in relation to liberation theology, an ethic of human "flourishing" indebted to Aristotle and Aquinas can fill out and extend philosophically the liberationists' trust that the humanity and claims of the oppressed will be recognizable and compelling, both to their oppressors and to "outsiders" who are in a position to apply power against power in favor of those on the bottom.

Aristotelianism and Kantianism are the two main philosophical traditions of moral thinking which have been targeted by postmodern thought, because they are reappropriated often in modern versions and because these reappropriations tend to be in some way realist, foundationalist, essentialist, objectivist, or cognitivist – in other words, because they claim transcultural insight into human goods and moral obligations. "Antifoundationalists" usually presuppose as an opponent a model of knowledge which grounds objectivity in a concept of reason as abstract and "autonomous." In other words, the current philosophical critique of foundations reacts more against hypothetical Kantian adversaries, than against Aristotelian ones.[59]

Some nonrelative forms of Aristotelianism (including Thomistic ones) generalize from human experiences of basic needs, of fulfilling goods, of well-ordered societies, and of human happiness. They draw not upon abstract rationality, but upon reasonable interpretations of historical existence, to make global and normative proposals about the goods human action should seek to realize, and the ends to which it ought to conform. A vision of the essential elements in human "flourishing" is inductively inferred from the data and facts of human experience and held out as a standard for action. Kant, on the other hand, believed that the categorical imperative for action must be derived a priori from the structure of moral reason itself, and will have a formal character. While Aristotle and Aquinas do not hesitate to enumerate substantive goods to be pursued in concrete realms of life, such as government, the family, education, and war, Kant focuses most of his attention on the universal obligation to treat others equally and as oneself would wish to be treated, i.e., as "ends in themselves," and never merely as means to the ends of others.[60] Discourse ethics has reinvigorated Kantianism by reinterpreting equal respect as a criterion of open, equal, and reciprocal communication, and by locating respect for persons in historical processes of community-building.

Another response to moral deconstruction and plurality, one which has *not* had wide appeal among feminists despite its success with theologians, is communitarianism.[61] More or less persuaded that standards of truth and justice can be neither objective nor cross-cultural, communitarians answer social disagreement on the true and good by building up particular communities with internal discourses and practices faithful to their own conceptions of the good. For some communitarians, such as philosopher Alasdair MacIntyre[62] and theologians George Lindbeck[63] and Robin Gill,[64] the authority of the community's vision is associated primarily with its coherence and historical transmission. For theologians such as Karl Barth,[65] H. Richard Niebuhr,[66] Stanley Hauerwas,[67] and John Paul II,[68] the historical community is the bearer of an authentic and reliable revelation of divinity, truth, and goodness. But this knowledge, however secure to those who participate in the community which it shapes, will never be fully intelligible to outsiders, nor amenable to establishment on philosophical or interreligious grounds. Although ethicists such as Hauerwas, Gill, John Howard Yoder, and Ronald Thiemann[69] are concerned to elaborate models of public discourse which permit religious ideals to influence secular culture, the truth of Christian ethics is premised first and foremost on the conviction that faith in Jesus Christ transforms the moral life.

The failure of communitarian theology to attract feminist proponents is undoubtedly due to its impermeability to radical critique, and its tendency to perpetuate the biases of some as the identity of many.[70] As we shall see, it was precisely dissatisfaction with the limited ability of traditions to sustain correction of the distortions in their own communication that led Habermas to depart from the tradition-focused neo-Aristotelianism of his mentor Gadamer. Given the fairly deep-seated hostility to women's equality which historical Christianity has transmitted, and its exclusion of women from the revisionary process, Christian feminists tend to reappropriate the tradition only after Christian communal history has been engaged by other sources of identity, such as philosophy, the natural and human sciences, and the contemporary experiences of women.

However, the work of feminist biblical scholars and of historians who use the tradition "against itself," countering warrants for oppression with liberating themes, figures, and practices, furnishes partial parallels to communitarian ethics. Examples are the writings of Phyllis Trible[71] on the Hebrew Bible; of Elisabeth Schüssler Fiorenza on the earliest disciples of Jesus;[72] the revival of interest in medieval women mystics such as Julian of Norwich;[73] Kathryn Tanner on the political genesis and transformative potential of doctrine;[74] and the recovery of evidence of popular religiosity, which has often been the sphere of women's unwritten religious contributions.[75] At the same time, feminists who creatively reinterpret the elements of communal tradition tend to rely either implicitly or explicitly on some "external" criterion for the continuing validity or authority of what the community hands on. This criterion, never thoroughly separable from the ongoing identity formation of the tradition itself, is often "women's experience" *as* representing women's equal worth and full humanity. As Schüssler Fiorenza expresses it, "The personally and politically reflected experience of oppression and liberation must become the criterion of appropriateness for biblical interpretation and evaluation of biblical authority claims."[76]

PRACTICAL REASON: A WAY FORWARD

Postmodern thought in its more historicist and relativist strands is highly skeptical about an Aristotelian–Thomistic project of discovering universal and generalizable moral values in the Greek *polis,* medieval Christianity, or any other specific and perspectival tradition; it is equally skeptical about the Kantian claim that moral reason everywhere has a consistent, recognizable, and reliable structure. At the same time, the practical commitment of postmodern thought to social justice and the development of strategies to transform social institutions or to intervene in situations of human suffering requires judgments of right and wrong.

Richard Bernstein urges that a "new conversation" about human rationality, and a new way between "objectivism and relativism," be built on the recognition in many disciplines, including the natural sciences, that knowledge is acquired through practice or action.[77] For some feminists, the turn to practical reason can yield a historically sensitive recovery of common moral ground which is more explicitly concerned with intercultural exchange than either the Aristotelian or the Kantian traditions have been in the past. The renewal of practical reason also can facilitate the move from *theoretical* equality or universality to the concrete, effective means necessary to equalize social *participation.*

From the Habermasian side, Seyla Benhabib concretizes Kantian "respect for others" by distinguishing between the generalized and the particular other, and allowing that equal respect will recognize differential particular needs and the importance of including concrete persons and their needs in ongoing communication about social justice. From the Aristotelian side, Martha Nussbaum develops the thesis that the need for judgment, consensus, and practical action toward justice both permits and requires some generalization about experiences and values which are "essential" to the moral life cross-culturally. She moves clearly toward concrete specifications of such values, without claiming infallibility for her formulations. (Nussbaum's work will be treated at greater length in the next chapter.)

The work of these feminist philosophers can be complemented by that of theologians who, on the one hand, advance the meaning of communal solidarity by linking it with New Testament solidarity and compassion; or, on the other hand, advance communication among traditions by accounting for basic experiences via shared human nature as created by God. In feminist liberation theology, experiential participation, communal solidarity, a sense of common humanity, and intercultural transformation are blended when very concrete human sufferings and needs are at stake.

HABERMAS'S THEORY OF COMMUNICATIVE ACTION

Rejecting the Enlightenment opposition between rationality and the authority of tradition, Gadamer sought a return to the sort of practical philosophy which Aristotle rooted in *praxis* and *phronesis*.[78] Genuine communication does not happen on the modern scientific model of unbiased and unprejudiced inquiry, but only in the historical traditions which shape the identities of speaker and interlocutor. Yet, although we always begin intellectual and moral inquiry within the horizons of tradition, those horizons are not fixed and impermeable. In confronting a text or commitment which emerges from a contrasting horizon of meaning, we reflect on our own prior assumptions and achieve a "fusion of horizons" with the text or conversation partner. Gadamer saw practical knowledge and decision as keys to truth and to liberation from the narrow modern rationality and the dominating technology of the natural sciences.[79] Gadamer was confident that tradition could have a positive and critical effect when engaged with the modern horizon. Tradition, which consists in "all the circumstances of concrete experience," is neither static nor exhausted in heritage from the past; it "exists only in constantly becoming other than what it is."[80]

Gadamer's student, Jurgen Habermas, who grew up during the rise and demise of Nazi Germany, was less sanguine about the positive role of tradition and about the potential to gain understanding and truth through conversations which seem to fuse worldviews, and bring partners to new understanding and renewed identity. Conversation can be so systematically distorted that real communication never occurs, assumptions are never challenged, and a false consensus is produced. This is especially likely when the horizons engaged exist at different points on a continuous traditional spectrum.

Think, for instance, of Christian interpretations of women's role in marriage which persist in holding up the biblically derived notion of "headship" (Eph. 5:23), interpreting it toward greater respect and "love" of husbands for wives, but still retaining a basic assumption that women are to be "submissive" to men. In this case the tradition does not have a benign face if viewed from an anti-patriarchal perspective, and yet, if the tradition is itself intransigently patriarchal in its self-interpretation, adequately critical revision will be impossible. Habermas wanted a critique of ideology within tradition, a critique of situations in which communication is distorted into "pseudocommunication," with speakers unaware of their own intentions.[81]

Habermas thus proposed, as the guarantee of genuine communication, a normative "ideal speech situation" in which requirements of equality, respect, and open participation would prevail.[82] Perspectives otherwise excluded from tradition-formation would have an equal chance to participate in critical conversation about its norms, and no norm would be valid which was not acceptable to all those who would in practice be affected by its authority.

A more practically oriented version of Kant's principles of universal respect, impartiality, and universalization, Habermas's theory also echoes the commitments of Marx and Foucault to ideology critique, to "resisting" domination, and (learned from Gadamer), the turn to praxis, action, or ethics as the locus of discourse. Unlike Kant, Habermas sees both the subject and rationality as radically intersubjective, communicative, and practical. Intersubjective communication originates in solidarity. While Kant tested norms monologically, in terms of the individual subject's willingness to universalize, Habermas tests them intersubjectively and dialogically, within the process of actual argument and consensus. This presupposes the relevance of all the concrete needs and interests of the participants, not just their abstract status in a kingdom of ends.[83]

Yet abstractness still dogs Habermas's project in three ways: communication is abstracted from specifications of the good or the good life; equality and reciprocity as supposedly universal regulative ideals of communication are abstracted from the Western political and philosophical traditions which have brought them into the modern consciousness; and communication is abstracted from concrete relations of power which do not at all conform to Habermas's noncoercive ideal of community. Habermas would undoubtedly say that such conditions are "distorted"; yet he does not specify how the ideal of egalitarian and consensual emancipation from distorting ideologies is to come about in practice, given social situations in which justice as equality is not already in place, or in which violent forms of power aggressively prevent its realization. While the ideal of open communication seems potentially amenable to substantive contributions from many cultural and moral perspectives, the values assumed by the process itself are not as clearly universal as Habermas (and Kant) assume.[84] For some other cultures, where strong familial and communal identification, and conformity to social roles, define the good life for individuals, freedom and equality as indispensable requirements of praiseworthy social life may themselves seem "distortions" of human happiness, well-being, and duty.

The only sure way to break the hold of distorted communication is to constantly engage perspectives from outside any given tradition. Intercultural communication and mutual critique may be a more essential element in discourse ethics than Habermas explicitly acknowledges or illustrates in practice in his writings. Feminist and theological interpreters of Habermas move in this direction.[85]

An outstanding example is Seyla Benhabib's *Situating the Self*.[86] First of all, aware of the crisis postmodernism presents for feminism's emancipatory ideals,[87] Benhabib defends a redefined universalism. Following Habermas's revision of Kant, Benhabib's universalism is respect for equal worth expressed as a concrete process of moral deliberation in which everyone's standpoint is taken into account, and in which controversy is settled by "the open and unconstrained discussion of all."[88] This process is not merely intellectual, but depends on moral imagination. Imagination enables empathy with the other, and permits us to redescribe our own situations and actions in ways which can be understood within other people's narratives.[89] The congeniality of such an approach to Christian morality lies in its resonance with the Christian ideals of compassion and solidarity, and the impetus of Christian discipleship to reach across boundaries in the formation of inclusive community.[90]

Benhabib's achievement may be measured against its Kantian baseline in three ways. First, Kant located equality in universalizability and a conception of persons as ends. Habermas alleviated Kant's abstractness by introducing a concept of undistorted communication which, as a concrete process, actually presupposes the specific characteristics of the dialogue partners. Benhabib makes this presupposition explicit in her distinction of the generalized from the concrete other, both of which must be taken into account. While, as generalized others, all are considered to have the same moral rights as we ourselves, each person, as a concrete other, is also approached "as a unique individual, with a certain life history, disposition and endowment, as well as needs and limitations."[91] Second, both Kant and Habermas view equality and respect as part of the rational and self-evident structure of morality. Benhabib, on the other hand, recognizes the modern, Western provenance of such values. They must be legitimated "from within the normative hermeneutic horizon of modernity," where the recognition of equality has been so recently achieved.[92] Benhabib universalizes this value to today's global context in light of the "processes of modernization and rationalization which have been proceeding on a world scale since the seventeenth century."[93] In other words, equality is not self-evident by virtue of the unvarying structure of moral reason, but it is universal *de facto* and *a posteriori*, on historical grounds. The critical question here is what such a defense of universality is worth – is it too tenuous to make equality a reliable ground of intercultural critique? It amounts to saying that, although equality is the recognized criterion of morality today, we have no basis on which to use it against social systems of the past – or, conceivably, of some future time when consensus about it has eroded. More immediately, Benhabib may be too sanguine about the extent of the *de facto* consensus on equality now. Debates about just treatment – of women, of ethnic groups, of races or classes – carry on just because human beings use many and controverted standards to define some in, and others out, of a common class of social and political belonging and of access to goods.

Thirdly, both Kant and Habermas opt for a formal, procedural ethic, and this is a commitment which Benhabib explicitly retains. She recognizes that the values undergirding the very process of communication – equality and respect – are substantive, but she declines to go further. Consensus on the nature of the good life is not a goal of open communication; Benhabib is wary of "value homogeneity."[94] In addition to the problem of the status of equality and respect as *substantive* premises of the formal process of communication, we now may reintroduce the problem of judging the virtue (or viciousness) of any given practice which open debate might produce. We might inquire whether convictions about better and worse ways to live do not prompt critiques of distortion in the first place, and provide the motivation for communication about improvements. Social ethics in any concrete instance – economic reform, war and peace, civil rights – certainly depends on inclusive debate, but would hardly be possible without some centering vision of the good life which draws community members together, and enables movement from one state of affairs to a better alternative.

When Habermas and even Benhabib concede an egalitarian procedure as their normative limit, they get less mileage than might be possible out of what actually happens when dialogue goes on in the concrete. Suspicion of the latent coercive power of distorted traditions undermines their trust in the potential of open and mutually critical dialogue to result in consensus about goods that can be appreciated from a variety of standpoints. Yet it is invariably through interactions on a common problem or concern – one that requires some practical resolution, not just perpetual conversation – that we do adopt the other's point of view and move to agreement on goods to be preferred or actions to be taken. In such a process, we recognize not only egalitarian reciprocity as a procedure, but some common human experiences, needs, and values, respect for which is what equality means in practice.

The question which may be pressed more fruitfully out of the Aristotelian emphasis on practice, prudence, and inductive knowing, is whether human experience as bodily, intersubjective, and social can yield any substantive goods, recognizable and realizable across or among the cultural traditions which will still shape them quite differently. In order to be reliable and effective, intercultural critique may need to go beyond the merely fortuitous historical universality of modern equality. When actual difficulties throw multiple traditions' interests together, it may require the assumption that one tradition's deepest values in the basic realms of practical living will strike a responsive chord in any other tradition simply on the basis of shared humanity.

A further issue will be how to move either from an ideal of respect, or from agreement on common goods, to an actual change in social conditions. The empathy that underlies equal respect is the emotion that humanizes and concretizes Habermas's discourse ethics; it is present in Benhabib's appeal to moral imagination. How can we create and sustain empathy and solidarity, so essential to change at the practical level? This issue will arise for Aristotelian–Thomistic ethics as the question how to prompt moral agents who share culturally mediated versions of essentially similar experiences to recognize and act on that fact, to actually behave as though one another are in morally relevant respects "the same" (despite differences of gender, culture, race, ethnicity, class, or religion). Christian ethics, to be addressed in chapter 5, as shaped by a New Testament vision of community, focuses exactly on the formation of communal bonds of solidarity characterized by the capacity to care for strangers and enemies as for oneself, one's family, one's friends.[95]

CHAPTER 3

Particular experiences, shared goods

The ethics of Aristotle and of Thomas Aquinas are teleological, eudaimonistic, and realist. Both are also practical and prudential. Human activity is purposeful; it aims at happiness. The goods which are constitutive of happiness, as well as the activities and virtues which realize those goods, are not mere social constructions or psychological projections. They are objective, stable across cultures, and knowable by human reason. The way in which they are known is not by examining the structures of reason itself, but by inductive reflection on, and generalization from, human experiences of need, of lack or deprivation, of fulfillment and flourishing, and of social cooperation. Moral knowledge, in this view, is not read directly from experience as sheer fact; the existence of a practice or its wide acceptance cannot as such yield a moral law. Morality requires reasonable reflection on human existence, fine discrimination of goods whose possession truly constitutes happiness, and judgments about which activities lead to those goods and which do not. Real understanding of the natural law and its practical demands requires virtue and prudence.

In a Thomistic perspective, the concept "nature" is a means to establish moral goods or ends on the basis of human experience itself, to give goods a morally compelling character by presenting them to choice as a "law," and to set human goods and morality within the larger scheme of divine providence by defining the natural law as derivative from the divine reason or the "eternal law." In the "treatise on law" of the *Summa Theologica*, Aquinas is indebted to the Roman law tradition as well as to Aristotle. Aquinas defines the natural law as the inclination of every creature to the proper ends and actions intended for it by God; in human beings this inclination is not just physical or instinctual, but also intellectual and rational.[1] Reason rules the appetites and sense, and is ruled by the Eternal Law (God's plan for creation). There is no ultimate conflict between what God wills and what is good or reasonable for humanity.

Aquinas lays out the order of inclinations by proceeding from those shared by all creatures, to those shared by animals, and finally to those which are distinctively human. Human beings like all things are inclined to self-preservation, so they protect human life; like animals, they mate and educate their offspring. Humans as such have a natural desire to know the truth about God and to live in society. Hence they shun ignorance, avoid offending members of the community, "and other such things ..." This is not an exhaustive list of moral obligations nor even of the general categories into which they fall, but an illustration of the sorts of generalizations which can reasonably be made from basic moral experiences which instantiate what it means to do good and avoid evil.[2] For Aquinas, humans may be sinful, but they also have a surviving ability to know and do good. *Synderesis*, a habit of the intellect, possesses and disposes us to act in accord with the first principles of the natural law.[3]

For Aquinas, the ultimate purposes of human life reflect the will and intentions of God, in whose image humanity is created.[4] Although actual human existence is "fallen," we can discern in and through it an "integral" or normative nature, especially with the support of revelation.[5] In the recent tradition, a competition between "autonomous ethic" and "faith ethic" interpretations of Catholic moral theology[6] may have obscured the fact that Thomas thought that morality was reasonable and that its requirements could be stated in terms of natural justice, without thereby implying either that it is possible in any simplistic way to read the "ought" off the facts of human existence, or that faith is irrelevant to Christian moral discernment. Knowledge of the natural law requires prudential evaluation of human activities which respond to genuine human needs, realize human goods, and hence are conducive to happiness and excellence.[7] Virtue, according to Thomas, is an inclination or disposition of the agent to act excellently by realizing goods through action.[8] Christian faith helps illumine moral goods for us, and educates us in moral virtue.

The recent revival of "virtue ethics" highlights the historicity of human agency, and the dependence of moral goodness on communities of practice in which the good is discerned and chosen.[9] The notions of virtue, of acts, of goods, and of principles are interdependent, insofar as agents act toward ends which they apprehend as good, and can be guided in their choices by principles and norms which generalize about goods to be sought and about priorities among goods. (For instance, "Sexual pleasure is good." And, "Sexual pleasure should be sought only in a context of mutual consent, of responsibility for procreation, of marital commitment, etc.") The virtuous person has a consistent tendency to make good choices. Virtue then defines the active, willing relation of agent to the natural human goods that reason apprehends.

Some forms of Aristotelianism fail to provide a convincing account of moral objectivity because they deliberately or inadvertently extrapolate conceptions of goods, of flourishing and of virtues and vices, from the preferences of circumscribed historical communities. Some forms of Thomism fail in the same task by treating specific historical formulations of goods and obligations as invariant first principles from which almost equally absolute conclusions can be deduced logically. Examples are rife not only in sexual ethics, but also in definitions of permissible and impermissible killing. A moral theology manual of the 1940s states as a general principle that "The body may not be mutilated unless mutilation is the only available means of saving the rest of the body, i.e., its life or health." The author subsequently derives the conclusion that "When vasectomy, fallectomy or ovariotomy or any other operations are employed simply for the purpose of producing sterility, in order that sexual intercourse may still be used without issue, the intention and the operation are both grievously sinful and forbidden."[10]

Little do the writings of Aquinas himself, and less so those of

Aristotle, warrant the rigidity of neo-scholastic Thomism, heavily influenced by the Kantian investment in the moral a priori, as well as by the apparent certainty and rigor of scientific method. Aristotle has written that discussion of action according to right reason "cannot be more than an outline and is bound to lack precision." After all, "one can demand of a discussion only what the subject matter permits, and there are no fixed data in matters concerning action." Moreover, on any particular problem, "the agent must consider on each different occasion what the situation demands."[11]

Like Aristotle, Aquinas admits that the practical reason, since it is "busied with contingent matters," does not achieve the truth "without fail" or necessarily. Where the natural moral law is concerned, "although there is necessity in the general principles, the more we descend to matters of detail, the more frequently we encounter defects." Hence, "in matters of action, truth or practical rectitude is not the same for all, as to matters of detail, but only as to the general principles."[12] Prudence or practical wisdom (*phronesis*) is the intellectual virtue which disposes reason to discern the right means to specific ends or goods,[13] and is concerned with what is "just, noble, and good for man."[14] Prudence determines which activities bring virtue (a habit or *disposition* to act excellently) down to the concrete level. It finds the best means to the human ends or goods to which virtue directs us.

Several recent interpreters of Aquinas have stressed that he offers resources for a model of moral thinking which is practical and analogical. As Jean Porter notes, our basic moral notions, moral rules, and ideas of the virtues are all essentially empirical, in that we generalize them from experiences we have had and apply them analogically in new situations.[15] Moral cognition, which moves imaginatively from precedent to new application, relies on the emotions, the affections, one's personal history, and a community of discernment. It is tested, not by the articulation of a moral concept or rule, but by the ability to act intelligently in the relevant sphere of life. Thus Stephen Pope concludes, "a proper grasp of the natural law can only be attained through training in the virtues and especially the exercise of practical wisdom."[16] Knowledge of the natural law depends on and is proportionate to the habit of prudence.[17]

Aquinas outlines principles of the natural law which reflect basic spheres of human moral experience and social living; then cautions that more particular determinations of right and wrong will be less certain; before moving on to make such determinations as clearly as he can, given the information and authorities at hand, and the analysis of which he is capable. Although in the latter task he is sometimes overconfident, the full effect of his method can be appreciated only if his initial reservation about contingencies is kept in view, as well as the indispensability of prudence to knowledge of what the natural law means practically.

These caveats are important, because Aquinas' own perspective on matters of sex and gender is quite limited by his cultural setting, and by his tendency in these areas to forget that the most distinctive human capacities are intellect and will. He is predisposed to focus the "natural" on physiological function.[18] He takes it for granted, not only that sex has above all a reproductive purpose,[19] but also that woman's existence, as supposedly the more passive and less rational sex, is to be explained primarily in relation to this purpose.[20] To retrieve Aquinas as a resource for a feminist and historically sensitive approach to sex and gender requires a readiness to develop in a more complete and egalitarian mode his inductive epistemology and his vision of the human person as embodied and social. This allows us to look critically at and to situate historically or culturally his reductionistic assumptions about sex and women. This being said, Aquinas's general theory still can provide "a foundation for a theory of morality that grounds moral norms in an account of the natural human good."[21]

Several Roman Catholic authors have converged on, and in various ways revised, an enumeration of human goods proposed by John Finnis. Finnis identifies seven goods as those which all societies in some way observe: life (including procreation), knowledge, play, aesthetic experience, sociability or friendship, practical reasonableness, and religion (questions about transcendence).[22] Many do not accept the further claim of Finnis and Germain Grisez that these goods are equally basic, "incommensurable" in the sense of being impossible to prioritize, and absolute in the sense of precluding any direct sacrifice of one for another in a conflict situation.[23] But their list does represent the conviction of many Thomistic authors that moral debate and even consensus are reasonable intercultural goals, because all peoples and all cultural differentiations have at their core a shared human way of being in the world, one closely linked to our bodily nature; to our abilities to reflect, to choose, and to love; and to our intrinsic dependence on a community of other human beings, not only for survival, but also for meaning. Justice consists in establishing social relations which are conducive to the flourishing of all human persons. Justice goes beyond the assertion of their personal rights, by encouraging and supporting each person's participative contribution to all the conditions of social living which further the common good, including fulfillment of duties to other individuals and to the community as a whole.[24]

Reinforced by liberation theology, Roman Catholic social ethics today identifies practical reason in strongly social terms. Many authors use the term "praxis" to render a sense of practical reason's social and structural implications. Both theory and action are included as dialectical moments within praxis, and praxis includes all the social relationships that determine consciousness, of groups as well as of individuals.[25] Insofar as theory reflects on the precise nature of social relationships, it illumines oppression and is the first step toward transformation. Yet, as the experience of both feminist and liberation theologians shows, the reflective moment often emerges precisely because of a concrete experience of injustice and the already-beginning mobilization of forces of change out of the experience of oppressed peoples themselves. Gustavo Gutierrez has given this dynamic a classic expression: "The praxis on which liberation theology reflects is a praxis of solidarity in the interests of liberation and is inspired by the gospel."[26] An example of Christian praxis which is already and intrinsically liberating for women is Latin American base communities. "A genuine perspective of solidarity and equal participation gives rise in the church base communities to an awareness of the grave problems suffered by women and encourages them to take the necessary action to uproot *machismo*."[27]

As I drafted this page on June 29, 1994, the *New York Times* carried two stories which poignantly illustrate the transcultural nature of some basic human experiences, both of value and of evil, as well as the necessity to ground practical moral response in a sense of solidarity which in difference comprehends sameness. The first, titled "Fear Is Still Pervasive in Rwanda Countryside,"[28] featured a photograph of a man captioned, "A father whose wife and 6-year-old son were badly wounded by shrapnel from a rebel mortar was comforted as he collapsed outside the Red Cross Hospital in Rwanda with his infant child." The man sits slumped on the ground, braced up by one arm. Two people lean over him, heads bent, arms outreached in a gesture of support. The man cradles a blanketed baby; the wordless grief and despair contorting his face capture the abstractions "genocide" and "death" in an icon of personal suffering. Any parent can know that suffering by gazing at his face; I instinctively cover my own face in my hands as I turn from my computer screen to look at it again. Its power to evoke this reaction is why the *New York Times* printed it.

On another page of the same issue, two women sit smiling on a sofa with a children's book, their arms around one another, a little girl, and a cat. They read together, while the child strokes a golden retriever. The group is described as, "Dr. Susan M. Love, center, and Dr. Helen Cooksey with their daughter, Katie; Sugar the cat, and Brownie the dog." The article, which is about Dr. Love's pioneering work in breast cancer treatment, explains "The couple have been together for 13 years. Five years ago, by artificial insemination, Dr. Love had a daughter, Katie Love Cooksey. Dr. Cooksey left surgery to stay home with the child. Last September, the couple won a legal battle that allowed Dr. Cooksey to adopt Katie."[29]

I respond to the women in the picture as people who love one another, as mothers, as professionals committed to service. I recognize the moment they share as they read to their daughter, much as I have often read to mine. In many ways they are more like me – a white, educated, privileged, Western mother whose position in life brings many advantages to her children – than the African man a world away whose countenance breaks with waves of pain, pain which my emotions comprehend more readily than the categories I can build from my own daily life. Neither lesbianism nor artificial birth technologies are *my* experience, though; no more than blackness, maleness, or survival in a country where hundreds of thousands are being killed by their neighbors. Yet the photographed subjects and I are all parents, we have mates in raising our children, and we sense fearfully what loss would mean. We know the security of home and family are good; we know violent deaths of our children are evil. We all would agree that a good society encourages the hospitality to children that we enjoy in the one photograph, and avoids the endangerment from which we recoil in the other. No one would say that the inhabitants of the photographed worlds and I are "just the same" – but we are all human beings and we are parents.

This example shows why it is not true that really quite general perceptions of common human nature are too "watered down" (in Kai Nielsen's phrase[30]) to be of any use. It is a mistake to believe that such perceptions are of value only if they can function as premises from which specific action-guides can be deduced. In the first place, they can function to establish the spheres or parameters within which, or the ideals and limits against which, our moral considerations ought to proceed. Especially with current dispute of the very idea that there are basic forms in which moral goodness will be found, this function is not as otiose as it may once have seemed.

Second, the recognition and articulation of forms of common human goods and evils have more than a prescriptive function, especially when we move them from books and articles about moral theory to human interaction in the face of opportunity and suffering. At the affective and emotional level, as well as at the cognitive, "counting the ways" of our common humanity can bring us into sympathetic relation to our counterparts, can help create the practical bonds of connection without which moral reasoning is cold. To look at newspaper photographs does not resolve ethnic violence or analyze African kinship patterns. Nor does it give us a full-blown response to lesbianism or to the wisdom of using anonymous donor sperm to create families. But it does establish that when we talk about such moral issues, we are talking about human beings' lives, and encourages us to see that those lives are somehow knit closely with our own, and that they matter as much.

What is most important to a feminist and intercultural retrieval of Aquinas (and Aristotle) is his openness to an inductive objectivity and realism, perhaps better phrased today in terms of shared framing experiences and moral common ground, than of moral "universals." While Thomas Aquinas certainly differs from Aristotle in the theological context he establishes for his ethics, he agrees that moral insight into human goods and excellences, and into the obligations they establish, is in a basic way available to human wisdom. The needed revision of Aquinas' natural law theory was foreshadowed by one of his interpreters, Bernard Lonergan, who wrote two decades ago of a transition from a "classicist" worldview to a more historically minded one. In the latter view, human meaning "is not fixed, static, immutable, but shifting, developing, going astray, capable of redemption."[31] Although one might see the concepts of history and of natural law as inimical to one another, Lonergan is suggesting that the idea of a natural moral law can and should be reappropriated in a more historically sensitive and flexible vein. Ethicists using Aquinas follow out the experiential and realist directions of his theory, while noting ever more forcefully that the specifics of a natural law morality are subject to historical variation. John Finnis sees Aquinas as "saying that any sane person is capable of seeing that life, knowledge, fellowship, offspring, and a few other such basic aspects of human existence are, as such, good, i.e., worth having." Yet Finnis, a quite traditional interpreter of Aquinas so far as the specific moral norms of Catholicism are concerned, can still set off as a separate issue "all assessments of relative importance, all moral demands, and in short, all questions of whether and how one is to devote oneself to these goods."[32] It is in the latter category that considerations of historical change and historical diversity in the *practical* demands of the moral law could have valence.

The essential point to emphasize for an ethics which begins with, and remains respectful of, differences in experience, while not giving up the possibility of normative ethics, is that the "shared" is not achieved beyond or over against particularity, but rather in and through it. Especially in the course of practical, problem-solving, conflict-mediating, or society-trans-forming activity, common footing can be found on which moral communication, and eventually judgment and action, can take place. But the participants in communication, judgment, and action will always be irreducibly concrete and historical char-acters who recognize humanity in one another, without leaving their own individuality behind.

MARTHA NUSSBAUM: TOWARD A FEMINIST ARISTOTELIANISM

The Aristotelian philosopher Martha Nussbaum moves to a less tentative and more substantive defense of moral objectivity and universality than discourse ethics provides. Hence her work is a resource for resolving some of the questions about moral objectivity posed in the last chapter. Taking practical rationality in an "essentialist" direction, Nussbaum advances confidently toward intercultural debate, evaluation and policy. Part of her program is to elucidate substantively, not just procedurally, what experiences and needs, and therefore values and rights, human beings have in common. This step is not only consistent with the development of Aristotelian foundations within Roman Catholic Thomistic ethics (as a morality of "natural" experiences and values), it also offers a possible way in to a contemporary, feminist, Christian, intercultural ethics of sex and gender which is historical and inductive, revisable but nonrelativist.[33]

Nussbaum unabashedly insists that "human life has certain central defining features."[34] Yet she insists on the practical nature of moral knowledge, and specifies that, as practical, it will be highly differentiated according to individual circumstances. She skillfully displays the importance of moral imagination, of the emotions, of perception, and of finely tuned ethical attention, in her analyses of Greek drama and of nineteenth-century novels, especially by Henry James.[35] General principles fall short in accounting for unanticipated features of situations; even repeated features are embedded in their own contexts; and moral situations do not exist apart from relationships among particular persons, relationships which have their peculiar and morally significant texture and intensity. The emotions in fact have a "cognitive dimension in their very structure," so that fully rational judgment requires their ancillary function to bring us to full understanding of that about which we deliberate.[36] Situational particularity gives the final shape to individual choices. Our ability to perceive and respond to other persons depends on our recognition of them as, like ourselves, aiming at a good and complete life for a human being. Like Aristotle, we all ask, "How should a human being live?" What that might mean is not infinitely variable nor incommensurable among cultures.[37]

Nussbaum refuses to succumb to the notion that "the whole idea of searching for the truth is an old-fashioned error." "Certain ways in which people see the world can still be criticized exactly as Aristotle criticized them: as stupid, pernicious and false," she says, granting that the standards for such judgments must be known from within practice. Although contentious relativists like to overestimate disagreement, we can and do sit down to discuss hunger or justice or the quality of women's lives with people from other parts of the world and still find it "possible to proceed as if we are all talking about the same human problem."[38] Human experience can disclose goods which constitute a full human life, and practical reason can guide action toward them. There is a convergence across cultures about the areas of experience which constitute humanness (exhibited for instance in myths and storytelling).[39]

Programatically, Nussbaum sees Aristotle's ethics, centered in the human good and on values, as carrying out investigations into the form of life of a being both needy and resourceful, with certain capabilities and certain sorts of incompleteness, and a certain sort of body in which all of this takes place. They are attempts to describe the limits and possibilities of that species-specific form of life, saying where, within those, good is to be found.[40]

The foundation of her social ethics is a revisable list of shared experiences: mortality, the human body (hunger and thirst, need for shelter, sexual desire, mobility), capacity for pleasure and pain, cognitive capability (perception, imagination, thought), early infant development, practical reason, affiliation with other human beings, relatedness to other species and to nature, humor, and play, separateness, and strong separateness (the peculiarity of a whole life, not just spatial and temporal separateness).[41] Of these, Nussbaum believes, the most distinctively human are practical reason and affiliation (corresponding to Aristotle's definition of "man" as a rational and social animal), and they give a shape to the whole.

Positive human functioning in these areas is valued cross-culturally, and grounds morality. The "basic human functional capabilities" are being able to live to the end of a complete human life; to have good health, to avoid nonuseful pain and enjoy pleasurable experiences; to use one's five senses and to imagine, think, and reason; to have attachments to others, to love, to grieve, and to feel gratitude; to form a conception of the good, and to plan one's life around it; to be concerned for animals and nature; to laugh and play, to live one's own life, and to do so in one's own surroundings and context.[42] The task of politics is accordingly to structure social life around labor, property, political participation, education, and some pluralism and choice in individuals' specific approaches to the good life.

Virtuous action, Nussbaum admits, will to some extent vary locally: "a good rule is a good summary of wise particular choices and not a court of last resort."[43] The aim is not absolute formulations, but a wide and recognizable working consensus that is "fully international."[44] Truth claims can be asserted from within an inductive, historical approach to the universals or essentials in moral experience, even though our perception and articulation of these is subject to constant cross-cultural revision.[45]

Nussbaum's work contains many illustrations of the importance for women of commitment to intercultural standards of well-being and of justice. A favorite example of hers comes from a development project in Bangladesh, which was unsuccessful as long as its sponsors approached rural women with liberal assumptions and values, failing to engage these women's own participation in nuancing aims to their particular situation. Like the women in *Silent No Longer*, they worked harder, ate less, got sicker, died earlier, and were less respected than men. An international agency tried to provide the women from a village with literacy materials to improve their uniformly low status. However, these women had no interest in education, since their imaginations were unable to encompass what an educated female life would be like, or what advantages it would bring. They had no role models. The situation called for some standard of change external to the community itself; but it also called for concrete engagement with the community women's experience.

Change did not begin until the researchers began to look at women's actual functions and opportunities in more depth, asking what might be important to them over a complete life. At last, the women themselves became involved in women's cooperatives in the village, which led to transformations on a number of levels, including gender relations and production, as well as education. The Western women and the rural women in Bangladesh were finally able to achieve results because, despite vast differences in culture, they "recognized one another as fellow human beings, sharing certain problems and certain resources, certain needs for fuller capability and certain possibilities for movement toward capability," as well as having the imagination and humor to identify with one another and envision mutual change.[46]

The liberal enhancement of access and liberty was in this case an inadequate foundation for real structural revision. The Bangladeshi women failed to take advantage of access to education because they could not see why it would matter. The

Western women had to learn that educational access might not matter much unless other factors changed too. Change required from both "an inquiry into the goodness and full humanness of various functionings, and into the special obstacles faced by deprived groups."[47] Beginning from different experiential and cultural standpoints, including differences of ethnicity, nationality, and class, they were able to undertake this inquiry together once they engaged at the practical level.

Reflecting upon the Bangladeshi women, we might question whether Nussbaum's own list of basic human experiences and goods reflects a liberal bias. Two further categories might supplement her Aristotelian rendering: religion and kinship. As would many other US citizens, with their traditions of church and state separation, Nussbaum explicitly excludes religion, though she allows for religious freedom. Kinship is dealt with only indirectly, and in ways which tend to minimize its social content, and to present it rather in terms of bodily realities (especially of individual bodies) and of freely chosen interpersonal relationships.

Particularly striking is the omission of kinship as a basic experience, one whose social dimensions and moral interpretation are certainly at the root of many feminist concerns. Nor does Nussbaum interconnect kinship with sexuality as realized socially in parenthood and family. She categorizes "sexual desire" under "body," then characterizes it as a "need," albeit one which can ground "recognition of others different from ourselves as human beings."[48] Missing here is the vast importance of marriage and family – the institutional arenas in which sexuality is endowed with significance for the whole fabric of human society.

Although it would be simplistic to say that sexuality is a trajectory of identity along which Bangladeshi women, Asian women, or women in general, are always systematically devalued, it is certainly true that women find their options drastically circumscribed in many cultural mediations of marriage and parenthood. Poor Bangladeshi women are a case in point. Take just one descriptive statement from Chen's study:

A young woman is contracted in marriage without her consent, often at a young age. Traditionally, marriage is universal and early marriage is preferred. Upon marriage, a young wife usually moves to her husband's home. Her husband and his family assume responsibility for her protection ... The marriage is often tentative until the birth of the first child, preferably a son. Many women face the possibility of divorce or the prospect that her husband will take a second wife.[49]

To reduce human sexual and reproductive capacities to the individual's sexual "need," much more so to "desire," is grimly farcical under such conditions.

The fundamental question is whether sex is *inherently* communal and relational (and not necessarily in oppressive or gender-biased ways). Sex or "sexuality" is not only a matter of individual sex-drive or sex-desire; indeed, desire itself is a drive toward another. Sex as a bodily reality grounds biological connections to other human beings (minimally, for every human being, to one's intergenerational family of origin). It is always socialized in institutions which channel its expression, recognize the alliances it creates, and protect the children it engenders. As such, it yields social forms of family, clan, tribe, ethnicity, and even nationhood.

Nussbaum puts human relationships in general in the category of "affiliation," which might include kinship, but tends to connote consensual relationships (and hence a "liberal" model of family). She does mention infant development as a separate category of basic human experience, though it is better placed with other human stages of growth and aging, as a subcategory of embodiment. Perhaps placing infancy as an experiential sphere of individuals *as* infants is a way of getting at the parent–child relation without elevating parenthood to the status of an indispensable experience; and of getting at the general requirement that infants be nurtured, without engaging the issue of upon whom that responsibility should fall (i.e., whether men and women are related to infants in the same way). But the oddness of this solution is that it individualizes and desocializes the infant stage.

Because patriarchy survives in and through the social media-

tion of biological reproduction, especially by enlarging reproduction and attendant duties into women's virtually exclusive
function, a feminist social agenda is not well served by neglect
or denial of this dimension of experience. Gender-based socialization of reproduction is not adequately addressed by
speaking as though sex and birth have no intrinsic social
dimensions at all.

Similarly, religion is a basic, cross-cultural human reality. If
we take Native American, Latin American, Asian, and African
societies into account as strongly as contemporary European
and European–American ones, it is evident that religious
experience and communal worship are not clearly demarcated
from the commonality of human experience, the public, and
the social. Religion is woven through the social fabric and
through the categories by which humans understand their place
in the world. They are open to an experience that could in a
broad sense be called "religious," in the sense that all human
beings wonder about the origin of the world and an intelligent
purpose behind its fortunes, about the human fate after death,
about a larger order of reward and retribution for good and
evil, about salvation from their own wrongdoing and suffering,
and about a unity of all persons and of the natural world in a
dimension transcending history. Has there ever existed a
civilization which did not recognize religious experience and
institutionalize it as an avenue from our historical existence to
the inexplicable mysteries which surround, sustain, break in
upon and sometimes afflict it? Needless to say, the institutionalization of religious experience is also of interest to any feminist
perspective because it is among the spheres in which women
are devalued by patriarchal traditions.[50]

CORRESPONDENCES WITH FEMINIST THEOLOGICAL ETHICS

Among the constitutive aspects of being human named by
Nussbaum, many feminists see affiliation and the body as
having special impact on women's experience as moral agents,
or note that a strong sense of separateness is often lacking in

women's identity, though it is necessary to their well-being and mature agency.[51] The concern with affiliation is often expressed in terms of relationality and sociality, as well as the inclusion within justice as fairness of a standard of "care."

In *Hispanic Women: Prophetic Voice in the Church*, Ada María Isasi-Díaz and Yolanda Tarango name six presuppositions of their approach, four of which explicitly mention community.[52] Contrasting with the predominance of equality, rights, and choice in the approaches of many liberals (including liberal feminists), the word "compassion" titles theologies in at least two volumes by Third-World women.[53] An African-American, Delores Williams, defines "womanist" thought as based in community, beginning with the care of mothers for children, extending to a sistership of all women, and including both men and women in community building.[54] Correcting an imbalance between autonomy and relationality, Margaret Farley develops justice and care as correlative norms. Feminism can appreciate that, against modern rationalism, "autonomy is ultimately for the sake of relationship," while, against postmodern diffusion of the self into language and social systems, relationship without autonomy is destructive, and, historically, especially so of women.[55]

However substantively defined, the assumption that human embodiedness and sociality provide a common platform from which to dismantle dehumanizing oppressions is quite pronounced in feminist theology. This is most true of Roman Catholic feminists who reflect a Thomistic heritage. Rosemary Radford Ruether's manifesto has become the motto of many: "The critical principle of feminist theology is the promotion of the full humanity of women." Whatever denies full humanity to women "must be presumed not to reflect ... the authentic nature of things."[56] Feminist theology begins from the standpoint of women's subordination, and promotes a pro-woman liberating agenda.[57]

Roman Catholic feminist theology often upholds an ideal of full human moral agency and well-being which presumes a common standard, and understands justice neither procedurally nor as protection of individual rights, but as egalitarian partici-

pation of all human beings in the common good. As Margaret
Farley has put it, feminism makes a case for a "common
morality" which goes beyond the feminist political agenda as
such. Whatever the differences of culture and history, the
experience of what it means to be "a human person" makes it
possible, even "across time and place," "to condemn commonly
recognized injustices and act for commonly desired goals." In
her own experience of listening to women from parts of Asia
and Africa, and from Central and Latin America, Farley writes,
she has encountered feminist theologians who "are as opposed
to unmitigated moral relativism as to false and inadequate
universalisms."[58] Elizabeth Johnson describes a dialectic of
"contrast and confirmation" that often propels social change.
This dialectic is grounded in lived experience, and envisions
"the *humanum* of women" over against situations of oppression
to which women say *no*. "Indignation generates the energy for
resistance, an act grounded on an equally deep and lasting *yes*
to women's flourishing."[59]

Examples of substantive ethics from Roman Catholic feminists reflect the same concern with identifying basic human
experiences within a social context.[60] In *Body, Sex, and Pleasure*,
Christine Gudorf criticizes the tradition for its overemphasis on
procreation, and its devaluing of pleasure, but approaches her
subject-matter in a way akin to Aquinas' generalization from
human "inclinations," to normative statements about goods.
Gudorf too works inductively from human bodily experiences.
She derives a moral norm from the capacity of both women
and men for sexual pleasure: mutual sexual pleasure is a
standard for moral sex. She is more than willing to apply this
standard cross-culturally, insisting that practices such as genital
mutilation are immoral on that score.[61]

FEMINIST ETHICS AS LIBERATION THEOLOGY

We have seen that at least some Western, academic versions of
feminism owe much to postmodern thought, with its celebration
of pluralism, and its resistance to moral uniformity. Liberation
theology reflects this concern for the different and the parti-

cular. But it also appeals for social transformation on the basis of the human dignity, rights, and potentials of those held captive by very particular forms of structural oppression. The liberationist call for social equality is no doubt indebted partly to modern, liberal, democratic forms of social organization, which empower individuals to advance their own social rights. But liberation theology has drawn more self-consciously on Marxist critiques of economically secured class distinctions and Marxism's call for action by those who suffer.

Feminist theologies frequently incorporate all these elements, bearing special affinity to the liberation theologies of Latin America (and now of other continents). Feminist theologies of liberation take the side of the "poor" or oppressed, and call for economic and political equality, appealing to biblical themes such as Exodus, to Jesus' socially radical treatment of women, and to neglected female leaders in the biblical accounts. Feminist liberation theology and ethics counteract the rationalism and individualism of liberal cultures by locating moral criticism in communities of identity and action, and by drawing attention to the social, political, and historical character of supposedly "private" and "personal" relations in marriage and the family.

Liberation theology, including some feminist theology, also counteracts the relativism explicit in post-modern philosophy and theology, and the relativism implicit in liberalism's practical absolute of free choice. Liberationist voices originate in concrete social and political communities, but they appeal across social groups and traditions to a sense of common humanity and justice. Unlike Marxism and postmodernism, liberation theology neither sees ideological differences as unsurmountable, nor views violence and the alternating victories of opposed power alliances as the only way to social transformation.

In practice, feminist liberation theology generally assumes a *substantive* and not merely procedural appeal – to common human needs, capabilities, and forms of well-being or dehumanization. These shared realities unite the sexes and all cultures, notwithstanding the indispensability of their differential realization. Introducing her collection of Third-World women's theology, Ursula King describes this theology as "fed by the quest and determination to seek the full humanity of women – and ultimately that of all people: women, men, and children."[62] She names specific evils which that humanity would exclude: "the plight of the poor, rural women, women laborers, oppressive customs and marriage structures, sexual exploitation or genital mutilation, prostitution or sex tourism in Asia, or the oppressively hierarchical structures of the churches and their traditional ideas about women's confined role." The feminist theologians whom she presents move beyond pain and struggle to "a sharing of hope, of a new empowering vision born out of the sense of *solidarity* among women," no matter what their nationality, class, color, or faith.[63]

María Pilar Aquino, a Mexican feminist working in the US, insists that the "perspective of women accords priority to the achievement of women's human integrity and emphasizes the right of humanity for all women and men," especially as threatened by the poverty and dehumanization which result from capitalism.[64] Rebecca Chopp, a Methodist, sees liberation theology as continuing modernity's view of the human subject as a "meaning-seeker" who must be brought to "higher consciousness." But liberation theology remedies modernity's distortions of rationality and moral judgment, insofar as it emphasizes praxis, questions the fact of massive human suffering, and explicitly aims at social transformation, not only at understanding or dislodging authority.[65]

In feminist liberation theology the epistemological or philosophical premises of a universal recognition of women's full humanity, and of the goods and rights it would entail, remain largely implicit. Martha Nussbaum offers a philosophical complement to Christian feminist ethics in that she elucidates how substantive rational discourse about general human well-being can commence. Although Seyla Benhabib accomplishes much of the same work with discourse ethics, she remains reticent about consensus on the concrete goods open and reciprocal conversation can accomplish. The exception is the value of equality itself, a potential structuring characteristic of all speech which has been accorded what Benhabib thinks is universal recognition only in the modern world.

Benhabib and Nussbaum come together in endorsing a concrete, practical, dialogical model of rationality. But Habermas and his interpreters tend to conclude that, although all participants' "needs" must be recognized, heard, and discussed toward agreement or compromise in all practical situations, there can be no universal, biologically or socially based conception of "need" or "good." Concrete and specific needs and the forms of life which fulfill them are too culture-dependent for the kind of generalization Nussbaum proposes.

The communication model for ethics is postmodern in that it moves away from any abstract and ahistorical point of judgment. Gadamer's "first wave" of communication theory, an Aristotelian revival, was attracted by practical reason (*phronesis*) in a historical context and nurtured by tradition. Habermas's "second wave," shifts the foundation of the communication model from Aristotle to Kant, and can be read as a historicizing of the Enlightenment model of universal and equal rationality. Both Habermas and Benhabib object to the potential for ideological distortion which will occur when communication and understanding within a tradition are supposedly self-guaranteeing. As an antidote to distorted traditionalism, they propose universal equality and respect within every concrete process of communication.

What we might call a "new wave" of Aristotelianism, epitomized by Martha Nussbaum, would certainly accept equality and respect in concrete dialogue as normative. It would be less likely to ground equality in an a priori procedure or structure of communication, and more likely to see it emerging experientially and historically out of practical encounters where shared humanity is recognized, sometimes in a flash of new awareness, sometimes as incremental respect. Moreover, this same practical process permits – indeed, requires – generalization about actual goods to be sought or evils avoided in personal choice and social interaction.

A critical ethics of sex and gender requires such generalizations, and in reality has always worked with them. Some sexual practices (for example, rape or wife-murder) are to be condemned as dehumanizing and hence vicious, and others (mutual pleasure, consent to marriage) praised as excellent in the sexual, parental or familial spheres. Generalizations about sexual morality and about gender roles are always historical, inductive, and revisable in proportion to their specificity. But no consistent feminist critique can maintain that practical good and evil in matters of sex and gender are culturally constructed to their very roots and in value utterly relative to social approbation.

FAITH COMMUNITY AND MORAL REASONING IN RECENT CATHOLIC THOUGHT

The ethics of human nature, virtue, and prudence tracing back to Aquinas' interpretation of Aristotle has been most prevalent and influential in Roman Catholicism. My argument is that this fundamental approach can provide a critically realist and reasonably objective model of ethics for Christianity in general, and even for interreligious and intercultural discourse. It is well known, however, that Roman Catholic moral teaching, especially about sex and gender, is often perceived to be an inflexible prescriptive system, centered on exceptionless absolute norms. Therefore it is important to examine the recent history and current state of natural law morality in Roman Catholicism, before proposing it as a useful resource for contemporary thought.

While the *Summa Theologica* of Thomas Aquinas has been a standard resource for Roman Catholic moral theology since the sixteenth century, it has been interpreted in manifold ways. The Kantian influence was undoubtedly strong among the neo-scholastic moral theologians who authored the seminary manuals used in the late nineteenth and early twentieth centuries. They proposed an abstract system of moral classification and a deductive application of principles to cases. Reading Aquinas' love for distinctions and orderly reasoning (a medieval scholastic achievement) through Enlightenment eyes and with a misplaced respect for scientific method, the manualists presented an abstract and rigid casuistry which was preoccupied with sexual matters.[66]

One revisionist response since Vatican II has been to nuance moral reflection more deliberately to concrete experience, and to show that innovative applications of or exceptions to "absolute" principles may be justified.[67] But other Roman Catholic moralists have shifted away from interpreting natural law as knowable either by reason or through experience, and have tried to locate morals more strongly within a faith commitment, revelation, and, for some, more firmly within the guidance of authoritative teaching. A good example is the 1993 papal encyclical, *Veritatis Splendor*, which acknowledges natural law as knowable by reason[68] but ultimately privileges revelation and church teaching as arbiters of moral knowledge which need not conform to, and may even contradict, consensus-building discernment of moral value and human well-being.[69] The drafters of *Veritatis splendor* may be among those who fear "a creeping secularism which would hand Christian ethics over to moral philosophy; and, they would argue, the vagueness and uncertainty of current moral philosophy offers a foundation far too insecure for the needs of the Church's teachings."[70]

A form of anti-foundationalism that is at once anti-Kantian, anti-secularist, and anti-deconstructionist has had impressive appeal, even for many who stand in traditions (Anglican as well as Roman Catholic) historically hospitable not only to natural law but to some form of natural theology. Some have re-emphasized the idea (noted at the outset of this chapter) that Aquinas's ethics belongs ultimately in the context of *faith*, rather than placing the emphasis on the inherent *reasonableness* of obligation, and hence on the inclusive and potentially public character of moral discourse. The emphasis on faith is a corrective both to Kantian interpretations of morality (which depict moral reason in abstract, ahistorical terms), and to postmodern critiques of objectivity (which maintain that, since Enlightenment reason is untenable, moral truth cannot be obtained). Yet, in my view, they do so at the unacceptable price of moral sectarianism. Like the biblically oriented communitarians who have more typically been Protestant, such theologians see the meaning established in Christian faith as objective but not visible without the light of faith.[71] Those who accentuate faith rather than the reasonableness of belief are more concerned with confirming divine transcendence as the object and cause of faith, than with developing the impact of a fideist *moral* epistemology on theological contributions to public discourse.[72] Interpretations of Christian ethics which rest objectivity of morals in a revelation to a particular faith community seem to preserve truth while escaping the attacks aimed at Kantian foundationalism.

To reject postmodernism because Christian revelation seems to depend on premises that are a priori incompatible with it; or to accept it because we hope a faith story of universality, ultimacy, and transcendence will save us from its consequences, does not satisfy me either as an ethicist or a feminist. It is no real solution to the truth question to locate truth and its criteria within the believing community in such a way that external or "objective" criteria become irrelevant to its own confidence in the message it bears forward out of its internally coherent traditions. This is not to say that *faith* in God can be justified or produced on rational grounds, but only that the *morality* that goes with Christian faith is intelligible on reasonable as well as on religious grounds. Affirming the self-sufficiency and final incommunicability *for ethics* of communal revelation is itself an essentially "postmodern" move, and as far as public moral discourse is concerned, has strongly relativist consequences.

If feminist ethics is to base social change on anything other than the acquisition of enough power to shove aside those who formerly monopolized it, we will have to rediscover or reinvent a reasonable account of knowledge and truth, and of the "universals" in human experience. This is what the "Catholic" (Aristotelian–Thomistic) ethical tradition is essentially about: a confidence that reasonable reflection on human experience can lead us not only to recognize and condemn injustice, but to persuade others that they can recognize and condemn it on more or less the same terms we do. To flee into dogmatic assertions as a refuge from postmodern indeterminacy has serious consequences for any natural law ethics, and "risks isolating the theological notion of reason from the wider intellectual conversation."[73]

Catholic ethicists, as well as the social encyclicals, typically work on the assumption that any two traditions with the occasion for conversation can have a meaningful exchange. When a matter of justice is at stake, criticism, argument, judgment, and action are required to transform specific situations toward objectively greater human well-being. As we have seen, this is precisely the way feminists and other liberation theologians approach "foreign" traditions and engage them in moral exchange toward political results.

Communitarian epistemological privilege fails because it is a start down the path of sectarianism. The community's ethical critique forfeits outside effectiveness and even intelligibility; and it weighs in in favor of a dominative approach to apologetics. What Christian feminism needs is not the reactionary fideism to which deconstructionist epistemology can lead, and which is already all too evident in defensive retreats into moral "tradition." What we require is a better account of moral *rationality* which takes particularity seriously without giving up on generalization.

The work of the Catholic fundamental theologian, David Tracy, is helpful in arriving at a model of intercultural ethics which assumes the possibility of communication without concealing its historical nature. Any text (or myth, event, work of art, or ritual) comes out of a particular tradition; but a classic text is one which has disclosive power beyond that tradition, an "excess of meaning" able permanently to address the great human questions in an indefinite succession of historical situations.[74] The theory of the classic goes beyond the theory of communicative action in a significant way, insofar as it presupposes, as indispensable to communication among traditions the *concrete* experiences, emotions, judgments, and virtues which are embedded in the narrative, visual or performative projections of a *specific* way of life (especially narrative, but also music, visual arts, dance, religious symbols, etc.).

Moreover, the concept of the "classic" envisions truly intercultural communication, not just the critical revision of one's own tradition; and it presupposes that a "classic" by definition has a reliable communicative or disclosive potential for any and every "foreign" culture as the culture of "other" *human* beings. The classic will never be definitively interpreted by any culture, but its ability to span cultures (always in and through particular, determinate expressions of culture) is never exhausted.

Tracy proposes "analogy" to capture the way in which conversation partners from different cultures, traditions, or experiences build bridges of empathy and understanding to one another. As noted above, analogical models of knowledge have a prominent history in the Aristotelian and Thomistic tradi- tions. Analogy affirms similarity in difference, and true knowing without reduction.[75] As Tracy cautions in *Dialogue with the Other*, we should be "suspicious of how easily claims to 'analogy' or 'similarity' can become subtle evasions of the other and the different."[76] Yet, though dignity in the family, adequate health care, a decent education, and fair gender roles in the public realm may not all amount to exactly the same thing in every culture, we *can* understand justice and injustice in different cultures by virtue of their resemblance-in-difference to our own experience.

Although Tracy seems to accept a postmodern situation for theology, he is in reality working toward an expanded definition of rationality.[77] He warns against "capitulating to foundation- alist [Kantian?] notions of rationality," but goes on to speak up for the "modest but real defense of reason" which he finds both in Hilary Putnam and in Bernard Lonergan, and which he even traces back to Aquinas.[78] The theologian must not be afraid to ask the "transcendental question" of "the nature of ultimate reality." But he or she can expect only "relatively adequate answers" judged by "ethical-political criteria," i.e., by their ability to transform.[79]

Tracy no doubt adopts the self-characterization "postmo- dern" because he wants to avoid the kind of foundationalism which is well-characterized by Thomas Guarino as centering on a true, unitary, and unchanging revelation which is but "grasped" historically and whose articulations always bear finitude as " 'scars'."[80] But Tracy should not finally be classified as a nonfoundationalist if by that is meant a relativist who deems judgments of objective truth impossible. The model he suggests, especially as exemplified in the classic, is not "relative" in the strong, deconstructionist sense. Tracy wants even more than Habermas's "non-repressed universal communication"; he wants "a universal conversation about the truth of reality and even Ultimate Reality," and he expects it to take place in a global conversation about human solidarity.[81]

Such a model of conversation would not back away from substantive goods, though it would exercise vast caution about naming the "natural order" of things, and would admit that truth is something persons, groups, and traditions come to know together. Yet it would assume in principle, and not merely hope for, meaningful and productive intercultural ethical exchanges which secure real results for human well-being. Given the crying injustices worldwide of poverty, war, hunger, neo-colonizing oppression of whole peoples, and of women among all peoples, we cannot afford to let intercultural debate be merely accidental or serendipitous, nor our agreements merely a matter of luck. The next chapter will investigate further the ways in which human embodiment and its common forms of socialization can serve as the beginning point of intercultural reflection on shared experiences, values, and norms.

CHAPTER 4

"The body" – in context

"The body" has come up for much attention in recent philosophical and theological work.[1] Just why is an interesting question. Surely it is not that the relevance of the body to moral judgment has never before been recognized. Thomas Aquinas and Roman Catholic moral theology have given, if anything, too much attention to the body in defining sexual and gender norms. Hence the frequent charges of "physicalism" leveled against both.[2] Indeed, ethics always has to do with the body in one way or another, for morality refers to human action. Most of the subdisciplines of ethics can be named according to the way they impinge on the human body – from sex and gender, to bioethics, to just war theory, and even to theories of economics, political organization, and government.

Current interest in the body seems to take one of two directions: affirmation of the body as constitutive of personhood or deconstruction of the body as produced by social discourse. Different as these two streams may seem, both flow from the Enlightenment, and their courses may not lie far apart. Both react against Enlightenment reason as universal and abstract; and against the modern scientific ideal of control over nature, including the body.[3] Those who insist that the body is the environment of the mind – that embodiedness is constitutive of human consciousness – are correcting a tendency to see thought in ahistorical, and morality in intellectualistic or voluntaristic, terms (for example, as rational self-direction, existential choice, or I–Thou intersubjectivity). For example, against such biases, Mark Johnson argues that we know our world only through embodied structures of understanding and imagination.[4]

This nondualist agenda regarding the body is conspicuous in theological writings on sex, since to dualism is attributed much Christian negativity about sex, traceable at least to Augustine and possibly to Paul. James Nelson and Sandra Longfellow define sexuality broadly as "who we are as bodyselves," and as involving "our minds, our feelings, our wills, our memories, indeed our self-understandings and powers as embodied persons." These theologians would not, however, agree to define the bodily meaning of sex in terms of procreation. The sexual body is for them above all a mediator of interpersonal consciousness and an avenue of the subject's fulfillment in intimacy. Sexual pleasure, enjoyed and shared, is the physical axis along which the meaning of sexual embodiment is primarily interpreted. Because of the ways in which procreation as a bodily dimension of sex has in the past been used to control sexual behavior, restrain and subordinate sexual pleasure, and restrict sexual identity, especially of women, the importance of procreation is downplayed. Religiously, embodied sexuality can be seen as "most fundamentally the divine invitation to find our destinies not in loneliness but in deep connection."[5] Clad in a new generational guise, then, these thinkers are heirs of the Cartesian premise that truth is discovered by looking inward, and of the Kantian dictum that morality consists in the perfectly good will with which one respects one's fellow agents. This stream bears forward the modern concern with interiority, consciousness, and the thinking, knowing, willing self.

A more historicist stream of thought about the body resists the assumption that the body or embodiedness are givens which set parameters within which consciousness, identity, and morality are defined. Similarly to Foucault, a second set of authors, often writing on gender and on sexual orientation, see the body as constructed by social consciousness. Joan L. Griscom concludes her critique of patriarchy by remarking, "As I contemplate the nature/history split ... it becomes clear that our history is inseparably part of our nature, our social structures are inseparably part of our biology."[6] Disputing that there are determinate lines dividing homosexuality and heterosexuality, Carter Heyward, citing Foucault, asserts that, "A historical reading of sexuality will move us beyond sexual essentialism as explanation of anything ... Understanding our sexualities historically involves understanding ourselves as people whose sexualities are in flux."[7] In a more direct way than authors who affirm the body as context of selfhood, authors like Griscom and Heyward privilege consciousness as defining the human reality. They would, though, be likely (with Foucault) to locate consciousness historically, and to see its effects in terms of shifting power relationships among persons, not in terms of unambiguous liberation from confining "traditions" and brute "nature." The historical deconstruction of embodiedness is "postmodern" in that it is a late manifestation of the modern concern to free critical reason from illegitimate authorities; like modernity, it is an attempt to reclaim (sexual) freedom and moral autonomy.

What is modern, then, in both these trajectories is that human intentionality (conscious or unconscious, individual or social) shapes, directs, uses to its own ends, the material substratum or aspect of human existence, including the body. What may be distinctively *post*modern in both is the recognition of freedom's limits and of its perverse potential to consolidate at those historical pressure points which permit opportunistic limitation of liberty by dominant power alliances. The medium of domination and constraint is the body. Examples are race mediated by colonization, reproduction mediated by the patriarchal family, and food consumption mediated by economic and social class. Interpretations of the body which are more truly opposite to these two developments than either is to the other are varieties of biological determinism: traditional sexual moralities which derive normative judgments from physical functions (to be addressed further in chapters 6 and 7), and sociobiology (to be addressed later in the present chapter).

Obviously, an Aristotelian or a Thomistic approach to ethics depends on some biological continuities. Yet to speak of bodies does not excuse us from the complexities of social interpretation. As Judith Butler, a strong critic of gender, plaintively confides, "I tried to discipline myself to stay on the subject, but found that I could not fix bodies as simple objects of thought."

Not only do bodies open out to worlds beyond, but movements back and forth between the body and its social world seem to be intrinsic to the meaning of body itself.[8] Hence to speak of the body means, on the one side, to stand up against moralities which take for granted a physical body which can "determine" social roles as norm and rule preceding them; and, on the other, to take up the question of social relationships (especially gender relationships) from the standpoint of human concreteness and presence. The project before us, then, is to achieve a theory of morality in which the body and culture are in reasonable balance.

In and through the most basic and widespread forms of our materiality, human beings have "common sense" access to the experience of other human individuals, as well as to a number of cross-cultural social relations, which derive from bodily needs and capacities. Fundamental to our embodiment is the fact that each person in his or her individuality is both body and the "more" which selfhood entails (intellect, will, emotions, "spirit," and relationality, especially to other embodied individuals). Similarly, society consists both in material conditions and in the cultural institutionalizations of materiality which give the society of members of our species its human quality. In society, physical life and instinctual mentation become "humanized." They are incorporated and sublimated into forms of association distinctive of the species precisely *as* knowing, choosing, feeling, and self-transcending. Human socialization of the body and its internal and other-directed capacities introduces a huge component of cultural variety.[9] In searching human social institutions for strands of common experience, we assuredly will encounter variation exceeding that of experiences drawn closer to the individual body. Yet the specificity and the relative stability of the human body make it a good place to begin moral and intercultural analysis. The human body provides the specific nexus around which social relations are built.

What is it that "the body" yields to our moral perspective? The recognizable "humanity" of the bodies of our species; the body's status as prerequisite of our species' intellectual, emotional, and spiritual distinctions; and the intrinsic social interdependence of human bodies as the foundation of social life: these all lead us toward nonrelative definitions of goods necessary to human flourishing, and of the virtues which social relations should realize. For instance, the basic needs of the human body for survival and the similarity in human experiences of deprivation or fulfillment of these needs ground moral notions such as equality, compassion, and rights. These needs also require that all societies will institutionalize the distribution of food and other resources; sex and reproduction; and education of children for future social roles.

There is, however, imperfect correspondence between the body and social relationships expressing human excellence. First, bodily needs and capacities, even universally similar ones, do not "demand" equally similar social recognition across cultures. Monogamy and polygamy as institutionalizations of heterosexuality are more disparate than the physical "fact" of sexual intercourse for reproduction. Second, physical inclinations of the human species (sexual desire or emotions like aggression and fear, for example) are not purely and simply oriented toward human goods, since goods exist concretely in complexes of needs and goods to be harmonized. Hence, the "humanization" of the species is a *task* of civilization, of morality, of religion. The human moral project (in Aristotelian–Thomistic terms) is to work upon, with, and out of, our innate bodily needs, capacities, and tendencies (whatever and however we may discover those to be) in order to achieve the virtuous and happy life for human persons.

ASPECTS OF BODILY EXISTENCE

In the preceding chapter, a couple of different renditions of the basic forms of human experience, individual and social, were provided by John Finnis and Martha Nussbaum. Rather than reducing common human experiences to a "thin" set of comprehensive categories, one might instead proliferate shared physical experiences and their social recognitions in as many directions as possible. The resulting list could display the complexity of embodied experience, and the broad, deep reserves of human potency for communication. We could say, for instance, that the following bodily experiences are shared by individuals in all the world's cultures: being "one in many," as mind or spirit and body, as bodily parts in a whole, and as qualified by identity and change over time;[10] sexual differentiation (male–female); sexuality; kinship, both vertical and lateral; birth; infancy; aging; eating; need for shelter; need for protective clothing; autonomous mobility; physical action upon the environment, physical skill; sensuality (five senses); pleasure and pain; communication (expressiveness and receptivity); emotions; mind-altering states of the body and bodily states caused by the mind; sleep and dreams; health and illness; inflicted injury, up to and including killing; death, being a corpse, decay.

These interlocking and overlapping items could be broken down and regrouped in other ways. To list the items does not settle their level of cultural ductility, their relative value, or their lines of interdependence. All demand socialization, and that fact produces both parallel institutions among cultures, and the tremendous diversity in the ways bodily realities are experienced within cultural institutions. Religious symbol systems build on common physical experiences but contribute to diversity of meaning as they encourage some bodily experiences and relations but sanction others.

The axes along which bodily experience is socialized are axes of social control, not necessarily as dominance, but as conferral of form and significance. For example, such an essential physical function as eating is highly subject to cultural elaboration of what is eaten; how it is prepared; and when, where, and with whom one eats. All of the above are subject to differentiation by age, gender, and class (for example, adults feed infants, women serve first and eat last; eating disorders afflict upper-class women disproportionately). Virtually all religions ritualize eating or the sacrifice of food as mediating divine presence. Christianity's central ritual is a sacrificial meal in which the elements are symbolic; Christians also give religious meaning to fasting, feasting, and feeding the poor.

Pleasure and pain, certainly elemental experiences, are

subject to a very wide range of social meanings: leisure and relaxation, often in a social context where physical pleasure is cultivated in company (eating, drinking, sports, arts, dancing, drugs, sex); punishment and torture; competition and endurance for sport or test. Religious traditions, including Christianity, give special meaning to pleasure as sin, but also as religious experience, as in the bodily ecstasies of mystics. Pain can be interpreted as a sign of divine wrath, tutelage, or even favor (stigmata), and can be cultivated as part of an ascetic discipline conducive to experience of the divine.

An ordinary but little examined bodily capacity, such as autonomous mobility, also gives rise to important realms of social significance which appear cross-culturally and are subject to recurrent religious elaborations. At the social level, the ability of the body to initiate movement grounds delimitation of home or of familiar territory; adventure, discovery or conquest; personal aversion to and political use of imprisonment, capture, and slavery; and race, class, or gender constraints on movement. Religiously, the body's aptitude for motion gives rise to cultural variations on the themes of journey (to discover or announce religious insights), pilgrimage, imprisonment for religious beliefs, "liberation" as a metaphor for salvation.

BODY, SOCIETY, AND SOCIAL CRITIQUE

In studying, from an ethical perspective, the trilateral relation of body, personhood, and social institutions, there are three fundamental moments. An ethics of sex and gender must pass through these three. The first is to recognize *the human body*, which, as such and in its physiology, is relatively invariant over space and time, despite periodic and geographical adaptations (such as race and other genetic fluctuations) and cultural interpretation. Examples would be differentiation of the human race into two sexes (not as clearly demarcated, perhaps, as we once would have thought); male–female sexual union to produce children; birth; and infancy.

The second is to note that certain *cultural institutions* engage and give form to persons' bodily experience. Some are virtually universal, though varied in form. Examples from the sex and gender sphere are regulation of sexual relations, through marriage and the incest taboo; parenthood, or the regulation of progenitors' responsibility for children, also primarily through marriage; kinship, or the social recognition of intergenerational biological connection, augmented by marriages which unite kin networks; and gender, or the institutionalized expectation that men and women will be differentiated and will cooperate socially by fulfilling distinct roles, minimally in reproduction, roles which are almost always elaborated patriarchally.

The third moment is to take a *critical and normative stance*. This means, first, to question whether the cross-cultural social relations which have been realized historically are in fact implied by the human body (the person as embodied), or by embodied individuals who begin, survive, and flourish socially. Second, it means questioning the degree to which actual institutions enhance or inhibit human flourishing and to envision preferable alternatives. Four social relations which recently have been subject to particular controversy because of reformist (including feminist) demurrers are gender, monogamy, sex orientation, and family. These categories are obviously interlaced, an assumption or counterassertion in one having ramifications in the others.

This chapter thus far has been primarily devoted to the first two moments. It has been concerned to re-establish the body's stability in response to the proposition that cultural institutions have a major role in defining what we think of as "our bodies." The latter insight is important and true but does not obviate the need to investigate the commonalities of human experience furnished by the irreducibility of our bodily existence. In moving to the third moment – critique of specific institutionalizations of the sexually differentiated body – we will continue to examine the ways bodiliness and consciousness can be played off against each other. Where appropriate, we will attempt to redress imbalance of these poles.

The critical question about *gender* is the question whether bodily differentiation of reproductive function, as male and female, is either so clear and certain as supposed, or so indicative of social roles extending beyond conception, pregnancy, and birth. The question about *monogamy*, at least as currently posed by evolutionary biology, is whether the channeling of sexual relations and of parental responsibilities into stable male–female social units is supported or undermined by an evolutionary process driven more by "genetic success" than by interpersonal commitment. The question about *sex orientation* is about the exclusive role or interplay of biological and social factors in setting the object of one's sexual desire; and whether reproduction and sexual desire/pleasure tend to be "natural" complements in humans as in most other mammals, or are normatively separable in human culture, due to the distinctive humanness of our capacities for reflection, emotion, and choice. The idea that sexual intimacy and procreation are fundamentally separable rather than fundamentally interdependent has helped make the moral defense of homosexuality possible. The validity of this idea must be considered in view of its implications for the meaning of human sex in general, including its placement within marriage as institution.

The question about *family* involves the relative importance and possible interdependence of intentional commitment and biological kinship in forming families. "Nontraditional" families, including homosexual unions, single parent families (usually headed by women), and blended families created by remarriage after divorce, are increasingly prevalent. They prompt consideration of whether biological parenthood creates or should create a lasting social commitment to one's children, and, conversely, whether a biological basis is really necessary for family or parental love and commitment. To an extent, this question has always been around in the form of adoption. But modern reproductive contracts, often involving infertility technologies which ally as biological co-parents persons who have no intention to share social parenthood or marriage, make the question even more urgent and pointed.

In order better to understand the nature of human experience (and hence of common ground) in the areas of sex and gender, we will consider in turn some aspects of the body and gender, the body and monogamy, the body and sexual orientation, and the body and family. (Greater attention from a specifically Christian ethical perspective shall be given to all these topics in following chapters.) Critical discussions of gender tend to emphasize the social determination of the body, while the implicit sociobiological challenge to mono-gamy derives from the premise that genetic characteristics determine social behavior. Debates about sexual orientation often put both the bodily and the social aspects of sexual experience under question, asking whether sexual orientation is itself biological or psychosocial in origin; and asking whether human sex is primarily for biological reproduction, personal expression, or social ends. In much literature on homosexuality, the issue of freedom is particularly acute, both as freedom from social condemnation and constraint, and freedom for the construction of one's own sexual identity. On the family, virtually all modern authors see culture and choice as taking precedence over "merely" biological rela-tions. But they differ on the extent to which the latter should still remain significant in defining the family and its moral relationships.

THE BODY AND GENDER

Although not absolutely beyond dispute by radical thinkers, cross-cultural differentiation of the human body into the male and female sexes which cooperate for reproduction will here be assumed. What must be granted at the same time is that sexual dimorphism need not provide the basic category for organizing human persons into social relations, and especially not for establishing social hierarchies.[11] If we can acknowledge male–female reproductive function as a cross-cultural universal, we must still ask whether the physiological reproductive coopera-tion of the sexes necessarily establishes social roles. Much feminist social criticism depends on the proposition that mascu-line and feminine gender need not follow from male and female sex, and in fact is no more than a socially constructed mechanism for ensuring male power. Gender should be dis-mantled, some argue, while equal and parallel participation of women and men in both public roles and domestic ones should be established.

Susan Bordo points out that the gradual acceptance in the 1980s of academic feminists and of women into the professions (in the West) has helped to produce this emphasis. Aspiring to the "male" model of academic and professional behavior prerequisite to career success, such women sense danger in "otherness," and in any distinctively "female" ways of knowing, thinking, or behaving. In the institutional contexts into which they have been integrated, "relational, holistic, and nurturant attitudes continue to be marked as flabby, feminine, and soft . . . We need instead to establish our leanness, our critical incisiveness, our proficiency at clear and distinct dissection."[12] Such a situation leads to a distancing from parental and domestic roles in which the former qualities are an asset. Their appropriateness to women's "nature" threatens (and in the past has functioned) to keep women in "their place." Susan Moller Okin illustrates this development:

A just future would be one without gender. In its social structures and practices, one's sex would have no more relevance than one's eye color or the length of one's toes. No assumptions would be made about "male" and "female" roles; childbearing would be so conceptually separated from child rearing and other family responsibilities that it would be a cause for surprise, and no little concern, if men and women were not equally responsible for domestic life or if children were to spend much more time with one parent than the other. It would be a future in which men and women participated in more or less equal numbers in every sphere of life.[13]

A similar prophetic ideal seems to motivate the work of *psychological theorists* who argue that few cross-cultural cognitive and emotional differences between men and women can be substantiated,[14] or that the patriarchally structured mothering relation perpetuates an alienation of sons from mothers which could be overcome if men and women shared equally in parenting infants;[15] in that of *feminist anthropologists* who strive to show that while patriarchy is virtually universal, it is based in cultural systems which are neither invariant nor inevitable;[16] and in that of anthropologists[17] and *historians*[18] who try either to uncover the existence of egalitarian societies or to identify a series of events or practices by which patriarchy came into existence, in order to show that nonpatriarchal organization of sex is possible. What all these have in common is the dissociation of hierarchized gender from biological reproductive function; many also reduce gender itself to as minimal and socially marginal an existence as possible. While a gender-neutral feminist theory of virtue had been represented by Mary Wollstonecraft, against Rousseau, in 1792 (*A Vindication of the Rights of Women*), the loosening of gender from women's bodily distinctiveness has become widespread as twentieth-century women gain access to traditionally male roles.

Others, though, sustain the interest of an earlier generation of feminists to elucidate a distinctively female, even "maternal," way of being in the world. Examples – to different extents and in different ways – are Carol Gilligan, Nell Noddings, Adrienne Rich, Sara Ruddick, Mary O'Brien, Luce Irigaray, and Mary Daly.[19] Experiencing themselves as outsiders to the dominant male discourse of politics, professionalism, and the academy, some nineteenth- and early twentieth-century feminists also associated gender difference with sex differences, even advocating separate or superior forms of women's virtue. Women's special moral assets, especially altruism, were interpreted in terms akin to their domestic and maternal contributions, and were contrasted to the competition, violence, and self-interest of which the world of men was accused. Such views are represented in the writings of Elizabeth Cady Stanton, Catherine Beecher, and Charlotte Perkins Gilman (*Herland*).[20]

The issue for contemporary feminists is whether, in a non-dualist perspective, the differential embodiment of men and women must be assumed to make a difference in their way of being in the world, even if not a difference which implies hierarchy, or even very extensive or firmly demarcated role allocation. The hypothesis that male or female embodiment does make some difference in one's identity and view of the opposite sex is reflected in competing theories about whether it is man's natural physical superiority – symbolized by the penis of which woman is supposedly envious – or his envy of woman's power to give birth and his own uncertainty about paternity which give rise to male domination of women in the first place.[21] Surely women's diffuse and receptive sexuality, cyclic reproductive capacity, and deeply connective relation to their children both born and unborn, contribute to women's sense of self. Women's embodied experience could not be identical to that afforded by men's sharply focused but uneasily controlled sexual response, perennial but momentaneous capacity to impregnate; the necessity to do so by means of an externally borne and hence vulnerable member; and a man's need to work out a social relation to his children without the easy and ready support of natural bodily relations (pregnancy and lactation) which place their mutual consciousness within the context of primal need fulfillment. Part of the point of feminism is that one's sense of self and relation to others does not or should not reside solely in one's sexual and reproductive experience. But to the extent that such experience is one component of one's self and one's social relations, gender infuses these realities along with many other factors.[22]

Decrying the exclusion of women's embodied experience from the social construction of the world, some feminists represent the female body as engendering its own, socially disruptive discourse. They claim that the language that we have used to describe the body, to relay its functions and capacities into social space, and to identify personhood – our own and that of others – as "embodied," has been intransigently, onerously, and now unacceptably, rendered from the male point of view. Human language of the body, and in fact of all (gendered) social relations treats male embodiment and male sociality as either the "norm" for all humans, or as the singular and exclusive form of humanity whose predominance renders the female "other," invisible, or defective. French feminist theory features *l'ecriture feminine*, women "writing from the body," devising new linguistic representations of women's experience as specifically embodied, to disclose that which has remained silenced and unnoticed between the lines of men's writing, men's language and men's world.[23]

This linguistic adventure brings into full confrontation the historical mediation and the material facticity of the human experience of "body." After all, theirs is a seemingly paradoxical enterprise: to write of some authentic and even presymbolic feminine experience from a body which has been mediated in "phallogocentric" terms, and with language tools honed originally with the erasure of that experience in mind. One wonders, having taken Foucault seriously if not finally, what sense it makes to talk of a "feminine" body and its "writing," as though women, embodied as women, have experience that is the same "feminine" (and not just biologically female) experience. The answer, perhaps, is that "writing the (feminine) body" is above all else a declaration of independence from generalizations about the body which do not apply to women, and hence of women's *specificity* – of particular women's determination to write, speak, resymbolize the world, from the specific space, time, and personal history of each.[24] The tangibility and "hereness" of one's physical presence, when brought to the center of consciousness, force recognition of a self not assimilable to the reality of different selves, especially selves who promote their own embodiment as universal (however true it may be that selves share realities in common).

For feminists who weight mind–body nondualism toward the social relations which produce what we think of as our "physical" experience, it is still a contentious question how far the "social construction" of the body can realistically be taken. Even Judith Butler, who has spearheaded the attack on gender, concedes that "bodies live and die; eat and sleep; feel pain, pleasure; endure illness and violence," and that these are "facts" which "cannot be dismissed as mere construction."[25] She goes on though to warn that the "irrefutability" of these facts "in no way implies" what it might mean to affirm them in practice. In no way? Such realities surely do fail to dictate at the most specific level what loves and pleasures are to be sought, which deaths, pains, and violences are to be avoided; or under what conditions we should prefer health to food or sleep to pleasure. It is indeed true that not only the content of such priorities, but even the definitions of their constituent terms (love, pleasure, pain), are highly subject to cultural resolution.

And one must agree when Butler says of "sex," that to grant its facticity or its materiality ("as sexually differentiated parts, activities, capacities, hormonal and chromosomal differences") is always to assert it in some *version*.[26] But if sex (or femaleness) is versicolor, pluriform, and in some ways unique to each individual – does that mean it is infinitely malleable? Or that a reliable and lasting sense of the moral relations among sexual (or male and female) bodies must forever elude us? Or that such a sense must be irrelevant to ways in which we might actually behave? I think not.

Undoubtedly gender has been illegitimately exaggerated in its significance for roles which are neither sexual nor reproductive. This has happened specifically to maintain role-constraints (for both males and females) which sustain social hierarchy. But Susan Bordo is right that gender is at least as structuring of identity and consciousness as is race, and should not become the quick casualty of an overly zealous politics of equality-as-sameness. Women's sexual and, more so, reproductive experiences have not only set them apart from men, but have bound women together historically. Why are we so willing to deconstruct them now?[27]

Another Rwandan vignette: The setting is Lake Kivu, near the border of Zaire, in a garden with "a large cactus and a mango tree." A woman in late middle age, head and shoulders swathed in traditional patterned scarves, mouth in determined, downcurved half-smile, kneels on the ground. She bends forward to reach sinewy arms across a younger woman, curled in the posture of sleep; she puts her hands around a baby, tiny fists waving before its face. The caption reads, "A Rwandan woman carried a baby yesterday away from its dead mother." The younger woman is among thirty-five people killed by mortar blasts as they rested in flight from rebel fire. The older woman, quite possibly a stranger, leans through the horrors of war to rescue another's maternity from obliteration, to respond to infancy's sheer need.[28]

Women, of course, experience motherhood in numberless circumstances of fulfillment and deprivation, freedom and coercion, hope and desperation, reward and disappointment.[29]

Yet just as the Rwandan savior rises out of pitiless material circumstances to honor the bonds among women and their children, Adrienne Rich can cry forth, from a spiritually suffocating domesticity, of her painful, ineradicable, redeeming tie to her sons. "*I love them.* But it is in the enormity and inevitability of this love that the sufferings lie."[30] Rich was to rebel against the expectation that mothers ought to love "unconditionally," at every single moment and without further identity; as well as against other patriarchal trappings of institutionalized motherhood; against marriage; and finally against heterosexuality. But she invests intrinsic social power in women's biological capacity for motherhood,[31] a power which unites mother and child "by the most mundane and the most invisible strands"; unites mother and mother, as "we" are "flooded with feelings both of love and violence," even with murderous rage toward our own children; unites women in their peculiar sins of powerlessness turned against the less powerful child; and provokes in men an "ancient, continuing, envy, awe, and dread."[32]

To argue for motherhood as a distinctive experience of women is not to argue that women are defined only or primarily by motherhood; that authentic mothering has to begin with genes and pregnancy (not adoption); that women who are not literally mothers cannot be fulfilled; or that men's fulfillment does not integrally involve sharing parenthood with women. Paternity, if different in texture, should still be as strong a component of male sociability as motherhood is for women. For neither should parenthood mean ownership or control, but rather for both care-filled connection to and responsibility for mate and child.

In some cultures, for instance in Africa, motherhood can be a greater source of independent power for women than it has been in the industrialized nations. Adrienne Rich's recollections choke with "the turmoil of the elevator full of small children, babies howling in the laundromat, the apartment in winter where pent-up seven- and eight-year-olds have one adult to look to ..."[33] But Mercy Amba Oduyoye, a Ghananian and an Akan, can say, "Motherhood has not made my mother poor.

My mother is rich. She has a community of people whose joys and sorrows are hers. I am rich because I have this community and hold a special place in it. I am not a mother but I have children."[34] Oduyoye does not romanticize motherhood in Africa – where women's lack of control over marriage, polygamous marriage, pressure to bear children for status, need for purification after childbirth, oppressive mourning customs for widows, and male control over land and property can still make motherhood onerous.[35] But motherhood in her culture is an open and broadly familial undertaking, generally empowering for those who achieve it, often combined with traditional women's economic activities, and certainly not enclosed in the hot-house of intimacy represented by the Western nuclear family. A Nigerian, Rosemary Edet, while not viewing rituals for women uncritically, can still say that "[t]he mystery of giving birth is the woman's discovery that she is on that plane of life which amounts to a religious experience untranslatable in terms of masculine experience," and that the "maternal symbols" which appear in childbirth rituals are those "of primordial totality, of universal harmony, of the vital source of happiness."[36]

Insofar as it is a relation to one's children, motherhood is in many cultures, and perhaps universally, an avenue of fulfillment and flourishing for women – as fatherhood should be for men – though patriarchal control over motherhood and economic deprivation as a condition of it are most certainly not. Gender understood as a moral project entails the social humanization of biological tendencies, capacities, and differences, including the social ties that they, by their very nature, are inclined to create. Biological sex differences and male and female parenthood – both the sexual cooperation it necessitates and the social partnership it sponsors – are more opportunity than limit. They provide a ground and content for the human virtues of love, commitment, respect, equality, and the building of social unity toward the common good. It is true enough that they can be perverted by domination, infidelity, objectification of fellow humanity, and division not only of the sexes, but of families, clans, and races. The feminist critique of gender, often focused on motherhood as constraint and delusion, envisions this possibility all too clearly. But if human physicality is to be fully integrated with reflection, emotions, choice, and social relations, then the mutuality and equality of men and women must be carved out partly in relation to those very qualities by which we distinguish those two human constituencies.

BODY AND MONOGAMY

Monogamy has long been institutionalized in Western cultures as best protecting the welfare of women, and as stabilizing mother and father in responsibility for their children. The Hebrew Scriptures permit divorce and concubinage, but hold marital faithfulness to be ideal (Mal. 2:14–16); the New Testament interprets the "one flesh" unity of Genesis 2:24 in monogamous terms, and enjoins spousal fidelity (Matt. 19:3–8; Mark 10:2–9). In the twelfth century, indissoluble marriage as a Church requirement of marriage overtook in practice the custom of dissolving marriages to enter politically or economically more advantageous unions.[37] Thomas Aquinas defended monogamy as more naturally just than either polygamy or childbearing by unmarried women, because the former ensures the ongoing support of children by fathers and protects women whose beauty and fertility have disappeared.[38]

In modern times, monogamy is praised as appropriate to the interpersonal union and commitment of spouses. Paul Ricoeur places a "wager" on monogamy as our best chance for tenderness in sexuality and for the duration of an intimate sexual bond.[39] Psychologist Sidney Callahan believes only a pair of "bonded mates working full-time for their mutually shared progeny" can produce the "concerted care and parental altruism" children require. Moreover, "the most intense and complete psychosocial bonding, attachments, and intimacy are made possible by pair-bonding."[40]

Despite the idealization of monogamy, however, it is far from the exclusive form of marriage worldwide. In Africa, polygamy is common, while in Asia, concubinage, sometimes with legal recognition and protection for "second wives," is still widely accepted. In Western countries nonmarital cohabitation, adultery, illegitimate births, and free divorce and remarriage, permit loosely regulated, and hence socially disruptive, forms of polygamy and serial monogamy to continue and increase. Many Christian commentators are alarmed and call for social reforms.[41] But the discrepancy between ideal and reality has led some evolutionary biologists, evolutionary psychologists, and sociobiologists to theorize that human beings are just not cut out genetically for the unique and intimate pairings that Western cultural and religious traditions extol. The tacit moral argument implied by some of this research, as well as its popularity, is communicated by a cover of *Time* magazine (August 15, 1994), which pictured a broken wedding band, and blared, "Infidelity: It may be in our genes."

Donald Symons, Robert Wright, and others, maintain that human males and females, like other animal species, diverge in their reproductive strategies and behaviors.[42] It takes a much greater investment for a female mammal than a male to produce surviving young, since she can bear few at a time, must devote considerable physical energies to pregnancy, and will ordinarily nurse her babies for some time thereafter. Thus she must be choosy about the assets of any male she allows to impregnate her. He will have to win that privilege by a display of strength, of his general fitness as a genetic contributor, and of his possible willingness to contribute to family maintenance. Males, on the other hand, invest a trivial amount of time and energy in each conception, biologically speaking, and so it is to their evolutionary advantage to spread their sperm around.

Sexual selection favors male ability to be aroused at the mere sight of a female, especially a new or young female. Young, attractive females are universal symbols of male status. Excellence in hunting and fighting are forms of competition for females and lead to control over them.[43] Thus natural selection also favors "calculated risk-taking in male–male competition, hence the evolution of large body size, strength, pugnacity, playfighting, weapons, color, ornament, and sexual salesmanship, which often are interrelated in that displays can function both to attract females and to intimidate other males."[44] Males tend to be polygynous and promiscuous, but experience intense sexual jealousy of mates or potential mates, whose time they do not want tied up with competitors' reproductive investments, and of whose offspring they desire certain paternity.

A female's reproductive success would, on the contrary, be "seriously compromised by the propensity to be sexually aroused by the sight of males," or by an inclination to accept the first offer.[45] Females' reproductive advantage lies, not in mating as often as possible, but in provoking male competition for their precious reproductive resources. They are not interested in casual sex, care little about sexual variety, are not prone to sexual violence, and see a long-term acquaintance with a male's individual characteristics ("intimacy") as assurance of his reproductive fitness and cooperation toward ensuring the survival of young.[46] Females need males to provide stable protection and resources.

Yet, despite their innate sexual differences – differences with marked gender implications according to the sociobiological account – males and females both "compromise" in order to gain the reproductive relationships they seek. Donald Symons thus turns to homosexual behavior, both male and female, as a magnifier of the sexes' sexual proclivities. He notes, for instance, the absence of any market for lesbian pornography. But, on the other side, and not to put too fine a point on it, "heterosexual men would be as likely as homosexual men to have sex most often with strangers, to participate in anonymous orgies in public baths, and to stop off in public restrooms for five minutes of fellatio on the way home from work if women were interested in these activities. But women are not interested."[47] I should say not.

Note, however, that some feminist evolutionary biologists have countered with claims that females of other species, including primates, can be aggressive, competitive, and non-monogamous too. Sarah Hrdy calls the activity of female primates in seeking out a variety of males for copulation exceeding that necessary for fertilization a "vast category of behaviors" which has been "ignored by evolutionary theorists." Such behavior could offer females evolutionary advantages, such as extracting male investment in or tolerance for infants who are not genetically related to them.[48] One could also see assets for females in other tendencies which sociobiologists dissociate from their nature, such as periodic switching to younger, more fit mates, or living cooperatively in groups rather than in a long-term liaison with one male. The identification of male promiscuity and female fidelity to mate and young as the "best evolutionary strategy" seems to confer on these roles a normative status encouraging social acceptance if not exactly moral defense. But these behaviors may not be as nearly universal in animals as some theorists would like us to believe; nor is it self-evident that humans will naturally behave in parallel ways. Moreover, to the extent that humans do have similar tendencies, that fact should be viewed more as the simple *de facto* legacy of our history as a species, than as a clearly superior "strategy" of adaptation.

Another dimension of our animal inheritance, which tends to get sidelined in the gamy high-color portrait of male sexual abandon, is that neither competition nor conquest are merely sexual – a matter of the most handsome plumage feathering the most nests. In fact, the sexual and biological kinship relations that humans institutionalize as family function for both animals and humans as pervasive and consistent lines between the in-group and the out-group, and between those with higher and lower status in the kin group itself, whether pack, herd, troop, tribe, or clan. First of all, as both Reinhold Niebuhr's concept of "collective egoism" and the theory of "kin altruism" recognize, individuals sublimate their own interests to those of the group, then take virtually any form of aggression toward outsiders as warranted in defence or promotion of group interests. Racist and nationalist pride or hatred are elaborations of this tendency. As this chapter's final section on the family will indicate, and the fifth chapter will further expose, the patriarchal family is a social means of defining and furthering group interests. Within the family, men maintain dominance over women, and adults often do over children, by means of group classifications as well as by overt threat or use of violence. Moral evil, in religious terms "sin," is precisely the reversion to animal survival behavior unintegrated with the human virtues which have empathy as their ground. Domination in animals is natural; in humans, it is wrong.

Yet the fact that both men and women often fail to integrate their biological urges with their distinctively human capacities for love, commitment, fidelity, and compassion is no indicator that biologically driven behavior is more "natural" to humans than behavior which reflects their unique capacities for reflection, choice, commitment, and respect for the needs of others as worth one's own consideration. Sex and reproduction are more than simple "biological" matters for either sex. Sociobiologists' analysis of our evolutionary past and present is in some ways true and in others ludicrous. There is both tragedy and humor in the prospect that either men or women would act as puppets of supposedly innate drives: men as inseminating Lotharios or women as coy gold-diggers half their mate's age. In real life, the stuff of paperback romances and TV sitcoms is generally modified by more than the unfortunate necessity to compromise with the opposite sex's agenda, or by the rational planning of routes to satisfaction of sexual self-interest. In both males and females, biologically based interests related to sex are also related to, and ideally subsumed by, our needs and capacities for affective and emotional intimacy and stability, as well as for a social life which enhances such bonds.

The philosopher Mary Midgley once wrote wisely that humanity's moral achievements are realized within – not beyond – the cluster of structural and emotional tendencies which give us continuity with other animal species.[49] Our biological inheritance furnishes us both with tendencies to selfishness (self-interest) and the capacities for empathy and altruism. Culture and morality build upon and channel the assets and liabilities that nature provides.[50]

From an evolutionary standpoint, survival advantages accrue from symbiotic exchanges of care among close kin, within larger groups, and even among nonrelated groups.[51] And it is worthwhile – more "fulfilling" – to humans, male and female, to behave sexually in ways which produce such relationships. One study found that even male homosexuals were happier when they were "close-coupled," i.e., living in a "quasi marriage." Such men did less cruising, spent more time at home, maintained higher levels of affection for their partner, had higher levels of sexual activity but fewer sexual problems, and less regretted their homosexuality, than did the typical homosexual male respondent. The researchers characterize them as enjoying "superior adjustment."[52]

Often enough, human affairs are governed by self-interest and fear of outsiders, perhaps rooted in an ancient biological substratum of our instinctual and emotional life. When integration fails, especially in sex and family, it is usually to the disadvantage of women, who are bested by the physical strength of men, their propensity to violence, and their relatively small interest in the ongoing welfare of their young. Yet in trying to reduce the social disasters that accompany such scenarios, we have a genuinely *human* ideal to which we can and do appeal. Human beings are not *only* interested in genetic self-perpetuation, or in maximizing their sexual and reproductive opportunities. They care about the establishment of long-term interpersonal relationships, especially to mate, children, and family members.[53]

Moreover, humans aspire to altruism and care for reasons beyond either kin success or personal reward. It is a mark of distinctively human excellence – and happiness – to recognize that potential sexual partners are beings like unto oneself with whom to establish interpersonal and social reciprocity for the sake of the other's intrinsic value and welfare, not for one's own advantage only. The ability to extend respect and care beyond the sphere of those whom we can expect to reciprocate is itself qualitatively human.[54] Unlike animals, humans can recognize competing desires in themselves or interests among self and others, interpret ambivalent situations from the perspectives of all the affected parties, and reduce conflict in practice by implementing compromises and envisioning alternatives.[55] Chapter 5 will show that Christianity, in its moral dimension, symbolizes, gives transcendent validation to, and educates for, empathy and altruism toward "outsiders," especially those occupying lower status ranks and suffering deprivation of the basic necessities of life as a consequence. It is these abilities which the New Testament ideals of compassion, mercy, forgiveness, and service aim to elaborate and empower (Matt. 5–7).

The big issue which the evolutionist or sociobiological approach to human behavior engages is the relation between humanity's embodiment, as introducing a strongly biological component into the parameters of our moral sentiments and capacities; and human morality, which calls for self-transcendence and the integration of capacities shared to an extent with other animals into the realms of existence which distinguish our own species. Sociobiology offers to theological ethics a stronger appreciation of the fact that both sin and virtue are conditioned by our embodiment, and not only by our freedom of will. Sociobiology can tempt those who see moral convictions as religious dogma, evanescent intuitions or cultural ideologies to abandon moral critique for a "scientific" resignation to our genetically programmed social destiny. Some sociobiologists see moral duty as the denial of true nature and natural desires: "We are potentially moral animals – which is more than any other animal can say – but we are not naturally moral animals. The first step to being moral is to realize how thoroughly we aren't."[56]

But to refer back to genetic development as a base of our capacities does nothing to undermine their moral character.[57] Their rootedness in our embodiment neither requires nor guarantees that any one capacity will in reality govern the integration of our multiple bodily, personal, and social potentials. The human capacity is to order, shape, prioritize, and encourage certain dispositions over others. Morality consists in making choices and deliberately establishing practices which resist dominance and keep the needs of all in perspective.

In an Aristotelian–Thomistic perspective on human flourishing, a complex array of needs and capacities innate to our embodied existence grounds the moral perspective and even accounts for the fundamental ordering of our moral obligations.[58] And there is no avoiding the fact that the variety of human needs and tendencies may include internal tensions, especially between distinctively human needs and capacities (those aspects of human flourishing which we most prize) and the biosocial working material with which evolution has provided us. The potential for *intrinsic* conflict among human needs and goods has been underrecognized in a tradition which, while tending now perhaps to reduce the claim of "higher" goods in view of the biological counterpull, has in the past dismissed biological tendencies as "sinful" and hence as not worthy of inclusion in a full conception of human nature.

It is neither true that what biological drives suggest, moral expectations must accept; nor that every bodily tendency which must be rearranged, sublimated, or even curtailed to accomplish moral excellence is an outlaw to humanity's true nature. Martha Nussbaum recognizes this when she says that the capabilities which define human functioning "may in principle conflict with one another as well as offering one another cooperation and mutual support." Care for our own and for other species, care for ourselves and for those close to us, may not always coexist harmoniously.[59]

Ethicists, Christian and humanistic, may need to acknowledge ambiguity and a certain "incoherence" to human life as embodied. Tension among the constitutive components of our nature gives morality and culture the character of a *project of integration*, rather than of a *call to authenticity* to our "real" or "true" nature. The evolutionary struggle for genetic success must be integrated with the humanizing qualities of monogamy; kin preference must be integrated with disinterested compassion and altruism, responsive to need as well as to advantage; and aggression, dominance and territoriality, while retaining in some arenas a valid function, must be reigned in by a broader concern for "the brotherhood of man," the "full humanity of women," the unity of peoples, or the "universal common good" (in the phrase of recent social encyclicals).

BODY AND SEXUAL ORIENTATION

The notion that people have an intrinsic sexual "orientation" is a fairly recent development. Whether accepting of same-sex genital behavior (ancient Greece and Rome) or not (ancient Israel), our forebears for centuries did not relate sexual preferences to any innate and constitutive type of sexual desire or drive, or see homosexual and heterosexual preference as mutually opposed, invariant, or unchangeable. The world's cultures and religions have often established a place for persons of unorthodox or ambiguous sex or gender identity alongside the institutionalization of heterosexual marriage.[60] It has been argued that overt homosexuality was accepted to a much greater extent in the Christian West through the middle ages than has generally been appreciated.[61] Even among those whose intense emotional attachments to members of the same sex are unlikely to have been consummated sexually, it is quite likely that homoerotic feelings are reflected in surviving correspondence, employing physical imagery of endearment, unity, and devotion. Examples can be found in the medieval monasteries (St. Bernard) and among the last century's American suffragists (Susan B. Anthony).[62]

It was not until the nineteenth century that European and American writers tried to develop a more precise nomenclature to describe types of homosexuality, and particularly to distinguish people who were so inclined exclusively from those who experienced alternating attraction to women and men.[63] Alfred Kinsey and his collaborators made a breakthrough in 1948 by arranging sexual object-choice on a seven-point bi-polar scale.[64] The genius of the Kinsey scale was as much political as scientific.[65] Its spectrum taught homosexuals that their "abnormal" behavior was well-represented in the population, while reasssuring heterosexuals that one homosexual experience was not enough to launch them from one end of the scale to the other.

At the same time, despite Kinsey's repudiation of dichotomies, his organization of sexual identity in relation to two opposite alternatives enhanced the impression that most people leaned innately toward one end or the other. This in turn led to the growing perception that moral condemnation of homosexuality was highly unlikely to effect anyone's sexual reversal. In 1974, the American Psychiatric Association took homosexuality off its list of mental disorders, reinforcing the liberalizing tendency of social scientific research into homosexuality's causes and characteristics.

More recent studies indicate a possible linkage of homosexual orientation, especially in men, to biological factors, especially genetic and hormonal. The discovery of biological factors would reinforce the understanding of sexual orientation as an innate condition, not susceptible to individual choice or re-education, and would further marginalize the notion that individuals are morally responsible for its basic direction. Confirmatory research includes investigation of primate parallels; studies of families with a higher incidence of homosexuality than in the general population, especially among identical twin brothers; studies of the sexual dimorphism of the human brain; and studies of the effects of hormonal abnormalities on psychosexual development.[66] Such research, like that of Kinsey, seems to warrant acceptance of what is, after all, a "natural" and irresistable inclination for some people.

But this resort to the deep psychological and even physiological fixation of psychosexual identity has not been welcomed in all quarters of the research community or the gay activist community.[67] First of all, reminiscent of Foucault, some argue that a cultural focus on sexual classification exaggerates the importance of sexual orientation for determining one's personal identity and social roles, and especially for determining how one is perceived by the social group. Secondly, an essentially bipolar differentiation obscures what is actually great similarity in the sexual behavior of gays and straights, as well as diversity within both categories. More importantly it hides the possibility that sexual attractions and self-identification can be ambiguous or fluctuate over a lifetime, especially for lesbians, and can include bisexuality. Thirdly, some, notably politically active lesbians, want their sexual identity to be understood as a moral and political choice and act, effective for the transformation of gender and sexual stereotypes – not a biological aberration or determination which permits heterosexuality to stand unchallenged in its own right.[68]

One author who objects strongly to the biologization of the

gay identity describes Kinsey and his heirs as acting with "misguided compassion ... to prove that homosexuals are born, however imperfectly, not made." In this man's experience, had there not been a political "idea of the 'gay identity' and a 'gay community' to foster it, most of us who have done so would lack the words, the occasions, the courage to make public disclosures of our homosexuality and, for many of us, to make it the core of our professional and scholarly endeavor."[69]

For political lesbians the "humanizing" socialization which lends sex its moral character, and assumes in sex a certain degree of plasticity, demands a movement away from patriarchal marriage. The option to identify socially, emotionally, and sexually with other women does not hang merely on claiming an "innate" sexual attraction to women (and *not* men). It is a matter of seeking a whole or pattern of sex and gender which is more fulfilling for women than the currently available alternatives; and so choosing those elements in women's sexual response, capacities for intimacy, and shared reproductive and social experience, which can best be molded into such a whole. Adrienne Rich's escape from marriage and motherhood *as institutions*, detailed in *Of Woman Born*, is an especially good example.[70]

There is no reason to conclude that male homosexuality and lesbianism are attributable to a single cause or to sets of causes which run parallel for women and men. While male same-sex attraction may tend to originate in the confluence of biological predispositions with other factors, at least some female homosexuality underlines the importance of freeing male–female sex from patriarchal enclosures. Male homosexuality and female homosexuality are examples of different reasons for, and ways of accommodating, the biosocial and the interpersonal/institutional sides of morality. For gay men, the issue is largely or commonly to integrate biological factors within a full human experience of sexuality, especially by bringing bodily-based sexual drives into line with the relational norms of sexual commitment. The difficulty is that society (and perhaps biology?) does not give commitment in the gay male context the same support that it receives in the heterosexual or even lesbian one.

Some gay women do undoubtedly also experience an "innate" attraction to members of their own sex. Yet, for a significant number of others, the issue may be the more political one of reorganizing the human female repertoire of physiological experiences and capacities to address interpersonal and social deprivations and injustices. Women tend more consistently than men to experience bodily sexual desire within a prior context of interpersonal affection and intimacy. Thus oppressive and alienating organization of gender relationships can extinguish some women's sexual desire for men and facilitate the expression of sexual feelings in relations with other women. Both male and female homosexuality are about the socialization and moral integration of bodily realities; but, while male homosexuality is usually about sex, female homosexuality is often about gender. (This is not to deny that men also socialize homosexuality in styles of behavior and vocational choices that contradict masculine gender stereotypes.)

The innateness or social construction of homosexuality has bearing on its moral evaluation, including Christian evaluation, insofar as most defenders of homosexual relationships begin from the premise that the orientation is neither chosen nor socially reconstructible, and therefore should not even arise as an object of moral blame. As personally "natural" and a "given" to those who experience it, a sexual drive towards persons of the same sex should be channeled by the moral values which humanize heterosexual relationships, that is respect, reciprocity, love, and commitment.[71] If it is the case that sexual orientation is in fact pliable, then the question returns of the moral warrants which would make sexual object choice commendable, condemnable, tolerable, or neutral. The importance of male–female reciprocity and reproductive potential as enriching or completing sexual relations would return as contentious questions. We would also have to address the questions whether, if gayness is chosen as a political response to oppressive social institutions surrounding reproductive sexuality and gender, gayness is the best and most effective instrument of change; and whether gayness would have the same moral valence in the absence of the social injustices at which it is aimed.

Gay activists arguing against "innateness," far from finding orientation as neutral as left-handedness (a frequent analogy among proponents of the "natural and good" thesis), politicize it as a courageous moral choice. However, the context for such advocacy remains the long-standing persecution and exclusion of gays by the heterosexual majority. Indeed, advocacy for the moral neutrality of the orientation itself (accepted even by the Vatican[72]), if not of the acts confirming and expressing it, comes out of the very same context. It is difficult to settle the question of the voluntariness of homosexual identity, not only because of inadequate biological and social-scientific evidence, but because the question is constantly addressed, necessarily, in relation to intimate and urgent experiences held to be crucial to personal destiny and well-being. Both the claim that homosexuality is innate, and the counterclaim that it is willfully embraced, can function as strategies of resistance to oppressive structures of "heterosexism," i.e., to normative standards of sexual behavior which use sexual differences to create status divisions and exclusions. Without settling the fundamental question of the origins of homosexuality, chapter 5 will consider some of the implications of biblical discipleship for the stance of the Christian community toward homosexuality.

BODY AND FAMILY

All societies recognize human relations built on genealogical ties, beginning with lineages of mothers and children, and including men as fathers to the extent that biological paternity is recognized (which it usually is, granted variety in cultural explanations of the precise nature of male and female cooperation for reproduction[73]). We may call the institutionalization of such ties kinship or "family." It is important to remember that "family" in cross-cultural context need not refer to the modern nuclear family, consisting of a mother, father, and their children, who share a home or place of nurturance and close emotional ties.

In 1913, Bronislaw Malinowski developed a concept of the family[74] which was to be influential for social scientists but which has come under attack by other theorists, including feminists. At the center of his concept was the idea that family exists universally to fulfill a specific social function: the nurturance of children. In order that this purpose may be accomplished, societies set boundaries around the family as a social unit, allocating responsibility for children to specific adults. The family also shares a specific place ("home and hearth"), where daily care for children is carried out. And parents are rewarded for their investment by the affection and intimacy that prolonged association and interdependence bring.

Perhaps the most radical challenge to this model consists in the thesis that kinship simply does not exist cross-culturally, but is an anthropological construct which field workers impose on their evidence. This is the line adopted by David M. Schneider, whose opening salvo is "there is no such thing as kinship."[75] Schneider repudiates what he takes to be Malinowski's view that kinship as a cultural construct is always based on basic human needs, tendencies, drives, in short, that "kinship consists of bonds which are essentially psychobiological in nature."[76] Schneider takes particular exception to what he terms the "Blood Is Thicker Than Water" assumption, which holds that the biological component of human relationships always creates a cultural response, which, following from the universal nature of the lines of consanguinity created by sexual reproduction, is interpreted cross-culturally in ways similar enough to be compared.[77] Schneider seems to object both to the biological reduction of human society, and to the arrogance of culturally imperialistic anthropologists. However, in his own work among the Yap, inhabitants of the West Caroline Islands, he demonstrates variety, fluidity, even "strangeness" in the Yapese confluence of biological, marital, and land-based relationships – without ever showing that kinship as "blood" relationship is abolished as a factor in social organization, and as a point of departure from which analogous relationships are built.

Although Schneider is undoubtedly right that Western social scientists can be closed-minded both about the forms kinship will take and about its importance in social organization, Robin Fox (whose analysis tends, it is true, to be both functionalist and sexist) is still warranted in claiming for kinship historical and cross-cultural privilege. "There would have been nothing whimsical or nostalgic about genealogical knowledge for a Chinese scholar, a Roman citizen, a South Sea Islander, a Zulu warrior or a Saxon thane; it would have been essential knowledge because it would have defined many of his most significant rights, duties and sentiments."[78]

The issue for a feminist approach to the family is not so much whether respect for the embodied nature of our existence demands recognition of the bodily origin of some significant interpersonal relationships and social institutions; it is whether women's and men's similar, nonidentical embodiment dictates roles in the family (and in other social spheres) which are hierarchically organized, or even whether it dictates highly differentiated roles at all. From a feminist perspective, different family forms (different institutionalizations of embodied relationality deriving from sexual reproduction) must be scrutinized for their likelihood of fostering or inhibiting equal, reciprocal, cooperative interpersonal relationships.

The recognition of equality as an ideal may be a peculiarly modern development, but it is confirmed as a fundamental form of human excellence by movements for equality worldwide, especially the abolition of slavery, the emancipation of women, and the persuasiveness internationally of something like a concept of "human rights." None of these movements are unresisted or complete – but surely they provide evidence that the ideal of equality is more than an aberrant construction of a few post-Enlightenment cultures. The family, as both a material and a social network of interdependence, must accomplish the nurturance of children, but it should also respect the needs and encourage the virtues of adults, and sponsor the contribution of all family members to the social common good. Moreover, especially but not exclusively in "preindustrial" societies, the family can fulfill important economic and political functions.

Family forms which succeed in these goals can vary immensely across history and geography. Recent American rhetoric about "family values" is but one modern idealization of the nuclear family as the best and indeed the "traditional" type of family. Feminist authors rightly resist both the narrowing of family to this model and the exaltation of a family type which is based on and perpetuates the post-industrial, capitalist public–private split, and the confinement of women in the domestic sphere.[79]

Kinship cross-culturally is often or even usually institutionalized more in view of the organization of labor, exchange of goods, and inheritance of property. The nurturance of children is subsidiary to these purposes, rather than an end in itself. Contrary to modern, Western expectations, marriage and family cross-culturally are not exclusively focused around or dependent on the fulfillment of parties who may contract in and out at will. The broader social goals of family, and of the linking and creation of families through marriage, often has functioned to the detriment of women, who are treated as the equivalent of property to be exchanged. Yet these goals represent the social importance of lineage and kin more effectively than does the idealization of the modern, consensual, nuclear family whose adult members claim the right to reorganize or terminate family constellations when emotional rewards run low.

A more social and communal view of the family allows us to appreciate more fully that the family is a set of alliances which is in its genesis dependent at least as much on biological linkage as on self-commitment and contract. As in the above section on sociobiological studies of kin behavior, we see from anthropological studies cross-culturally that, whether organized patrilineally or matrilineally (and in both cases, power is held primarily by men[80]), societies place family relations in the context of genealogy or biological relationship. Families may be large and complex; their boundaries may be flexible; family and marital ties may or may not be a primary factor in the social organization of authority and goods; and the roles of "kin" may be exchangeable or extendable so that persons with no biological tie may function in the family as "fictive kin," that is, analogously to blood kin or relations-by-marriage.[81]

But "family" has a basic and constitutive relation to biological relationship (including reproductive partnership to produce the next generation), for which other relations, however valid, are analogues, not replacements. Families cross-culturally are based on the biological realities of sex, reproduction, shared male–female parenthood, being the child of two older parents, and being biologically tied to other children of one's mother and to a wider range of relatives. In the words of Sidney Callahan, family is a kinship system "which consists of interrelated roles and identities – mother, father, husband, wife, sister, brother, grandparent, cousin, and so on." Only the human brain can image and retain the abstractions that extended kinship systems require, can maintain enduring attachments beyond immediate gratifications and frustrations and beyond distances of time, space, and generations.[82]

In summary, family is a biologically based, cross-cultural phenomenon, which may, nonetheless, vary widely in form, especially as to the flexibility of its boundaries and as to the intimacy and equality of its internal relations.[83] Families can also fulfill several purposes, that is to say, can secure a variety of the goods important to human flourishing, and the combination and interrelation of these will also vary culturally. Families, and the alliance by marriage of families or groups, are certainly the place where both reproduction and care for children are socially recognized and promoted as duties, even though the duty of care for children may not always be carried out in a bounded domestic unit of mother, father, children. Just as fundamentally, families, clans, tribes, or other kin groups are one medium through which individuals find and fulfill the social roles for which "nurturance" should prepare them; and through which the benefits of social participation redound back to individual members. It is not always by "leaving" the family that the young find such roles, for in societies in which economic and domestic spheres are more interwoven, one's identity as family member may be interdependent with one's economic, political, and religious identities and opportunities.

Since families fill social ends and provide social goods, these as well as the biological foundation of families provide their human significance. Contemporary debates about the meaning of "family" arise from the fact that the family's typical social ends, such as economic and domestic cooperation, physical and emotional nurturance of children, and sexual and emotional fulfillment of adults, can be met in groups which are analogous to the family in form and function, but which do not have a biogenetic or marital base. Social support for the formation of step-families and adoptive families has long indicated moral approbation for at least some surrogate family styles, and social willingness to offer these the encouragement and respect other-wise reserved for the biologically or kin-based family is a mark of their success.

The commendability of such families, however, does not yield the conclusion that biological and reproductive ties are irrelevant to family formation today, or that such ties need not be met by a strong social expectation of concomitant familial support and responsibility. The ideal family is not necessarily the nuclear family. But it is in the family that both biological parents nurture children physically and emotionally, and educate them by example for larger social roles; in which parents and children are supported by a "kin" network; and in which parents are fulfilled not only through sexually expressed love for each other, but through mutual and equal dedication to offspring, to family, and to the larger community. In the Christian perspective in particular, the "successful" family does not ensure only its own welfare, or even that of the clan, but is able to extend altruistic identification with, and sacrifice for, kin to include neighbors, more distant community members, and even strangers. It must do this sometimes by loosening the body's claim, and the claim of the "familiar," especially when familiarity and kinship serve the dominance of some persons and groups over others. The New Testament household churches and the metaphor of the family as "domestic church" in patristic writings and in Roman Catholic teaching, are examples of the power of Christian commitment to transform body-based family sympathies without eradicating them.

An interlude and a proposal

The first four chapters have undertaken to show that moral reflection on sex and gender need not become so befuddled at diversity that normative inquiry is a lost cause. With appropriate caveats and epistemological caution, we may consider sex and gender as representing human realities which are both bodily and social. If socialization is always culturally various, human existence in the body provides at least a base point for communication, empathy, and critical assessment of the relationships and institutions which mediate experiences of maleness, femaleness, and sexuality.

In the next several chapters, Christian socializations of sex and gender will be addressed. Primitive Christian practice exalted virginity and sacramentalized marriage to transform dehumanizing socializations of the sexual, reproductive body. Yet Christian tradition has been ambiguous. It has defended marriage as good, and in many ways protected the freedom of spouses and the dignity of women against familial control. On the other hand, it has also produced oppressive socializations of the body, some of which have denigrated the reality of sexual experience, especially sexual pleasure, and divided women's virtue between asexual and reproductive roles.

Even to offer this critical statement about Christianity as more than an expression of opinion or bias requires that one draw on some broad, inductive consensus about which expressions of maleness, femaleness, or sex are humanly fulfilling or vicious. My perception of these realities, and the goods and values attainable within them, has already, of course, been indebted both to the Christian and to the "modern" sensibilities. The latter prizes *equality and freedom*, and the former molds those values with *compassion and solidarity*, accentuating the insight that respect for others as one's equals implies a commitment to their well-being. In addition to sponsoring trust in the reasonable discernment of value in the first place, Roman Catholicism heightens my appreciation of the genuinely *social* nature of persons, of the importance of embodied sociality in turning equality, compassion, and solidarity toward a sexual ethic. When the material and social conditions of freedom are left out of the moral picture, the perversions of social relationship which undermine genuine freedom can all the more easily escape analysis. Roman Catholicism draws attention to the body as a locus of moral reflection on sex, and includes procreation as one of the morally and socially important meanings of the sexual body.

In these few pages, I will lift to the surface the convictions about human sexuality and about gender which coalesce in the outlook just described. Since they can be stated without any specifically religious rationale, and since they will in fact guide my analysis of the religious perspectives to follow, one might call them a portrayal of "human" experiences, emerging from the discussions of women's experience and of the body that shaped the preceding chapters. But – in perhaps a "postmodern" mode – I find it important to state explicitly that this particular discernment of the values inherent in sex has already motivated the inquiry up to this point, and in fact has been informed by the Christian materials which I have yet to present. This does not mean that they need be relative to Christianity, or nonsensical and irrelevant to the moral sensibilities of others who are neither Christian nor members of modern, Western societies. Moreover, the "proposal" has in no way been a solid "position," around which better evidence and clearer explanation had only to be marshalled. The refinement, expansion, and replacement of values once more inchoately perceived continues as I write; and will continue after writing, especially if I am fortunate in having the present text become a locus of collegial and even intercultural interaction.

My proposal is essentially that, while human sexual differentiation and sexual reproduction have no doubt been vastly exaggerated in their importance for identity and social organization, they do stand as experiences which begin in humanity's primal bodily existence, and which all cultures institutionalize (differently) as gender, marriage, and family. Human flourishing, as sexually embodied, depends on the realization of the *equality of the sexes*, male and female; and. in their sexual union, on the further values of *reproduction, pleasure,* and *intimacy.* The institutions gender, marriage, and family should *ethically and normatively* be responsive to and should enhance these values. Institutions embodying these values socially will vary immensely with cultures; the linkage of the values will not always be the same; evaluation must proceed with all appropriate modesty; but certainly not every cultural realization of sex or gender can be ceded equal moral status.

The defense of this proposal consists more in reflective persuasion, considerate of the demurrers of imagined interlocutors, than in statistical data or logical deduction. We begin with the fact that gender, marriage, and family are all social expressions of a more basic experience of embodied individuals. We may call that experience "sex." The designation of sex as a fundamental reality is, as we have seen, not unproblematic. It is already an interpretation to speak of sex as our object of consideration. Such language implies the gathering up in a single notion of identifiably different aspects of the body, its capacities, its responses, and its relations – such as sexual pleasures; the bodily surfaces, organs, emotions, and contacts or intimacies which produce them; reproductive acts or acts which follow the same basic form; even conception and birth. A critic will ask whether these elements occur with any inherent connection, and may well suggest that their "unity" in experience and as a topic of discourse is no more than an imposition.

Yet to void sex of all but "bodies and pleasures," as does Foucault, is, I think, to identify the experiential unit too minimalistically, to cut off too quickly a complex and *intrinsically relational* dimension of human being. It is only when the reading of experience is individualistic – even adolescent – that the discovery of "sex" is the discovery of sexual pleasure. Sex as a species phenomenon (and hence a social one) has definitive reference to reproductive capacity, including sexual desires or "drives," sexual release or satisfaction, and the potential of reproductive acts for reciprocity in pleasure. The distinctively human aspect of sex is that, among normally conscious human persons, the acute physical intimacy or "union" of sex entails an intersubjective interaction (falling on a scale from violence to love). This personal interaction can be deepened and augmented both by sexual pleasure and by procreation.

Neither personal intimacy nor sexual pleasure is limited to the kind of sex act required by reproduction. But when persons do interact sexually in that way – setting aside artificial birth technologies, which are arguably not "sexual" – intimacy and the potential for sexual pleasure are intrinsic to the experience. Sex, the sexual dimension of the human body, originates in and comes back to the reproductive or genital organs as at least a point of reference for a "sexuality" that may well extend itself in pluriform and diffuse ways. We can acknowledge that "sexual" experience is not strictly compartmentalized, segregated from other types of sensual and emotional experience. We also know that not everyone experiences their greatest sexual pleasure in sexual intercourse. But when all is said and done, the idea that there is no such thing as "sex," or that sex in humans has no intrinsic connection to reproductive physiology, is more rhetorical than factual. Such a claim could only be maintained on the basis of an abrupt break between humanity and other mammalian species.

If we view human sexuality comprehensively, then, sex has three bodily meanings, meanings which are realized and elaborated in personal relationships over time and in social institutions. These are reproduction, pleasure, and intimacy (the intimacy of close bodily contact and even interpenetration). *Reproduction* as a physiological process of conception, pregnancy, and birth is a human bodily reality. It is personalized in the immediate family relations between procreative mates and between parents and children. It reaches the status of a social institution through intergenerational networks of kinship. *Sexual pleasure* as a bodily reality involves sexual drives and attractions, and their resolution through orgasm or through less genitally focused experiences of sexual satisfaction. Sexual pleasure is personalized in the mutual pleasure of a sexual couple, but it is subsumed into personal identity when an individual recognizes and responds cognitively and emotionally to his or her capacity for sexual pleasure. Pleasure is institutionalized in socially reliable or predictable forms of sexual relationship, some of which can be focused directly on pleasure, most often male pleasure (prostitution, courtesans, lovers, and mistresses); and others of which socialize reproduction as well (marriage, concubinage).

Intimacy at a bodily level consists in the contacts of bodies which produce pleasure and children. Insofar as these are bodies of persons, such contacts will also be intersubjective or "personal"; their personal meaning is enhanced when physical intimacy expresses affection, mutual vulnerability, commitment, and understanding. It is distorted or violated when bodily sexual intimacy occurs in a relation of domination, manipulation, or violence. Intimacy is institutionalized in socially recognized partnerships of sexual couples, like marriage or homosexual covenants, which again can socialize more than one value. For the transition to the social level of meaning to be completely accomplished, it is important that such relationships be seen not only in terms of the couple's personal relationship, but also in terms of their social responsibilities and contributions.

It is important to note that a truly humane interpretation of procreation, pleasure, and intimacy will set their moral implications in the context of enduring personal relationships, not merely of individual sex acts. If human identity and virtue in general are established diachronically, then this will also be true of sexual flourishing. A problem with current official Roman Catholic ethical analysis of sex is that it truncates the meaning of reproduction by using the procreative structure of bodily sex acts to ascertain whether the value of parenthood is represented in a relation of intimacy. It ties the interpersonal and moral value of sex to the structure of separate acts. Sexual pleasure and its integration with intimacy is largely ignored. In the end the sex act as a "mutual self-gift" seems strangely disembodied, as well as severed from the dimensions of memory, trust, and hope that make human sexuality unique.

Deficient moral behavior or inadequate moral analysis can result from the truncation or division of the pleasurable, intimate, and procreative meanings. Human sexual experience is complex and complete when all three bodily dimensions of sex are developed through the three levels (bodily, personal, social) and integrated in relationships over time. The modern, Romantic ideal of mutual sexual fulfillment integrates at least pleasure and intimacy through the personal level, but overlooks the social, and sometimes the reproductive, meanings. Sex in the cultures of the ancient world was institutionalized socially, but along separate trajectories for sex's reproductive, and its pleasure-giving meanings. Intimacy could be integrated with either reproduction or pleasure, but in distorted forms: the mutuality of reproductive marriage was ordered in an emotionally restrained hierarchy of sexes, while the passion of extra-marital sex lacked the continuity of a community of lives, and thus also tended to exploit the female partner.

As will be illustrated in the coming chapter, the premodern sexual ethic was social but often impersonal with regard to the individual fulfillment of spouses; the modern sexual ethic is personal but individualist. Both ethics are symbolized in the body. The body in ancient Greece and Rome bore children for the state; even the form of intercourse and the attitudes of partners were prescribed for greater social benefit. Woman especially were defined by the social–procreative role. In the Augustinian Christian tradition, the meaning of pleasure stayed largely at the level of the body, was personalized only as a snare and a danger to virtue, and was not linked in a constructive way either to parenthood or love. Parenthood and love both received institutionalization in marriage, but were not well integrated, insofar as procreation was made the primary purpose of sex, while love was a secondary consideration; and intrinsic interconnection or mutual support of the two values was never developed. In medieval Christian culture and in many cultures today, marriage and parenthood are still understood more in terms of the good of the family, social group, or even species, than of the spouses in their own right.

The Protestant Reformers upheld procreation as sex's primary purpose, but did grant more significance to the social relationship of spouses and to the companionate value of marriage than did their predecessors. In the modern period, the meaning of sex to the individual has overtaken all other meanings. Sex as an expression of personal "authenticity" is consensual at least, and "loving" at most; and in either case is focused bodily on pleasure, not reproduction. Sexual pleasure becomes a means of personal gratification or interpersonal fulfillment, but the procreative side of sex, with its strong social dimensions, loses greatly in moral value.

Perhaps the major contemporary question about sexual morality – one certainly tied into gender – is whether the reproductive goals which control most of the sexual behavior of other species are still so relevant to the sexual virtue of humans. The question is raised particularly by the potential of human sexual intimacy and pleasure to contribute to the interpersonal relationships unique to our species. Sexual intercourse, sexual pleasure, and reproduction are distinct and possibly separable components of human sexuality globally understood, and of marriage. Just how necessary is the interdependence of these elements in an enduring relationship, in constituting the richest, most excellent, or ideal human sexual experience?

The capacity of intercourse to give mutual pleasure helps provide the possibility that what is in any event an intimate interaction may also be an occasion of interpersonal knowledge, affection, and commitment. Sexual delight engages the emotional and affective dimensions of the person, in proportion to the depth of the relationship between the partners. Pleasurable sex contributes to their ongoing social relation and commitment. Although these interpersonal goods may be accomplished, and often are, without either the intention or reality of conception, sex can also serve as the initiator of a physical process of pregnancy and birth which makes possible another interpersonal and social role, parenthood. Parenthood joins the relation to one's mate with the relation to one's children, through co-parenting. Sex has meaning *both* in relation to the personal union of sexual partners, including their social partnership as a couple; *and* in relation to parenthood as an expression of personal union and as a contribution of the sexual couple to the next generation.

The most complete and morally attractive experience of sex is at the intersection of its three sides – the pleasurable, the interpersonal, and the parental. Sexual union, mutual pleasure, and intimate affective commitment are expressed, reinforced, and given social magnitude by a joint parenting relation to the children of the couple. In the past, responsibility for children was offered as the key argument against pleasurable but transient sexual encounters. But if we see human sex in all of its dimensions as expressive of our ongoing personal identity and relationality, then we can also appreciate that the intense intimacy of sex and even the pleasure it can bring are best realized and nurtured in a personal relationship of commensurate trust and commitment, and that mutual parenthood can enrich the relation of the parents themselves.

There are many human circumstances in which the conjunction in a sexual relation of pleasure, intimacy, and reproduction is not possible or even desirable. A sexual but not parental relationship, or a parental relationship which is not initiated sexually, may be commendably and joyfully undertaken – as in the marriages of infertile or elderly couples, exclusive same-sex commitments, and the adoption of children. Separability of the intimate and the parental meanings of sex can be recognized in fact and justified in appropriate cases without implying that their unity can or should no longer function as an ideal for those who are reasonably able to meet it. To envision permanent personal union and parenthood as aspects of the human sexual ideal is neither to regard as morally pernicious, nor to withhold social approbation and support from, any and every realization of sexual commitment or of parenthood not characterized by this unity. We recognize for instance that there can be good moral reasons for ending a committed sexual relationship, just as there are for giving over the care of one's children to others. The question here must not be of a norm which excludes all it does not idealize. It is, rather, how to express the ideal as humanly excellent and attractive; and how and when to justify situations which from the standpoint of the ideal may be anomalous, but which from the perspective of many life situations are virtuous and satisfying.

My intent is not to use an ideal of committed, parental sex to condemn, exclude, or cast into the shadows "nonconformists," such as gay and lesbian persons, divorced persons, persons desirous of a committed relationship who enter tentative sexual liaisons hoping for eventual love and permanency, or those who settle for a probably temporary relationship because it makes available something of the intimacy and sexual fulfillment for which they long. Indeed, I am hesitant even to speak for such persons, well aware as I am that my own experience as a married, heterosexual, mother of five, may allow me to empathize, but not fully to appreciate what their experience is like. Convinced as I am that empathy itself is rooted in the fact that under great difference lies some commonality of experience, I have learned from the writings and friendship of those in sexually different situations.

However, my critical attention is focused primarily on the sexual experience of which I trust it is most my business to speak, and which is also the cross-cultural sexual "center": heterosexual, reproductive, and typically patriarchal marriage and family. My concerns here are twofold. First, the sexual subordination of women to men in marriage and parenthood is unjust, and women's equality needs a substantive, intercultural defense. For many women in the world, issues like lesbianism, extramarital sex, divorce, and even equal access to work, as "free choices," are quite secondary to their continual economic dependency on men, to their struggle to bear and raise children under adequate conditions, and to their difficulty in gaining anything like educational, political, or professional parity with the opposite sex. Second, I believe sex has been given a moral meaning in cultures like my own (North Atlantic industrialized nations) which is individualist and even narcissist, which has taken shape in the dissociation of sex from parental fulfillment and social responsibility, which has made commitment increasingly marginal to sexual meaning, and which has permitted sexual privacy and free choice to serve as a front for continuing oppressions of and violence toward, women (whose choices are in reality not always so free).

Focusing on issues like homosexuality, premarital sex, and divorce can very effectively distract attention from more fundamental issues of sexual meaning, and from critical renewal of the institutions of marriage and family. "Conservatives" assume a clear and intact model of sexual morality which allows equally clear judgments about wrongdoing; the dedication of "liberals" to tolerance and acceptance can sidetrack the project of developing a normative view of human sexual embodiment which takes all its dimensions seriously. In both cases, foregone conclusions about which acts and relationships will or will not be acceptable can become a "bottom line" which distorts and predetermines investigation of the human values cross-culturally available in sex, as pleasurable, reproductive, and an avenue of intense human intimacy, all of which are realized in diachronic relationships and are invested with profound social meaning.

In advancing a heightened appreciation of the ways sex and sexual differentiation can be realms of human flourishing and excellence – or of sin and suffering – I am not as interested in demarcating specific offenses against sexual virtue as I am in finding the directions in which sexual value and happiness generally lie. I do not want condemnations so much as a better *apologia* for a humane and Christian approach to sex and gender. And when we do mark off unacceptable kinds of sexual behavior, moral offenses within socially approved institutions like marriage and religiously vowed celibacy should be underscored.

More important than defining moral and immoral forms of sexual conduct is the fundamental NT concern to transform all human relations toward greater equality, compassion, and solidarity. There is a universal human tendency to make distinctions in the experienced world for the sake of organizing experience, and of facilitating activities and social relationships; it is this tendency that makes symbolization possible. But humans also have a tendency, just as universal, toward "sin" or evil, consisting essentially in denying the co-humanity of the "others" one experiences.

The social derivative of this denial is hierarchical organization of experience and society, motivated by the desire of individuals to affiliate with groups in which they can seek for themselves and their "own" a dominant (and not merely secure) position, especially under conditions of scarcity. As I will explain in the next chapter, relying on Mary Douglas, the body is a "natural" symbolic source of differentiation and organization. Yet it is also a site and symbol of *domination*. Bodily characteristics which are more or less innate will be the most obvious, permanent, and useful markers of social position; bodily characteristics (sex and race) which are least variant culturally will also serve as the most consistent social markers, i.e., as the designators of "class."

A further question is whether or why these reoccurring social markers always have similar meanings, i.e., whether race or sex is always in the same way associated with status. In the case of race, meaning varies considerably. Although racial groups are notoriously hard to pin down, it is still true that race and ethnicity – difference in recognizable physical type or in known group ancestry between "insiders" and "ousiders" – is almost universally used as a barrier to compassion and a rationale for social domination. But the particular internal orderings among racial groups in any given society will vary. Race is virtually everywhere used to define class (lower or higher social status), but, although it is still true that the white race often asserts dominance, no one racial or ethnic group will always have the same status in every culture.

In the case of sex, on the other hand, femaleness is invariably subordinated to maleness, though degrees and forms of subordination vary immensely. No single racial group always comes out on the bottom, but women always do. Since the male–female difference is also the condition of crucial forms of human relationship – sex, parenthood, kinship – those relations also become subservient to social domination. The obvious and most fundamental explanation for such consistent male domination along the axis of sexual difference seems to lie in men's greater size and physical strength, and perhaps in a mammalian and primate tendency to assert dominance sexually. Robert Wright points out that in primate species with marked sexual dimorphism, males are able to control a number of mates, which could be read as an indicator of male dominance over females as well as over weaker male competitors. It may be significant that in male primates, sexual success is associated with physical and social dominance, especially control of females. While the evenly sized male and female gibbon are monogamous, the huge male gorilla collects a harem. In chimpanzees and humans, males are about 15 per cent larger than females, and both species are polygynous in rough proportion to the degree of their dimorphism.[1] The size differential also permits men the option of violent force in controlling women, a tool which is especially effective in a domestic setting spatially or socially sequestered from public interference.[2]

All humans have sinful tendencies, that is, to dominate when and how they can. It is not that women are naturally more virtuous than men, as our own exploitation, abuse, and neglect of the less powerful, even our children, illustrates too well.[3] It is simply that size, strength, and hormonal readiness for aggression, including sexual aggression, give men in general a window of opportunity for dominance which is not open to women in general to the same degree. In the case of male–female domination, men's physical power exists in an unresolved competition with women's ability to give birth. Historically, the power to give life has been institutionalized to male advantage. The task of a Christian social ethic of sex is to imbue sexual and reproductive behavior with the qualities of respect, empathy, reciprocity, and mutual fidelity which would allow sexual and parental love to be transforming agents in society in general.

In the modern industrial and technological period, physical strength offers a waning social advantage. Political and economic successes depend in very few cases on physical size. The assets of strength have been translated into economic power. Today, it is lack of economic alternatives that usually keeps abused women dependent on men. And economic structures, especially the separation of the economic and domestic spheres and the definition of gender on the basis of that separation, perpetuate inequality even when individual men affirm and seek opportunities for women. But this very transformation of the mode of oppression also offers women their avenue of escape. With access to education, women are far more able than in centuries past to unite in ameliorating their own situation,[4] and to take advantage of intellectual, social, and even technological means of redressing the imbalance of power. Ideologies which maintain that women cannot or should not have full access to social, educational, political, and economic opportunities because of the constraints of their reproductive functions are more and more transparently a rationalization of the status quo. Just as important, to divide the sexes with gender-classifying roles is also to deprive men of the rewards of domesticity, parenthood, and family, and to exclude them from an important sphere in which the next generation is educated.

CHAPTER 5

Sex, gender, and early Christianity

The object of this chapter is to show what bearing the faith and practice of early Christianity had on sex and gender.[1] Its thesis is essentially that Jesus' preaching of the reign or kingdom of God represents a new experience of the divine presence in history, an experience which transforms human relationships by reordering relations of dominance and violence toward greater compassion, mercy, and peace, expressed in active solidarity with "the poor." Christian ethics today should encourage forms of behavior which serve an analogous function, without necessarily replicating the precise practices the New Testament records. The approach adopted thus represents a departure from a more familiar one of applying texts to issues; or of showing why the standard texts are not relevant to the issues as posed in our own time.[2]

The NT cannot be expected to specify a "sexual ethics" as such, for the same reason that it does not provide a comprehensive ethics in any sphere of human action. Ethics in the NT is not a topic of interest autonomous from the new relationship with God which Jesus initiates.[3] The gospel is about the good news of God's reign, and an invitation to live within it, not about a timeless system of moral instruction. The gospel certainly requires that all relationships be reconfigured by life in the new community inspired by the Lord. Insofar as the NT literature represents the concrete meaning of the gospel in relation to the life situations of the early Christian communities, it provides illustrations which remain provocative and even paradigmatic today. Yet NT authors do not investigate systematically all facets of any moral topic, nor develop a corresponding set of rules for the definitive resolution of future variations on any moral problem. Furthermore, not every NT moral example is equally adequate to the reign Jesus announced; nor would all have the same effectiveness in realizing kingdom life today as in the first or second century.

A constant NT theme is the *transformation or reversal* of ordinary human relationships so that they better reflect God's presence and power, as disclosed in Jesus Christ. NT authors assume the *de facto* reality of certain human institutions and patterns of relationship. They challenge human relations and values which perpetuate sin. They encourage emotions, virtues, and practices which embody the reign of God. So, for instance, the basic question to put to the NT regarding sex and gender is: how can Christian faith and life break or at least modify relations of dominance, and enhance solidarity across status boundaries in marriage and the family? We will not expect to discover that the NT answers this question completely or that the early Christians fully realized its implicit aim in their communities.

What the NT does provide is an ethos of discipleship with profound implications for patterns of moral relationship. Although the NT memories of Jesus are certainly marked by pluralism,[4] there is notable consistency in the ethos of the reign of God Jesus preached and illustrated by his inclusive behavior, particularly table fellowship and healing. This ethos consists in compassion for others, active solidarity among status groups, and a bias toward inclusion of "outcasts." In the words of Elisabeth Schüssler Fiorenza, the Jesus movement "had experienced in the praxis of Jesus" a God who called not Israel's righteous, but its "social underdogs." In Jesus' ministry, God is experienced as "all-inclusive love," a God who especially accepts "the impoverished, the crippled, the outcast, the sinners and prostitutes, as long as they are prepared to engage in the perspective and power of the *basileia*."[5] Negative moral judgments are leveled primarily at those whose behavior (sexual, gender or race related, economic, or political) creates or underwrites exclusive status hierarchies.

A crucial question for this chapter – and for Christian ethics in general – is whether the New Testament presents a pattern of values which, while not necessarily incompatible with "our" values, is also not reducible to them, and in fact implies a critique of the ways these values often take effect in moral attitudes and practices. The explicit philosophical and political recognition of values, such as equality and reciprocity, latent always in the humanity, individuality, and sociality of every person, represents an advance in human moral consciousness and a critical possibility for social reform. However, New Testament patterns of moral relationship can in no simple way be equated with modern, liberal values of equality, freedom, self-determination, and mutual respect (important though the distinctively modern recognition of these values is). This last point is important, for many interpreters of biblical sexual ethics position "obsolete" prohibitions within a larger context of transformed interpersonal relationship which looks remarkably similar to the liberal, consensual, individualist, pragmatic, yet often romantic, sexual ethos of twentieth-century North Atlantic cultures. Neither the Sermon on the Mount nor the parables of Jesus about God's reign focus the attention of the disciple on his or her own moral freedom and personal fulfillment. While the biblical reign of God or "kingdom" does entail equality and respect, the implications of those values socially are not so much the protection of personal choice and the furtherance of affectively fulfilling relationships, as the integration of all persons in a new sense of communal unity and inclusiveness in Christ.

Research into the social history of Palestine in Jesus' day, and of his followers in the next two generations,[6] suggests that Jesus and the gospels are responding to and challenging highly stratified social relationships, especially those installed by a *patron–client economy*, a religious ideology which organized economic and social status around *purity laws*, and by a gender hierarchy within the *patriarchal family*.

Early Christianity does not reject exchange relations, purity observance, or the family as such. But it does challenge and even reverse cultural criteria of inclusion and exclusion, and gauges all moral relations by their success in dislodging power elites and including "the poor."

Building on the work of Mary Douglas and Peter Brown, I will argue that the NT not only liberates from oppressive constraints on sexual and gender behavior, but proposes a new discipline of the body which symbolizes a reordering of relationships and is central to the liberative process. A Christian ethics of sex and gender today should replicate the radical social challenge of early Christianity, if not necessarily its concrete moral practices.

THE REIGN OF GOD AND CHRISTIAN LIFE

As the earliest gospel has it, "Jesus came into Galilee, preaching the gospel of God, and saying, 'The time is fulfilled, and the kingdom of God is at hand; repent, and believe in the gospel'" (Mark 1:14). The meaning of kingdom imagery for the historical Jesus is not uncontroversial, since Mark as redactor may accentuate its prominence, and since its eschatological and even apocalyptic framework has been debated since the advent of nineteenth-century historical criticism.[7] Nevertheless, the image of the inbreaking reign of God was certainly an important vehicle by which Jesus communicated his religious experience and its moral and communal implications. Jesus' words and actions make present and accessible in the present time an existence in relation to God whose nature is often disclosed in terms of a reversal of worldly values, hierarchies, and expectations, and in which disciples imitate the mercy, forgiveness, and compassion of God.[8] The Sermon on the Mount (Matt. 5–7; Luke 6:1–49) is perhaps the best paradigm of the moral meaning of kingdom life, but other classic texts, such as the parable of the Good Samaritan (Luke 10:29–37), Jesus' prayer for the coming of the kingdom (Matt. 7:6–15; Luke 11:2–4), and the command to love God above all and one's neighbor as oneself (Mark 12:28–34; Matt. 22:34–40; Luke 10:25–28; cf. Deut. 6:4), are also indispensable to a New Testament view of the quality of Christian relationship.[9] Recent research has highlighted the role of Jesus as a wisdom teacher who subverts cultural wisdom about a righteous way of life, purity, honor, and status, wealth, rewards, and punishments, and the character of the divine lawgiver, judge, and enforcer. Elisabeth Schüssler Fiorenza identifies Jesus and his experience of God with the figure of Sophia in Jewish wisdom theology (cf. Luke 7:33–35, Matt. 23: 34–35), and sees him as establishing an "alternative ethos" in which the despised are included as equal to the righteous.[10]

This includes, and, in fact, specifically implies as a first and most urgent step, the inclusion of those who are most marginal, outcast, and vulnerable in relation to community identity and access to material and social goods. Jesus was notorious in his own day for associating and even sharing meals with tax-collectors[11] and other sinners. Modern commentators note also that Jesus' approach to women, unmediated by any male authority and inclusive in terms of women's participation in at least some discipleship roles, was revolutionary for his time.

Compassion for others as the moral side of one's personal response to Jesus' revelation of God has as its social side a solidarity which breaks the ranks of stratifications in which the prosperous can turn a blind eye to the misery of the needy. It evokes an inclusive response in which the disciple recognizes the humanity of the other across social boundaries. In the parable of the last judgment, giving food and drink to "one of the least of these my brethren" is Jesus' criterion for inheritance of the kingdom (Matt. 25: 31–46). The same point is illustrated by the parable of Lazarus and the rich man (Luke 16:19–21); and by Jesus' instruction not to invite friends, kinsmen, and rich neighbors to banquets, but "the poor, the maimed, the lame, the blind" (Luke 12–14). The New Testament does not contain directives for a specific social program of reform, but it has clear and extensive social implications.

Even though Jesus did not concentrate his energies on social reform as such, and despite the apocalyptic overtones the symbol "kingdom of God" carried in first century usage, Jesus expected God's reign to have a present impact "in the midst" of us (Luke 17:21). Jesus acts out the presence of the kingdom through striking actions such as exorcisms (Luke 11:20: "If by the finger of God I cast out demons, the kingdom of God has come upon you.").[12] The early Christian communities began to embody God's reign socially. The Greco-Roman family is a critical factor in the background of NT views of sex and gender; but economics and purity laws also defined social structures which were highly relevant to the status of women and to the general moral ethos in which Christianity arose.

The Bible's interpreters are conditioned by cultural setting, academic specialization, audience, and even personal taste. "Yet, in one way or another, we claim that it is possible for us as human beings to understand the 'other' – a word of revelation, an ancient text, a foreign culture, a dead language."[13] This is despite the cultural distance of the text, cultural variety even within text, and greater cultural variety among the communities which receive and recreate it in an ongoing historical process. Biblical compassion builds on and expands a natural capacity for empathic identification with others, relying on universals in human experience, such as the body, the cumulative or narrative identity of the self within historical change, the formation of a life plan through the interaction of ideals and present practices, the counterpoint of self-affirmation and self-effacement which makes "the irruption of the other" and the availability of the self to others possible.[14]

Distinctive of the Christian moral vision is the centrality of compassionate beneficence to unity with the divine, and the image of a God who not only is imitated by neighbor-love, but who dies in the sufferings of the excluded. Yet the task – or mission – of Christian ethics is not to invent empathy, but evoke it in a reversal of our habitual attitudes, and to nurture it in a community of support. To live (even proleptically) in the kingdom of God is to grasp and live out of oneness of self and other as ultimate reality, human and divine, which human morality at best imitates and at worst actively suppresses.

ECONOMY

In the traditional peasant societies of ancient Palestine, the economy was enmeshed with religious, political, and cultural institutions to a much greater extent than in modern industrial and capitalistic economies. Moreover, since both material and nonmaterial goods were perceived to be limited (one person's gain is another's loss), the welfare of all was interdependent. The distribution of resources was largely determined by patron–client relationships which depended upon asymmetries of status and power. A few could deprive many of the basic necessities of subsistence, which resulted in high levels of anxiety, competition, envy, and subservience. This system of distribution intersected with purity and family, in that, as will be discussed below, purity could be a way of distinguishing the elite from the non-elite; and the family could be a means of pooling assets, both material and political, and channeling (or limiting) access to scarce resources. By bringing together people from diverse social strata, and indeed by attracting those from the social bottom rung, early Christian communities moved toward a communal practice of fellowship, solidarity, forgiveness, compassion, and sharing of goods which, even without ever having been perfectly realized, was extremely subversive of the expectations and relationships which favored the entrenched beneficiaries of the exploitative social order.[15]

Central to the Pauline letters, for instance, are a unity of fundamental interests and identity, and mutual service or "building up" through love.[16] These qualities of community are, for Paul, constantly expressed in terms of the metaphor of Christ's body and its members. Attention to real bodily needs, especially when deprivation is the result of group divisions, is key to Christian living. Acts 6 tells of the need to resolve a situation in which Hebrew were being preferred to Greek widows in the daily distribution of food. I Corinthians 11:17–22 treats social divisions at the Eucharist specifically in terms of the unworthy sharing of Christ's body and blood by those who eat and drink sumptuously, while letting the needy go away hungry.

A social-historical understanding of the milieu in which Jesus preached and Christianity took root has aided several NT scholars who draw contemporary economic and political implications from the symbol of the kingdom as instigating a new social reality.[17] Halvor Moxnes argues from the Gospel of Luke that Jesus was in conflict with Jewish community leaders (represented by the Pharisees) over community boundaries, status relationships, and control over resources. "Luke's Gospel represents a protest against the abuse of the needy by the rich."[18] Giving without expectation of return and a redistribution of goods to the needy (from the elite to the non-elite) is the practical implication of the "reversal" the kingdom brings.[19] Ched Myers uses Mark to suggest that Jesus sponsors subversive communities which oppose the dominant ideologies maintained by violence, and establish a new political and economic order. Richard Horsley claims that the communities of the Jesus movement, formed around the symbol "kingdom of God," replaced the patriarchal family with new "families" which were "tightknit and disciplined," and which fostered reciprocal generosity among households.[20] No doubt wealth was never abolished by full communism of property, either in Jesus' own day or among the first Christians. Yet it is quite evident that Jesus' teaching drastically undermined lines of power and markers of status which privileged a few and deprived many of the very conditions of a satisfying existence.

Christian ethics requires analogous, not identical, action.[21] Christians are responsible to identify and engage in moral practices which upset exploitative, oppressive, and dehumanizing relationships and institutions in their own cultures. For instance, New Testament scholar Seán Freyne asserts that Christian discipleship action today must "always be anti-ideological, that is opposed to all forms of discrimination: sexism, racism, ageism, classism, monetarism," even though we remain fully aware of the ambiguous nature of Christian history itself on these issues.[22] Richard Horsley and Max Myers target Western capitalism, especially huge multi-national corporations, as focused on the modern-day idols of money and commodities, whose priests oppress those who are induced to serve them, and enslave masses in the Third World who are forced to build their temples.[23] These authors render the gist of Christian ethics in the vocabulary both of an Aristotelian perspective ("the good consists in living according to the kingdom of or the will of God, which is the political-economic-religious liberation of people so that they are enabled to pursue the good life for mankind"), and of discourse ethics (an ethics of the kingdom as the politics of God "requires a universal community of equal participants").[24]

The essential and enduring relevance of the New Testament for ethics lies in its heightening of the human ability to recognize humanity in others, especially others over whom one may wield power. In a global context, Christian life and practice have converged on solidarity with the poor and oppressed as a universal imperative – however problematic it may remain that both solidarity and "globalization" are often defined (and exploited) from a First World perspective.[25] New Testament ethics not only enhances compassion, but prioritizes inclusive action in very specific and concrete forms. In our own social situations, we must seek out forms of behavior which challenge exclusionary and dominative social practices, and not leave the values of compassion and solidarity at an ineffective level of abstraction.

PURITY

Purity societies are organized around polarized categories of pure and impure, clean and unclean, which are the central way of structuring the social world. They apply both to individuals and to groups. Purity is concerned in particular with what passes in and out of bodily orifices, and these represent, in the words of anthropologist Mary Douglas, "the entrances and exits of society." The key axes of status in a purity system are intake of food and emission of bodily fluids, especially those related to waste products and sex.

Purity and impurity may result from birth (caste), behavior (eating, sex, washing, and so on), social position (including occupation), and physical condition (wholeness and health or disfigurement and disease, as well as sexual and reproductive functions). Social boundaries are established on gradations of purity, from the most pure, to temporary impurity, to the socially marginal, to the outcast.[26] Purity and economic systems are related, in that purity laws reinforce distinctions between the elite who control social resources and the nonelite whose power is marginal. In purity societies, women tend to be more identified with impure states, since sexual contact with women is stigmatized as impure for men, and both menstruation and childbirth are impure for women.

The social significance of purity has been examined by Douglas, who discerns in purity systems that control the body a natural system of symbolization of social organization. Bodily experience and its cultural meaning are closely tied to the social order, of which the body functions as a symbol. Concerns about the social order, especially the need to strengthen and preserve a certain pattern of social relations, are reflected in norms of bodily behavior, and even in the way individuals experience themelves as embodied. "The body is a complex structure. The functions of its different parts and their relation afford a source of symbols for other complex structures." As a symbol of society, the body can represent society's "powers and dangers."[27] The symbolic potentials of the body are to some extent culturally constant. To present the front rather than the back of one's body signifies respect. Physical closeness means intimacy. The casting-off of physical waste products (spitting, urinating) is incompatible with formal discourse and may be used to terminate it by insulting one's interlocutor.

In *Purity and Danger*, Douglas focused on the potential of the body to represent avoidance of social danger, an emphasis which has influenced theological interpreters of her theory. The heart of that theory, as she herself summarizes it, is "the purity rule," according to which "the more the social situation exerts pressure on persons involved in it, the more the social demand for conformity tends to be expressed by a demand for physical control."[28] Of special concern are bodily orifices, which represent the "exits and entrances" of society. And concern with reinforcing social boundaries will be particularly strong for an isolated and perhaps persecuted community, a minority in a larger society, against which the minority must erect barriers to ensure its own survival. Douglas specifically mentions the ancient Israelites as a threatened body politic which developed a complex system to control "the integrity, unity and purity of the physical body."[29]

In *Natural Symbols*, Douglas expanded her analysis with a

typology for comparing societies according to the degree of
social conformity expected (the factor of "group"), and the
degree of internal classification or regulation which characterizes relations within the society (the factor of "grid").[30] Both
grid and group may be strong or weak; in a strong group, high-
grid society, there will be high social pressure to conform to a
highly classified or stratified set of roles. Strict control over
bodily behavior, especially regarding sex, reproduction, gender,
food, and all bodily emissions, will reflect the closely guarded
boundaries of the society itself.

There is an ambiguity in Douglas's typology, however, for
she at once distinguishes between high and low grid societies,
and seems to maintain at a more fundamental level that all
cultures express social relationships by means of corresponding
expectations of bodily behavior. In *Natural Symbols* Douglas
maintains that, since "the human body is always treated as an
image of society," there thus "can be no natural way of
considering the body that does not involve at the same time a
social dimension."[31] She speaks of a universal human tendency
to express social experience "in an appropriate bodily style."[32]
Every culture is shaped by the human "drive to achieve
consonance between social and physical and emotional experience," which finds expression in the body's function as a
natural symbol of the social order.[33] All societies thus "construct" the body – not *ex nihilo*, but on the basis of embodied
sensations, capacities and relationships which are then
mediated in ways reflecting social values. Whether in more or
less formal and ritualized cultures, there is no real question of a
human body "free from" the function of social representation.
The issue is rather what sort of a society it is that the body
represents.

Douglas's own explication of this point can be misleading, for
she tends to focus on bodily control in societies which have both
high classification and strong pressure to conform, and to follow
in them the function of the "purity rule" by which social
intercourse can become almost disembodied or "ethereal-
ized."[34] She tends conversely to associate informal, anti-ritua-
listic societies with weak structure and weak social control (low

grid and group), as exemplified in her frequently cited contrast between "smooth" and "shaggy" forms of social behavior.[35] Artists and academics – fancying themselves social critics – display their looseness from social control by a "carefully modulated shagginess" of hair, dress, style, and choice of restaurants and home furnishings. Stockbrokers, accountants, and lawyers, on the other hand, behave smoothly on the same points, representing their commitment to structures which underwrite the social whole of which they envision themselves essential parts. Yet the contrast between smooth and shaggy also reveals the other side of the equation: behavior that seems like what Douglas refers to as "bodily abandon" is also in its own way highly structured and may be pressured to great social conformity. The informal but also intentionally iconoclastic and status-defining dress of my teenagers and friends is a case in point. ("*Why* can't I wear my cut-off jeans to the restaurant/ church/grandma's?" "Only losers [or current equivalent pejorative] buy their jeans in that store/wear that brand/patch up a hole in the knee.") What may appear to some observers as "low grid" social expectations may only seem so because the onlookers' criteria of control have been replaced. On another look, a deeper understanding, or a substitute grid, alternative criteria may surface which express just as firmly and clearly to initiates the social place of the actors observed.

Douglas notes that "high grid" controlled and formal behavior will be valued in societies in which there is a strongly defined structuring of the roles of individuals and groups.[36] Yet, conversely, freedom of physical movement and expression – the individual's "control" over his or her own body – can be in just as tight a symbolic correspondence to a set of social expectations about individualism, autonomy, and the contractual nature of personal relationships. Even in ostensibly unrestricted societies, the body and its movements still follow social norms, and are still ordered, even controlled, by the social ethos. This point is rendered in a contemporary context in Charles Taylor's critique of the modern "ethics of authenticity," which seems to present as moral compass nothing else than the freely chosen, original life-plan of each individual.[37] The ideal of authenticity to one's own, personal ideals is, on a deeper look, not so nonconformist. It bears the cumulative effect of a number of strands in Western culture, including Romanticism, existentialism, and the privatization of any rationality that is not "scientific." Modern individualism is hardly detached from group and grid, but reflects instead a quite strong social ethos, including an internal classification system.

A further point is that Douglas's analysis does not require that we see bodily symbolization of the social order in negative, restrictive terms. Peter Brown's discussion of early Christian virginity, to be discussed below in the context of the Greco-Roman family, operates on the insight that discipline of sexuality could be a positive expression of new Christian identity and could have a liberative function *vis-à-vis* social expectations about gender and procreation.

Similarly, purity laws were developed and systematized in ancient Judaism during the exile, a time in which a displaced people struggled to re-establish its identity over against the foreign cultures and cults among which Israel was forced to dwell.[38] Purity took momentum in Jewish history as a form of communal resistance to domination. In both ancient and modern Judaism, purity laws may be understood as a way of sanctifying the entirety of life and of ordinary life, of reminding the observant that every moment of every day is dedicated to God. Even the most daily and repetitious activities may be sanctified, especially those related to the renewal of the life process: nourishment, cleanliness, dressing, sex, giving birth, and encountering death.[39] Each of these ritualized practices sustains a symbolic connection of everyday life with the sovereignty and providence of God, contextualizing humanity within the entire creation and before its divine source. "Hence, when Israelites seek out and eat proper meat, they reinforce, emphasize and perhaps consciously recall the supremacy of God as well as their distinction from other nations."[40] Purity laws, especially ritual purification before Temple worship, were also a means of ensuring that the bodily processes most intimately connected with life and death be separated from the holy and unchanging presence of God.[41]

First-century Palestine was centered around the temple and an interpretation of the Torah elaborated by the scribes, a "retainer class" attached to the priesthood. According to this interpretation, holiness meant separation from everything that was unclean as defined on the basis of Leviticus.[42] Although this was not their original or only function, purity laws tended to serve as a sustaining ideology for elites who defined who and what is impure, who is thus of lesser status, and who consequently is excluded from control of material and political goods. The purity system in ancient Palestine upheld a positive ideal of holiness in community, and even resisted colonial domination. In practice, however, it also augmented the status of the high priestly families (which is not to say the majority of priests were rich[43]). The products of the peasants' agricultural labor were taxed to support the Temple and the clerical classes; in turn, the Pharisees, scribes and lawyers were dependent on the higher aristocracy. Purity laws did not affect all Jews equally, since observance was tied primarily to Jerusalem and to participation in the Temple cult. The importance of purity diminished outside of Jerusalem (for instance, in Galilee). The ordinary Jew, male or female and whether living in a rural area or in the city, was not expected to observe all rituals daily. So it would be just as wrong to see Jewish peasants as universally oppressed by purity expectations as it would to view all members of the priestly class as purity's economic beneficiaries. Nevertheless, to the extent that economic and social differences did exist between priests and peasants, purity laws could reinforce them.

The moral ethos of early Christianity took shape and had effect in light of Jewish purity practices.[44] It is doubtful that Jesus, as a Jew, rejected all observance of purity, a traditional form of holiness. Indeed, later controversies over the Pharisees' efforts to extend daily purity observance are probably projected back by gospel authors into accounts of Jesus' own lifetime. Yet it is clear enough that Jesus did behave in ways which upset social expectations created by purity, and that he did so precisely through practices which fell most firmly under its authority (eating, reaction to disease, association with women, and sabbath observance). John Dominic Crossan spotlights Jesus' iconoclastic table fellowship ("open commensality") and free healing as repudiations of the class-oriented aspects of the purity system of his culture. Anthropologically, conventions of meals and eating replicate the social rules of class identity and association. Table fellowship is "a map of economic discrimination, social hierarchy, and political differentiation."[45] Jesus had a reputation for eating with social outcasts, including tax-collectors, sinners, and whores (standard terms of derogation for groups with whom the elites found free association intolerable).[46] In the parable of the wedding guests (Luke 14:15–24; Matt. 22:1–13), Jesus commends to his listeners the inclusion at table of the good and bad, the "poor and maimed and blind and lame" (Luke 14:21). The social danger in this parable is its replacement of the map of the purity system with a radical eclecticism, and its abandonment of the "appropriate" social distinctions. Yet open commensality was for Jesus more than an *abandonment* of controls; it was the institution of a new way of behaving at table which involved specific, positive *practices* of invitation and inclusion.

Crossan uses Mary Douglas on the body as a microcosm of the social order to show how Jesus manifested social equality not only through table fellowship, but also through practices of itinerancy, healing, the raising of Lazarus, and exorcisms. In Jesus' world, disease often meant ritual impurity and social ostracism; healing reincorporates the marginalized, and challenges both the boundaries of community, and the authority of the priestly gate-keepers.[47] A particularly good example is Jesus' healing of the woman who had had a "flow of blood" for twelve years (Mark 5:25–34). If the hemorrhage involved menstrual blood, she would have been ritually impure, thus compounding by gender the stigmatization of physical illness.

Jesus undercuts the social effects of purity insofar as purity defines elite and nonelite status in terms of certain types of bodily states. However, this does not mean that the ethic of Jesus or a Christian ethic must renounce every form of bodily discipline which expresses or symbolizes social organization. This includes discipline of the sexual body. The NT's treatment of sex, though scant, is to be found largely in the Pauline corpus (especially 1 Cor. 6–7). An increasing number of biblical scholars[48] turn to Mary Douglas's work to illuminate ways in which early Christian social identity is given expression and reinforced by various norms for physical behavior, including sexual control. Some suggest that Paul's attention to sexual behavior has oppressive consequences precisely because it is governed by "purity" concerns, i.e., that restriction of bodily boundaries derives from concern about community boundaries. The aim is to loosen the authority of controls over the body by relating them to first-century social and religious concerns.[49] Many biblical interpreters who use Douglas's analysis of body and society tend to adopt a Foucauldian set of assumptions about the social construction of the body, downplaying its physicality as in some ways universal, and stressing the repressive effects of "regimes of knowledge and power." These latter themes are especially influential when sex and gender are at stake, due to interest in resisting social institutions with an oppressive history.

For instance, Jerome H. Neyrey sees Paul as advocating a purity ethic representing his concern for unity in the community; clear roles, status, and authority; and guarded boundaries. These values are symbolized by bodily integrity; hierarchy of bodily parts as metaphors for society, such as head and members; and regulation of orifices, especially in eating, drinking, and sexuality.[50] William Countryman interprets the effect of physical purity on sexual morality in negative terms and reads in the NT a break with Judaism on this issue. He maintains that the NT writers were "ethically indifferent" to what both the Jewish holiness code and later Christians view as "dirty" sexual behavior, and urges the sole authority of the "purity of heart" espoused by Jesus and Paul.[51] According to Countryman, the key to Jesus' sexual ethics is intention.[52] The corollary is apparently that all sexual norms beyond consent and equality are the illegitimate residue of a purity mentality. "Any claim that a given sexual act is wrong in and of itself will be found ultimately to represent either a lack of ethical analysis or a hidden purity claim."[53] Moreover, the gospel allows no rule against the following, in and of themselves: masturbation, nonvaginal heterosexual intercourse, bestiality, polygamy, homosexual acts, or erotic art and literature. The Christian is free to be repelled by any or all of these and may continue to practice her or his own purity code in relation to them. What we are not free to do is impose our codes on others.[54]

Countryman and others are undoubtedly right to argue that Jesus rejected control of the body, especially the sexually differentiated body, as a means of defining social in- and out-groups. Yet it would be rash to move quickly to the conclusion that control of the sexual body, even a highly socialized and communitarian control of the body, is inimical to the spirit of NT ethics. I will argue, to the contrary, that New Testament, especially Pauline, concern with the body is instructive for Christian discipleship precisely because of the kind of communal vision it represents. New Testament authors use sex and gender conduct to enhance solidarity, not as mere conformity, but as inclusion of the excluded and as unified resistance to oppressive social structures.

Neyrey contrasts Paul's cosmology (strong group and grid) to that of his opponents in Corinth (weak on both axes). In discussing the consumption of idol meat and behavior at the Eucharistic feast, Neyrey notes the problem of division among Corinthian Christians,[55] but the fact that the divisions in question were class-oriented is underdeveloped. Yet this fact is key to appreciating what Paul might have meant by control and authority – and how it differs from the purity systems envisioned by Douglas. After all, while Paul may have been concerned with order, authority, and status, he was not concerned to reinforce, but rather to disrupt, elitism of wealth, superior knowledge or gifts, affiliation with a high-status patron or leader, etc. He eliminated circumcision, a bodily mark of communal belonging, because it seemed to diminish equality within the community. The very imagery of body of Christ, and the metaphor of Christ as head, in whom members share unity, undermines the possibility of a highly stratified "grid," although it does not do away with the necessity of respecting Christian identity as defining the disciple's bodily behavior (1 Cor. 6: 15–20).

Moreover, while there was pressure to conform to group practices of solidarity and mutual forbearance; and while "group" feeling was no doubt also heightened by the prospect of rejection, persecution, and suffering; the "entrances" of the community were hardly closed. Noted above all for his mission to the Gentiles, Paul also founded churches which drew in membership from a spectrum of social classes (1 Cor. 1:26–29). In addition, it is conceivable that the "idol meat" controversy (1 Cor. 8, 10) arose out of a situation in which membership in religious communities was somewhat fluid. People may have attended Christian meetings without completely breaking off attendance at pagan rituals or participating as guests in feasts hosted by pagan associates.[56] We might imagine a middle- or upper-class Christian family today whose members not only attend weddings, funerals, and christenings in other Christian congregations, but see it as a part of social fellowship to join Jewish friends in the synagogue for a funeral or a bar mitzvah.

Needless to say, in a culture in which Christianity is well established, such looseness of ritual boundaries is less threatening to group identity than in one in which Christianity is a marginal sect. The point to be taken here is that it is not at all clear that Paul was at the far "strong" end of the axis of group conformity; and hierarchical classification of roles internally was something he opposed more than he upheld (though not unambivalently, as is evident in his approach to gender). One feminist interpreter, Ross Kraemer, notes that in early Christian communities, some women, such as the Corinthian women prophets, benefitted from a "comparatively strong group and minimal grid arrangement." In so doing, she rightly disputes Douglas's assumption that high or low group or grid will always tend to have consistent effects on women as a group (ignoring race or class, for instance). She takes particular exception to Douglas's view that, after all, traditional "high grid" societies are more protective of women's welfare because they ensure that, filling their proper roles, women will be guaranteed respect. "In relatively egalitarian low grid communities, women experienced increased autonomy, wider scope of public roles, increased access to education and information, decreased emphasis on childbearing and marriage, and so forth."[57] Women had enhanced opportunities for equality in communities like those of early Christianity, where group identity is strong, but the internal classification system is relatively loose, especially about marriage and kinship.[58] Yet Kraemer maps the benign consequences of early Christian community for women in disconcertingly – even anachronistically – liberal terms when she describes the value that low grid permits to surface as "autonomy as self-determination."[59]

A similar set of values motivates William Countryman, according to whom every "modern individual" owns his or her own sexual property. Each individual retains right of control over that property and should prefer "interior goods" like intimacy, friendship, counsel, and solace, over "exterior goods," such as security and children.[60] Kraemer interprets early Christianity as diminishing the importance of control over sex and reproduction for defining community boundaries. Countryman, on the contrary, finds Pauline ethics inadequate to the extent that it does retain or confirm contemporaneous gender expectations. But, for both, the criterion against which to evaluate early Christian morality is individual freedom from sex and gender regulation by a strictly bounded community exerting strong pressure to conform.

Shared assumptions about the function of the body as a social symbol appear to be operative in an approach to New Testament sexual ethics which authors such as Countryman, Kraemer, and Neyrey represent: (1) High social expectations of bodily control belie repressive societies. That is, control is equated with constraint; notions of "purity" and the social boundaries they represent are a function of the strong controlling the weak. (2) Control of sex represents in the body the order of a patriarchal society. (3) Where there is no visible, tight social classification system, and where bodily movements are relatively informal, individuals are free. (4) Liberal, democratic, and more gender-equal modern societies do not control bodies (embodied individuals).

Mary Douglas's perspective is compatible with more positive, constructive, nondualist reconfigurations of bodily meaning in

Christian tradition. Key to this tradition are the incarnation of the divine in the human, Jesus' suffering in the body and death on the cross as revelatory and redemptive, human healing and sanctification as resurrection of the body, the Eucharist as a sacrament of union with God, and feeding or eating with the poor as criteria of discipleship. Marriage and sexuality are seen as sacramental in some, though not all, Christian traditions. Sexuality and motherhood, as well as feeding (sometimes nursing) have been central symbols for Christian religious experience. Caroline Walker Bynum's captivating historical studies demonstrate the extent to which Christianity, along with other societies, sees the body (not only the spirit) as an avenue of transcendence and even of union with the divine. In fact, gnostic, dualistic spiritualities, while occasionally infecting the Christian tradition, have been consistently declared heretical. "Control, discipline, even torture of the flesh is, in medieval devotion, not so much the rejection of physicality as the elevation of it – a horrible yet delicious elevation – into a means of access to the divine."[61] Among the most universal bodily routes to the divinity are sex, food, and death, along with death's foretastes, pain and illness. Christianity and its mystics have invoked all three.

Both Taylor and Douglas are worried about alienation of individuals from the public order, and the interiorization and relativization of morals. In Douglas's view, the sincerity, authenticity, and personal success of the subject are in Western societies overriding respect for roles, duties, and social structures. Children, for instance, are educated to be interested in their own emotional states and the feelings of others. Douglas thinks "seeds of alienation"[62] are contained in the relocation of control to the personal system, and the lack of integration of the individual with the social body. Taylor predicts choices will be trivial if not referred to anything bigger than choice itself. Worse, unexamined choice leaves the chooser susceptible to manipulation by larger social institutions – like the state and the economy – which have taken on a life of their own. In relation to sex and gender, an insistence on pragmatic self-determination which is individualist and asocial can also permit exploitation by tacit yet tenacious sexist attitudes which survive under a veneer of women's rights, masking a deeper lack of public investment in the positive welfare of women, children, and families.[63]

The moral challenge for the first Christians was to devise a set of strategies which could break the grip of societal norms on the quality of their own communal relationships. Primitive Christianity appears in a setting in which not only women's sexual and reproductive capacities, but men's also (though to a far lesser extent) have been organized for the ends of a stratified, controlled, and dominative social order. The mode of organization is the patriarchal family. Resistance was a challenge which the early Christians did not always meet successfully. But neither, on the whole, did they fail.

FAMILY

The major argument of this chapter will be that New Testament instructions about sex and gender *often* functioned in the early Christian communities to challenge social hierarchy, especially as embodied in the Greco-Roman family. To the extent that androcentrism and even misogynism pervade biblical texts, suspicion must accompany retrieval. Yet the biblical text simultaneously communicates an alternative reality which can be reappropriated in a critical, historical hermeneutic fed by the New Testament's inclusive social vision.[64]

What should the New Testament view of sex and gender be set "against"? Jewish, Greek, and Roman families were assuredly patriarchal, but, as recent scholarship attests, with more complexity than may in the past have been acknowledged. Greater nuance is prompted by greater awareness that the legal codes and other normative texts from which impressions are drawn were written by men; may not reflect social practice as much as the way authors wanted their communities to be perceived; may indeed be intended to control discrepant social practice; and may be inconsistent with other evidence (like funerary inscriptions) about "what really went on."

Although historical study and archeology have provided us

with relatively little factual information about the family in ancient Israel, compared to Greece or Rome, the Hebrew Bible presents a religious community built upon the patriarchal family. In its biblical setting, the family is a kinship unit intermediate between the tribe and the household, the members of which claim descent from a common ancestor.[65] A network of families long before it was a state, ancient Israel depended on a kinship substratum to define social and political relations even during the periods of the monarchy and of two kingdoms.

The primary context of individual identity and the basic unit of the tribe was the ancestral household. A typical agrarian household might have included grandparents, grown sons, and their families, adopted children, a divorced adult daughter if the family could afford to support her, and servants or slaves. Households in an extended family lived in close proximity to one another. Biblical laws and regulations governing households and property envision a fairly prosperous population, although some proportion would at any given time have belonged to the landless underclass. But ownership of a plot of land was key to the survival of a typical agrarian family. An important economic function of the family was the cultivation and transmission of this land. Descendants, especially the first-born son, had the right of inheritance from the head of household (1 Kgs. 21:3). Loss of the land due to economic hardship and debt spelled ruin for the entire line, and safeguards existed to ensure eventual restoration of property to its original ownership (Lev. 25:8–55).

Marriage in ancient Israel was likewise institutionalized in view of economics and property. The laws forbidding marriage within certain degrees of consanguinity represent a concern to make alliances outside the family and to enhance the family's economic and labor assets. At the same time, marriage of select close relatives, as in cross-cousin marriage (for example, Jacob wed Leah and Rachel), was permitted in order to consolidate family assets. Choice of marriage partners was of interest to the entire household, but unmarried women had relatively little self-determination in the matter. The family, especially the father, was regarded as having a legally protected financial stake in marriageable daughters (Exod. 22:15–16, Deut. 22:28–29, Hos. 3:2). Property also was settled upon the woman at marriage, and thus contributed to the household for which she was destined (Gen. 30:20, 31: 14–16, Josh. 15:18–19, 1 Kgs 9:16). Adultery as well as seduction and rape were regarded as types of theft (Exod. 20:17, Lev. 20:10, Prov. 6:29–35).

Paternity was a consideration in marriage which was even more important than property. A man lived on in the religious community through his descendents, especially his sons. Thus he must be guaranteed that children borne by his wife were his genuine heirs, and needed assurance that female fertility be available to perpetuate his line even if he married a wife who bore no sons. Polygamy (in pre-Davidic times), concubinage, and levirate marriage all illustrate this concern to create and maintain a line of male descendents. A man's interest in offspring could be framed in financial terms (Exod. 21:22–23). Men were permitted to initiate divorce (Deut. 24:1–4), although the precise causes for which it was allowed remain unclear. Economic arrangements attending divorce are not specified in biblical laws.

Hierarchy and authority were important to the ancient Israelite family, structured around male prerogatives and favoring elder sons. Women outside the male support system were at a serious social and economic disadvantage. A woman's religious and social identity were primarily in relation to male family members, and her communal status was secured by marriage and the birth of sons. Little or no provision was made for unmarried daughters, divorcees, or widows to inherit fathers' or husbands' property. While an egalitarian interpretation of the creation stories in Genesis 1–3 can be employed as a critical norm against the subordinate status of women in ancient Israel, it is also possible to identify texts in which the rape and murder of women seems accepted as unremarkable.[66] Nevertheless, important women – Sarah, Rebeka, Rachel, Leah, Zipporah, Deborah, Naomi, Ruth, Abigail, and Judith – have major roles to play, at least in the biblical story. More recent readings, especially by Jewish women resisting Christian portrayals, have argued that women historically may have had higher status, more influence in the religious cult, and more independent spheres of activity in ancient Israel than is usually acknowledged.[67]

In the first century CE, Christians reworked their Jewish heritage in the context of Greco-Roman culture and the growth of churches in Hellenistic cities like Corinth (to which St. Paul directed the only extended remarks on sex and marriage in the NT).[68] In ancient Greece, the family had been much more controlled by the state than in ancient Israel. Although under the first-century Roman Empire, women had gained more legal rights, their influence in the family was, as traditionally, limited and usually indirect. As one historian states it, "Greek society was (and is) patriarchal: the master of the *oikos* was the head of the family, its *kyrios*, as its governor, governing the slaves as master, the children as a sort of king because of their affection for him and his greater age, his wife like a political leader ... the husband is always the head of the family."[69]

In the Homeric period and in Athens until the fifth century B.C.E., Greek society replicated a phenomenon common in many cultures: an aristocratic woman enjoyed considerable freedom within her husband's domain, but her position depended on his success, and on his good will or the ability of her relatives to exercise social pressure against him.[70] Women were sometimes well informed of family financial affairs, and could take charge of husbands' property in their absence. Sonless families could pass property through a daughter whom they would arrange to marry, if possible, to her paternal uncle. But women could never dispose of property in their own right. The upper classes, of course, depended on a huge population of slaves and serfs, where women no doubt suffered doubly, both by gender and by class.

Also largely outside the circuit of respectable women's lives (but not, of course, of upper-class men's) were the prostitutes. In the Hebrew Bible, references to prostitution imply pagan cultic practices or sexual immorality whose unacceptability for Israelites is almost taken for granted. Greek prostitutes, in contrast, had acknowledged social roles; they ranged from the

artistically trained and cultivated *hetairai*, or paid sexual en-
tertainers and companions, to the *pornai*, common prostitutes.
Some were slaves, and some were free foreigners residing in
Greek cities. *Hetairai* entertained men at all-male drinking
parties or *symposia*, in the men's quarters of an ordinary house,
in their own houses, or in houses rented for the purpose by the
clients. Some *hetairai* adopted the occupations of citizen women,
such as weaving and other domestic tasks, and occasionally
even tried to pass themselves off as respectable matrons.
Occasionally a Roman citizen would leave his wife to take up
residence with his mistress, and even legitimize her children. As
depicted all too graphically in vase paintings, however, the
more common fate of an aging courtesan was to specialize in
sexual services the younger competition found too degrading.[71]

Citizen women were married in their early teens to men
often many years older, with whom a betrothal was arranged
by the families. Although many were taught to read and write,
their education rarely extended further. A high social premium
on virginity before marriage and fidelity afterwards was part of
a culture of honor and shame, focused on women's sexuality.
The honor of men depended upon the sexual purity of their
women, which they protected ferociously. Linked to gender
through an ideology of women's uncontrolled and provocative
sexuality, needing well-guarded confinement within the home,
this culture produced a fairly strict separation of men's and
women's spheres.[72] Women in classical Greece did not even
dine with their husbands at home, much less at social events.
Nor did they participate in the political life of the city. Aristotle
mentions "superintendents of women," as though that were an
actual social office, though not a widespread one.[73]

Separation of women from the public and political spheres of
men, however, need not imply "physical sequestration, and
consequently utter subjection, as does seclusion."[74] Although
the rhetoric of women's virtue boasted of ingenuous virgins and
wives who never passed beyond the doors of their houses,
Athenian women participated in a range of activities which
brought them into contact not only with family and slaves, but
with neighbors, co-workers, and clients. For many, economic

survival while their husbands were away at war or in widow-hood demanded it. Women's economic endeavors may have included nursing, weaving, working in the fields or vineyards, and labor as midwives, innkeepers, or bakers. Women also met together in carrying water from the well, washing clothes at the fountain, and in religious festivals at which they not only participated, but in some instances were the primary organi-zers. In Athenian society, women played a central role in religion, and even held the public office of priestess.[75]

Since young girls were married at thirteen or fourteen, and men not until they were near thirty, younger men were motivated to seek nonmarital means of sexual gratification. The general unavailability of women, and some social disapproba-tion of association with prostitutes and courtesans, may have influenced some men to turn toward homoeroticism. Not that social attitudes were in that case entirely nonjudgmental. In a critique of Foucault and of others who theorize that the Greeks were only concerned about sexual roles, and not about the sex of partners, David Cohen characterizes Greek homosexuality as beset by contradictions and ambivalences.[76] Pederasty was not unequivocally forbidden. At the same time, adult men who had sex for money could be partially disenfranchised, men who enticed free boys with payment could be the objects of lawsuits by their families, and schoolboys were fiercely guarded from the advances of older males. Eventually, of course, all boys were expected to assume the "male" role; "permanent male–male sexual partnerships were not a socially legitimate substitute for marriage."[77]

It is clear, then, that the celebrated homosexuality and bisexuality of ancient Greece were hardly equivalent to a free-ranging and unrepressed enjoyment of sexual desire and plea-sure. Even the stages of male sexuality were quite strictly managed, and little nuanced to the personal preferences of those who were expected to assume reciprocal roles. "The Greek man had to go through his homosexual experiences at the right moment, with the right people and according to the right rules."[78] As a youth he might be receptive to the advances of an adult lover; but suddenly upon maturity was expected to assume the active sexual role, both with women and with younger boys.

During the period of early Christianity, Greek culture had come under the control and influence of the Roman Empire. Roman law, to be discussed shortly, had given women increasing legal rights, but it applied only to Roman citizens. Hellenistic cities largely followed their own customs, which would in many ways have been more like those of classical Greece than like those of the Roman elite, whose concerns the laws reflect. However, constraints on women began to loosen in Hellenistic culture as well, a process already in evidence in papyri and art works from Hellenistic Egypt (predating the Roman Empire).[79]

Even more in the case of the Roman family than of the Greek, recent literature has opened up the patriarchal family to show power dynamics that went in multiple directions. During the period when Christianity first arose, the state regulated marriage, divorce, and inheritance, and gave ultimate control to fathers and husbands, who had almost unlimited legal power over their children within the household (*patria potestas*), including the exposure of infants and the execution of adult sons for fairly minor insults to family honor. Recent work, however, has shown that actual paternal treatment of children could not have been as rough as such laws suggest. Not only do Roman authors write fondly of their children, but sons in particular were groomed to assume responsibility for the family in the next generation. Fathers attempted to cultivate in them a sense of worth and honor which set them far above slaves (for whom harsh physical punishment was an ordinary means of psychological as well as of physical control).[80]

As in Greece, women were married in their teens to older men. Although the Roman ideal was a companionate marriage, and women were highly praised for prudent and frugal management of slaves and household, the age differential in marriage and assumption of male superiority meant that young girls were trained essentially to be intelligent and faithful subordinates to their husbands. And neither social tolerance of male sexual infidelity, nor the custom of men keeping concubines before marriage, would have strengthened intimacy and reciprocity in their relationships with their wives.

In early Roman law, women who married passed directly from the authority of their fathers to that of their husbands, who assumed full ownership of the wife's dowry and property. But, by the middle of the second century C.E., this form of marriage (*cum manu*) had been replaced by one in which the dowry went to the husband, but the wife remained under the legal power of her father (*sine manu*), and could inherit property from him of which she remained the independent legal owner after his death. By this time, the dissolution of a marriage required no more from either party than a notice of intent, and did not carry with it financial penalties. Although the youth of wives in relation to their husbands no doubt resulted in psychological and social dependence, Roman women's independence in marriage had a legal asset in the availability to them of financial resources.[81] While the continuing interest of their natal families in the disposition of property would have resulted in certain restrictions or expectations for women, their families also had a stake in guarding its daughters and sisters from the influence or control of husbands. Indeed, divorce could result from pressure on women by birth families who desired to rearrange their social and economic alliances. After divorce, fathers retained custody of children, who almost always resided with him, usually with a stepmother and her children as well. In marriage, and even after divorce, however, husbands and children had reason to satisfy and placate women who might consider their interests when the wife, ex-wife, or mother came into her share of her birth family's estate.

Families in the Roman Empire tended to live in "nuclear" groups (father, mother, children, along with slaves and servants), rather than in extended kin networks which combined multiple married couples and their offspring. Relationships and emotional ties within this setting seemed important to men and women alike,[82] as attested from Cicero's letters in exile to his wife and children. But rampant divorce and remarriage, especially among the upper classes, could make household relationships complicated and vastly extenuate the so-called "nuclear" group. It must also have had the effect of destabilizing and often diminishing the affective bonds of parents to children. Mothers were separated from children after divorce, at least by residence[83]; fathers divided whatever affections they chose to bestow among the children of their old and new wives. Cicero himself was divorced after more than twenty years of marriage, remarried quickly to a much younger woman and divorced again. His correspondence reveals his closest social and familial ties to be to his blood relations, especially his brother's family.[84]

The absence of emotional investment in Roman marriage was both a cause and an effect of frequent divorce and remarriage. Keith R. Bradley observes that

any attempt to characterize the upper-class Roman family must proceed from the perception that marriage for the Roman elite was not a permanently binding institution, and that as a result the families brought into existence by the procreation of children after marriage were subject to a high level of impermanence and flexibility as the parents of children sequentially, and in some instances cavalierly, changed spousal partners and established new households.[85]

Bradley gives several examples, among whom is one L. Cornelius Sulla Felix, who lived about a century before Christ, and married five times (sometimes for evident political reasons), siring five children. One daughter had a son who was the contemporary of his mother's half-siblings. In addition, one of Sulla's wives brought three children by a former marriage. One of those children was already married and pregnant when her mother remarried; and the daughter herself was "compulsorily divorced and remarried," apparently before her baby was born. No wonder Bradley concludes that the members of Sulla's constantly recombining family must have experienced "a very diffuse set of personal relationships";[86] or that he speculates that "it may be the contemporary Western family, under the impact of the modern 'divorce revolution' that provides the best analogue for the upper class Roman family."[87]

In summary, marriage in the cultures in which Christianity was born were patriarchal, even though women had some recourse to independence and social power, especially through their right to control inherited property. While women under Roman law were able to divorce, this is less a sign of their autonomy or freedom from spousal control, than it is a sign that marriages were a route to social, economic, and political objectives. A woman's right to divorce preserved her natal family's stake in the social as well as financial assets of her marriageability, and her family's interests were prior to those of her husband in shaping her destiny. Loving, companionate unions were idealized and were not unknown in practice,[88] even though it was rare that a marriage be undertaken for sentimental reasons, or on account of the mutual attraction of partners. Becoming a parent did not necessarily signify long-term, personal devotion to offspring, even on the part of mothers. Even families of moderate rank gave children into the care of wet nurses; divorce reduced mothers' contact with their children. Marriage and the production of children were seen more as services to kin networks and to the state than as promising personal reward.

CHRISTIANITY

As was argued as a first premise of this chapter, Christian communities emphasized solidarity and sharing across the traditional status boundaries, such as sex (male–female), class (slave–free), and culture (Jew–Greek). They rejected ostentatious displays of wealth and conspicuous consumption which excluded the poor. In the new communities of discipleship, the outcasts were to be included, the poor cared for, and enmities forgiven. A new way of life was initiated (never perfectly achieved) which stood in criticism of the standard assumptions about legitimate power relationships and control over other persons. It was mediated by means of sharing of property, table fellowship, inclusion of slaves and women in the community, and the setting aside of religious practices which marked the boundaries of the Jewish community.

The early Christians were resocialized from the patriarchal family of society and the state to the new family of brothers and sisters in Christ. The bonds of holiness in the community required both economic and sexual self-restraint (1 Thess. 4–5). While Greco-Roman philosophers railed against promiscuity and economic excess too, the difference of their early Christian counterparts is that the focus of concern is the unity of the community, not the perfection of the individual. Members of the community are addressed as members of the body of Christ, or of the community in whom his Spirit dwells, not as individual citizens with control over their own bodies and households.[89] Christians' baptism into the new cult (Gal 3:28) influences their social behavior, including their bodily and sexual behavior.

In the reign of Augustus, in 18 B.C.E. and 9 C.E., two pieces of legislation were passed which exacted penalties against celibacy, childlessness, and adultery, while offering benefits to Roman citizens who became parents of children in marriage. Wealthy men protested the threat this presented to the accumulation of family property. Augustus was fond of quoting Metellus, who a century earlier had declared that "since nature has decreed that we cannot live at all comfortably with our wives, or live at all without them, we should consider the long-term benefit rather than immediate happiness."[90] Augustus feared that a decline in fertility among the ruling class would threaten its existence, and hence the empire's structures of social continuity, civic order, and political success. Norms controlling the selection of an appropriate wife, and about the conduct of sexual relations in marriage, had as their purpose the perpetuation and security of the governing classes, and were focused precisely upon the bodies of the elite.

Against this landscape, early Christianity's aversion to divorce (Mark 10:11–12, Matt. 5:31–32 and 19:9, Luke 16:18, I Cor. 7:10–11), downplaying not only procreation but family ties in any form (Mark 3:31, Luke 19:29 and 8:21), advocacy – however mild – of equality in marriage (1 Cor. 7:2–5; and even Eph. 5:28–33), identification of female worth in roles outside family duties (Mary and Martha, Luke 10:38–42[91]); and above all its idealization of celibacy (1 Cor. 7: 8 and 25–40), were dangerously countercultural.

Corinth, the setting for most of the sexual concerns addressed in the New Testament, had been refounded as a Roman colony

toward the middle of the first century by Julius Caesar, and
some of its citizens would have arrived there recently from
Rome. (The ancient city of Corinth had been destroyed in 143
B.C.E.) As has often been noted, Corinth was a cosmopolitan
city, a crossroads of cultures and religious cults, and would
certainly have been influenced by Roman marriage and family
practices. When Paul tells the Corinthians to exclude an
incestuous man from the community, and to avoid relations
with prostitutes (1 Cor. 5, 6:15–16), he has the communal
welfare in mind, especially solidarity in Christ. In the case of
the man living with his stepmother, it is possible that Paul is
reacting against status differences within the community. A
wealthy or prestigious convert might have been permitted to
remain in a sexual relationship which was forbidden to the
ordinary Christian, because he and others thought he deserved
special treatment (as evident perhaps in "boasting" about this
member [1 Cor. 5:6]). Augustan laws required the widowed or
divorced to remarry and decimated the inheritance of a
surviving spouse if childless. It is credible to speculate that,
under such circumstances, the union of a young widow and her
stepson – not outrageous by cultural norms – could have been
designed to produce heirs in the family that would improve the
couple's financial position and social standing.[92]

VIRGINITY

Peter Brown argues the thesis that permanent virginity as a
religiously dedicated and ideal sexual state was a distinctive
contribution of early Christianity, and that it operated not so
much out of a "negative" attitude toward sex, as out of a
commitment to communal solidarity and a rejection of the
hierarchical and state-controlled functions of the patriarchal
family. Virtually all sex in the climate out of which the New
Testament arose served social purposes; it seems unexaggerated
to say that it was virtually everywhere a symbol of domination.
Virginity for Christians could serve a contrary purpose.
"Sexual renunciation might lead the Christian to transform the
body and, in transforming the body, to break with the discreet

discipline of the ancient city."[93] For early Christians, permanent vocational celibacy was a stand against the civic-minded, and often kin-manipulated, procreation of standard hierarchies through one's children.

Virginity also represented the democratization of access to an "elite" way of life.[94] Without special training, religious mysteries and rites, money, or social standing, each disciple could elect and fulfill the highest personal and social manifestation of "singlehearted devotion to the Lord" (1 Cor. 7:35). Marriage is a distraction from preparation for the imminently expected end of time. But perhaps more importantly, virginity, as Paul recommends, was a way to elude the affairs of the world of family and politics which could cause so much anxiety, and so easily seduce a disciple into calculations of power and personal advantage.

There were no doubt many reasons for which Christians adopted a celibate life style, including asceticism, dualistic tendencies, an aversion to unruly passion, or even to the opposite sex. Yet virginity adopted as a path to religious excellence was also in effect an escape route from the patriarchal household and its duty to procreate, and a way into a new community of inclusive solidarity. This was especially important for women. Unlike their Jewish and Greco-Roman counterparts, Christian women did not have access to the community of faith only through the family, nor was their value defined in terms of procreation of male heirs. While the married life was still acceptable, the sexual subordination of women to men was eroded.

MARRIAGE AND PARENTHOOD

Heterosexual marriage and family are assumed rather than defended as the framework for sexual activity by New Testament authors. The dominative and sexist aspects of these institutions are, however, resisted. A first line of resistance was to place Christians outside the divisions of status and modes of control represented by the Greco-Roman family, both by offering the option of celibacy, and by disconnecting the religious "family" from the biological kin network, at least in the sense that family advantage and unity no longer controlled religious identity. A second line was to transform the marriages and families of Christians so that they could be hospitable to the new religion and even serve it. This transformation is visible in the households which became churches and in the married couples who served in the churches (for example, Prisca and Aquila in Acts 18:18 and 18:25; 1 Cor. 16:18; Roms 16:2); in Paul's acknowledgment that marriage could be a "gift" in the community (1 Cor. 7:7); in his belief that children of mixed marriages were holy, and that a Christian spouse might sanctify a pagan one (1 Cor. 7:14); and in the hope that God could be experienced in ordinary married life (Eph. 5:21–23).

Low attention is given to parenthood as a role or duty of Christians, both because of eschatological expectations, and because procreation in the culture did not represent what it may for a modern reader. As we have seen, parenthood in the patriarchal family was an effective axis of the social control of all persons' bodies and relationships. By the same token, the minimizing of procreation in the New Testament does not amount to a biblical defense of nonprocreative sex, or of affective, romantic love and bond-enhancing pleasurable sex separated from procreative considerations. It would be especially anachronistic to attribute such a position to biblical authors given the marginal place of interpersonal love in defining marriage as they knew it. To even seek freedom from, or adjustments of, imbalances of power within family structures which focused marital sex exclusively on procreation (for family and the state), and which viewed sex outside marriage not only as deviant from the ideal and all-inclusive married condition, but in terms of an extreme double standard, was already to muster an almost incredible revolution in social attitudes.

SEXUAL "SINS"

The positive biblical vision of sex focuses on faithful, heterosexual marriage, and sex outside of that context is clearly not part of the normative picture for the early Christians. Yet, the function of any moral vision is, from a biblical standpoint (as in I Cor. 13), to encourage and support community members in their relations toward one another (to "build up," I Thess. 5:11). This applies to sexual teaching, which has undeniably for much of the Christian tradition, been used to reinforce exactly the kind of boundaries of judgment and exclusion against which original discipleship stood. A Christian sexual ethics does not function first or most strongly to "mark off" and condemn, but rather to inspire and encourage the disciple to do good.

Jesus manifests solidarity with those whom society or the religious community itself brands as "sinners"; and his warnings of sinfulness are not usually aimed in the directions anticipated by his hearers. Jesus' response to the woman caught in adultery (Jn. 8:3–11) instantiates an attitude of compassion and forgiveness when concrete sexual "transgressions" are committed by the powerless. Transgressions must be marked, and their perpetrators separated, when an ongoing offense endangers the community or the vulnerable within it, and particularly when the sexual offense represents the hubris of the powerful (as possibly with the incestuous man). Among the few concrete targets of which we learn in the New Testament, especially from Paul, are prostitution, divorce, and homosexuality. All of these represent dominant power relationships in the New Testament context. In the case of prostitution, few Christians would debate its exploitative character today, and that is especially true if we look at its social causes and conditions worldwide. On divorce and homosexuality, however, the picture is somewhat more complex.

Both Paul and the gospels attribute to Jesus a prohibition of divorce (I Cor. 7:10–11, Mark 10:2–12, Matt. 19:9, 5:32; Luke 16:18). Both Mark and Matthew 19 portray Jesus as appealing to the "one flesh" unity of man and woman established at the creation. Both of the Matthean texts are addressed only to men, and accuse men of committing adultery if they divorce and remarry or marry a divorced woman. If a wife divorced by her husband remarries, this adultery is attributed to the man's responsibility (Matt. 5:32).[95] Some scholars theorize that the divorce sayings originated in the early Christian communities, as a response to divorce for ascetic reasons,[96] a theme which is particularly evident in Paul's instruction to couples to separate sexually for prayer only temporarily (1 Cor. 7:5). Although the early Christian ideal was celibacy, that ideal was not to be used to disrupt existing marital commitments.

Whatever its origin, if seen in broader cultural context, early Christian teaching against divorce would also have protected women from the Jewish man's unilateral right to dismiss his wife, and from the Roman man's tendency to use wife and female relatives as pawns in the game of political and economic power. It also protected all family members, but especially children, from the emotional distances, dislocations, and betrayals which must have resulted from the transiency of the Roman nuclear family. Although the biblical authors reflected contemporary philosophical and Jewish critiques of the legal and social realities of marriage,[97] they selected from the environment ideals of marriage which could help tranform that institution into a more adequate representation of Christian values. Paul's repetition of Jesus' divorce prohibition is already adapted to a Greco-Roman setting, for it assumes that a woman may have initiated the separation.[98] The appropriation and reformulation of moral teaching was an ongoing process, even within the New Testament. For instance, Paul does not take the anti-divorce teaching he attributes to Jesus as a rigid precedent, but adapts it on his own authority as inspired by the Lord's Spirit (1 Cor. 7:40). He warrants his own permission of Christian divorce from a rejecting pagan spouse by the "peace" to which Christians are called (1 Cor. 7:15).

Same-sex genital activity is certainly repudiated by both Old and New Testament authors (Lev. 18:22, 20:13; Gen. 19:5–7; Deut. 23:18; 1 Cor. 6:9; 1 Tim. 1:10; Rom. 1:26–27), whatever the unclarity of certain wordings, and however true it may be that the causes and contexts they envision differ drastically from our own. The size of that difference makes this a particularly vexing issue on which to derive a "biblical" position for our own time. Throughout the Bible, homosexual activity is associated with idolatry, with transgression against God, and with

contemptible habits of alien religious groups.[99] There is not the
ambiguity and tension among texts that we find on gender,
marriage, or family. Condemnations of homosexuality by Paul
(1 Cor. 6:9; Rom. 1:24–27) may owe at least in part to common
social assumptions, especially among Jews, about "natural"
behavior. When it occurs in a list of illustrative vices being
contrasted to the way disciples are supposed to live (as in 1
Cor.), it may simply represent a social norm Paul can count on
his audience to share. And Paul's and his audience's perception
of the unnaturalness of homosexuality could not have but been
colored by the exploitative conditions under which it occurred.[100]

As in his treatment of all sexuality, Paul reacted against a
particularly obvious symptom of the domination and control
which sexual practices represented generally in the Greco-
Roman world. The evil of homosexuality did not rest only on
the fact that it permitted the exploitation of some categories of
individuals (slaves and boys) by others (free adult men). The
practice of homosexuality rested on the institutionalization of
social control through the family, including misogynist attitudes
toward sex and marriage. It was one more instance of pressure
exerted on all by, as Foucault would put it, regimes of power
and truth which co-opt individuals' very self-understanding and
bodily experience. In the case of divorce, it was recognized
after Jesus' lifetime that particular circumstances can call for
justified compromises in practice. In some situations a rigid
insistence on the behavior the ideal would usually imply would
have destructive effects for the greater Christian communal
value of "peace." In the case of homosexuality, circumstances
have also changed since the first century. The primary kinds of
sexual conduct that are excluded by New Testament teaching
are status-marking, boundary-erecting, other-dominating, and
self-promoting actions and practices, especially when they
deprive others of what they require to survive and to "flourish"
as human beings. Unfortunately, stigmatization of homosexuals
has in the Christian community often functioned in just this
way. The biblical message about homosexuals probably has
more lasting pertinence to the way they are received in the

Christian community than with the nature of their sex acts. Flexibility in incorporating homosexual people in the Christian community does not necessarily denigrate the ideals of virginity (introduced by Christians) or faithful, mutual, heterosexual marriage (transformatively appropriated by Christians from cultural trends). Instead, it may redress a history of exclusion of and suffering by those termed "sinners" by others who are righteous according to the standards of those with greatest access to institutional power.

The sexual discipline of the body within Christian vision and practice serves, above all, to challenge hierarchy and domination, both in the family and in society. In the early church, virginity could have this purpose, as could respectful mutuality in marriage ("each has his own special gift from God, one of one kind and one of another" [1 Cor. 7:7]). In today's churches egalitarian marriage *should* have such a function, but interiorizes all too often the types of domination (especially domination of women) against which Christian virginity may originally have reacted. Hatred and excluding condemnations of sexual "sinners" is another distortion of marriage as a symbol of the presence of God. Nonmarital types of sexual relationship fall further from the model which biblical teaching presumes to offer the best opportunity for communal unity and service: mutuality in marriage. This fact is relevant to their moral evaluation. Sex outside of commitment, for instance, does not symbolize "solidarity" and may well be exploitative. An ethos of sexual experimentation and variety (gay or straight) militates against the intimacy and commitment that is human sexuality's fulfillment. Parts of gay culture can tend to centralize sex and sexual identity as the key to human (and Christian) identity for both women and men. Avoidance of parenthood by young professionals may represent social depreciation of families, consumerism, and individualism.

Still, it would be hard to argue on a solid biblical basis that the key to the Christian evaluation of sex is categorization of behaviors, rather than discernment of what is commonly upbuilding and what is not. Certainly not any and all kinds of sexual acts and relationships are equal in this regard. What the values of the kingdom mean in practice in any historical era must be re-evaluated in the light of their specific relevance to human goods and well-being, and to social practices which enhance or destroy the sharing of those goods in community. In the case of human sexual well-being, it is essential to take into account the relative concrete availability to persons of elements of sexual flourishing (sexual pleasure, intimacy, commitment, parenthood), as Christians define the appropriate bodily symbolization of Christian identity and community. But condemnation of types of sexual conduct is very far from being a major moral concern of the New Testament, and falls a great distance behind economic and class behavior in importance. (Also, note that when Paul excludes sexual sinners from the kingdom of God [1 Cor. 6:9–10], he is still at the level of exhortative attitude formation, not at that of someone's existential crisis.)

This interpretation does not, however, permit any quick move to liberty-oriented renditions of a biblical ethic of sex. Key to biblical morality in all spheres of life is a strong social sense, a sense of unity in Christ with demanding ramifications for the moral life. It focuses on the ability of each disciple to recognize the need of those whom society has deemed unworthy or even "nonpersons," and to meet that need as though the other were oneself. In the sexual realm, particular care is required to ensure that sexual liberty is not a screen for – and even a modern-day institutionalization of – manipulative and ultimately oppressive sex which demeans women; fosters the destruction, neglect, or domination of children; and permits a market-place mentality of free entrepreneurship, risk-benefit analysis, and survival of the clever and well positioned, to undermine this crucial realm of human interdependence.

Marriage and family, as important institutions for ordering human life and educating human agents, deserve critical attention and theological analysis, as much or more than sexual dilemmas which arise outside these parameters.[101] Yet Christian communities have expended disproportionate energy debating issues like homosexuality, which certainly affect a smaller number of their members, and are rarely enabled today by the ability of the "sinner" to wield social power, than are sins which lurk closer to the tradition's heterosexual, marital, and procreative heart.[102] Consider domestic violence; sexual abuse; marital rape; callousness of men to the daily burdens of their wives; wives' and mothers' emotional manipulation of husbands and children; sexual objectification or coercion by men or women; neglect and abuse of children; narcissism of family members in their relations to one another; narcissism of families in relation to those outside their family, church, or community; consumerism; drugs and alcoholism; sloth toward the commitment it takes to sustain a marriage and be responsible parents; and irresponsible divorce. Celibacy as the approved Christian counterpoint to marriage can also conceal perversions such as clergy who sexually abuse minors, and those who, vowed to celibacy, maintain sexual relationships, sometimes resulting in children. These are surely larger practical and moral concerns in the church, in the priesthood or pastorate, and in the "normative" heterosexual family, than are the sexual mistakes, failures, and often the sufferings, of those who lie closer to the margins of socially accepted sexual practice.

"HAUSTAFELN"

A perplexing and seemingly ever-present problem for a feminist interpretation of sex and gender in the New Testament is the *haustafeln* or "household codes," which commend to Christians the submission to the *paterfamilias* of women, slaves, and children, as was the standard expectation in the pagan culture (Eph. 5:21–6:9, Col. 3:18–4:1, 1 Pet. 2:18–3:7). Some scholars distinguish these codes as a later layer of accommodation by the Christian churches to social pressures to conform (or at least appear less subversive) in order to survive. As on issues of wealth, social status, slavery, and violence, it is doubtful that even the earliest followers of Jesus ever enjoyed a total transformation of their personal and social relationships. Elisabeth Schüssler Fiorenza says rightly that the early Christian communities and their moral practices can provide "historical prototypes," but not "timeless archetypes."[103]

What the *haustafeln* illustrate is that the early Christians were neither morally perfect nor socially sectarian. They engaged their religious experience with their social reality – in this case the patriarchal family comandeered by political aims – and transformed it with varying degrees of success. The Gospel of Thomas was non- "canonical" precisely because it pictured "sex and its consequences, the entanglements of family life and household responsibilities" as "the most dangerous snares in the world."[104] The churches whose testimony later generations accepted as authoritative saw the body and sex as problematic, especially in their social ramifications – but not as evil. They neither repudiated directly nor completely changed the status-structured family and community, but they did begin to transform them. One example is the leadership roles women assumed in the Christian community. These included Prisca, leader of a local church (1 Cor. 16:18, Rom. 16:2, Acts 18:18, and 18:25); Phoebe, a deacon (Rom. 16:1–2); Junia, called an apostle by Paul (Rom 16:7); and Mary Magdalene, a disciple whom all four gospels attest was one of the first witnesses to the resurrection.

As far as the household codes are concerned, the Bible's originality surfaces more in relation to slaves than women. The pagan parallels found in Aristotelian traditions of instruction on household economics are directed predominantly to the masters of the house, but the reciprocal address to women in the Christian versions is not in their predecessors absolutely unparalleled. (However, the Aristotelian delineations of women's proper submission are much more extensive and extreme).[105] The Christian household instructions not only address all the social groups, but, according to David Balch, they are unique in addressing slaves directly. This is evidence that the gospel had unusual power to integrate slaves into the house churches, even though Christians failed to repudiate slavery directly.[106] The deutero-Pauline Christian writers in the New Testament (Colossians, Ephesians, and 1 Peter) thus give two powerful twists to Aristotelian ethics and politics. They integrate slaves as moral agents to whom the gospel is preached directly. And, while pagan moralists demanded that wives conform to their husbands' religious preferences, the Christian communities supported women's rejection of the Greek and Roman divinities, even in the face of severe social consequences (especially 1 Pet. 3:1, 6).[107]

Certainly the social changes achieved in early Christianity are neither the final word nor a high water mark for subsequent efforts. We note that the changes they began worked in the direction of greater mutuality, respect, reciprocity, and solidarity. Although 1 Peter 3:1–7 represents a greater reversion to pagan gender expectations than most of the New Testament codes, referring to the woman as the "weaker vessel," and suggesting that holy women call their husbands "lord," the author adds, "Finally, all of you, have unity of spirit, sympathy, love of the brethren, a tender heart and a humble mind" (3:8). His sentiments may be admirable, but he no doubt expected his instruction to be interpreted differently for women and for men. The New Testament record reflects an ongoing *process* of transformation toward compassion (personal) and solidarity (social), a process which passes through higher and lower points. Rather than being scandalized at the latter (for example, the restrictions of women's activity in 1 Cor. 12 and 14, or 1 Timothy), we should be encouraged about our own ability to recuperate discipleship despite failures.

THE BIBLICAL VISION

Paul and other New Testament authors seek ways to express their new communal identity through bodily symbols as the appropriate occasions or problems arise. Hence the somewhat random character of the topics they address. Heterosexual marriage is certainly assumed to be the proper context of sexual behavior, but the New Testament does not particularly value procreation. It upholds the equal sexual reciprocity of men and women in marriage; it forbids divorce, unless a continued union destroys Christian peace; and, above all, it offers another alternative to marriage, vocational celibacy. Perpetual virginity avoids the ramifications of the patriarchal institutionalization of sex, and by implication challenges all social relationships based on coercive power.

The continuing norm of New Testament ethics is compassion and solidarity which brings into community those who have not been looked upon or treated as fellow human beings with interests, needs, and potentials for development and contribution which are as important as those of the "ruling class." Both the success of early Christian morality in its own setting and its authority for our own must be evaluated by this core moral component of faith. Although this core is not unique to Christianity, Christian faith, centered on Jesus as the inauguration of God's reign, throws it into relief and gives it ultimate moral importance.

To arrive at more expansive and detailed guides for moral action, we must move to the concrete, historical nature of human "flourishing." Biblical compassion and solidarity entail that each disciple seek the flourishing of others. The discernment of the components of human flourishing is a historical process, the justification for, and the outlines of, which were suggested in chapters 2, 3, and 4. The process engages Christian ethics with multiple sources of moral insight, including philosophy, concrete human experience, scientific descriptions of human being and its natural environment, and other religious and cultural traditions. This broad and dialogical view of Christian ethics, sponsored by faith but not self-enclosed, is warranted by biblical precedent. The image of the body and its members is reworked by Paul from Aristotelian and Stoic notions of the state as the body politic, to mean the living presence of the Lord through the community centered in the physical consumption of the Eucharist.[108]

New Testament morality, taking even the *haustafeln* as an example, could build on developments already occurring in the culture, such as increased legal independence for Roman women. New Testament authors chose what to incorporate and emphasize according to the Christian vision, what to criticize, and what to take further along a trajectory of solidarity, such as incorporation of slaves. There were few sharp divisions between the Christian community and its culture, though the pattern of

Christian life, taken as a whole, gave human relationships a different meaning. It could even be said that the entire Bible, from Mosaic religion onward, is both cross-cultural and apologetic, constantly weaving together elements from various religious and cultural contacts to create a distinctive view of God which challenges every culture.

Paul thus sews together various strands, including perhaps at the moral level, catalogues of virtues and vices taken both from Palestinian Judaism and from Hellenistic (Stoic) philosophical writings (Gal. 5:19–23; 1 Cor. 5:10–11, 6:9–10; 2 Cor. 2:6–7, 12:20; Rom. 1:29–31, 13:13), Jewish references to the moral law (Rom. 7:23), Stoic conceptions of natural law (Rom. 2:14), Greco-Roman assumptions about proper gender behavior (1 Cor. 11:1–16 and 14:34–36), and Aristotelian traditions about the ordered household (the *haustafeln*).[109] In some of this borrowing, he is not sufficiently critical of the potential of his sources to undermine his central message about unity in the body of Christ. This is a pitfall which is endemic to Christian moralities, whatever the political and cultural traditions in which proponents define their identity. Yet, on the whole, Paul and other New Testament authors achieve a reinterpretation of the body as symbol of a new communal discipline in which status hierarchies begin to break apart.

Far from a simple loosening of social controls on the body, the moral question for a Christian ethics of sex and gender becomes how to socialize the body – as male and female, as sexual, as parental – in ways which enlarge our social capacities for compassion toward others and solidarity in the common good. This means resistance to competing socializations, and hence "resocialization,"[110] but hardly the rejection of the idea that embodied behavior will reflect a set of social values, nor even a thorough rejection of values which inform the other communities in which Christians participate.

Contemporary Christians who seek equality for women and men typically seek to revalorize both men's and women's sexuality and parenthood so that they no longer represent structures of domination, but of reciprocity and fulfillment. The social situation of the first Christians was different, and the forms of resistance they adopted toward such problems as patriarchal marriage and divorce tended toward the loosening of personal identification with the family, marriage, and parenthood, and the appropriation of sexual norms, even within marriage, which resisted the standard institutions. Perhaps because of the almost universal cultural assumption that women and men were incapable of equal domestic cooperation, and because of the strong state-sanctioned social norms maintaining the patriarchal family, the first Christians may have found it difficult to envision the family itself as an axis of social transformation. Transformation of marriage and the family as institutions is, however, an urgent present task of Christian social ethics.

CHAPTER 6

Sex, marriage, and family in Christian tradition

Faithfulness to NT criteria of moral discipleship should yield a sex and gender ethics which is also a social ethics, including and protecting society's judged, outcast, and vulnerable. Has Christian teaching and practice about sex, gender, marriage, and family enhanced appreciation of all persons' common humanity, the value of each, and the interdependence of all? Has it led to the construction of ecclesial and social institutions which give such appreciation stability and material expression? As on most other embodiments of discipleship, Christianity has on these issues a mixed record.

The pre-modern cultures which contributed to the first centuries of Christianity set a high priority on the *social* functions of marriage and family, and assumed gender to be both hierarchical and highly differentiated. According both to Roman law and to the traditions of the Germanic peoples who immigrated into Europe in the fourth century and later, sex was largely defined by its reproductive function, and parenthood and family by their socioeconomic functions. Sexual intimacy was structured patriarchally, and sexual pleasure was not linked to the mutual affection of the reproductive partners, so much as to the accomplishment of reproduction itself, whose requirements it always exceeded. Hence sex's reputation as unruly and dangerous to its own social role.

As we shall see, certain developments in the Christian theology and of marriage and in its regulation under ecclesiastical law worked to protect the dignity, freedom, equality, and affective relationship of spouses. The Middle Ages, especially through the Christian ban on divorce for both men and women and its requirement of personal consent in entering marriage, provide some precedents for the emphasis on personal relationships in marriage and family which gained full sway after the Enlightenment. Yet it was not until the modern period that theologies of marriage and church teaching about marriage presented its interpersonal dimensions as primary and overriding. Today, Christians in most cultures idealize the personal functions of marriage and family above the socioeconomic. Sex, interpreted in light of the individual's intersubjective experiences, is valued for allowing intimacy as reciprocity, and as supplying mutual pleasure which enhances intimacy. Parenthood too is valued for its affective rewards. In sex, marriage, and family, there is a proportionately low differentiation of female and male roles and increasing egalitarianism of gender, compared to most premodern societies.

The twentieth-century heirs of Western Christianity thus discern and resist in the received institutions of marriage and family a "regulation" of sex which seems to violate its personal and "covenantal" significance, taming sex in favor of institutional interests, and submitting it to bureaucracies which embody resentment and fear of sex's vitality, its irrepressibility, even its sacredness. The French historian Georges Duby plainly embarks on his study of medieval sexuality with an anti-juridical attitude: "Regulation, officialization, control, codification: the institution of marriage is, by its very position and by the role which it assumes, enclosed in a rigid framework of rituals and prohibitions."[1]

The historical accession of the individual to key importance in defining marriage and its purposes, as well as the modern ideal of equality across gender and class, have brought momentous changes in the understandings of sex. Only with the impact of these sea changes in human consciousness could the notion of marriage as a full commitment of individuals gain ascendency, and the meaning of marriage take on the character of a personal covenant of woman and man. In the twentieth century, especially in the West, the interpersonal and affective replaced the institutional and economic aspects of marriage and family as paramount, leading to questions about the viability of the institutions themselves. These developments present modern interpreters with the problem of reinstating in relation to personal values the social and institutional realities, as well as the "sacramental" role of Christian marriage in mediating the "kingdom of God" in both the personal and the social spheres.

The present chapter will develop the dialectical, perennially uneasy relationship in Christian tradition among (1) the struggle to reflect radical discipleship by means of sexual teaching, and to use that teaching not just to delimit or reject family loyalties and hierarchies, but to transform them from within; (2) a persistent ambivalence toward both women and sexual pleasure; and (3) the newly enhanced personal and covenantal understandings of sex, marriage, and family, which exist in some tension with the biological and parental meanings so important in the past.

The interplay of these strands will be examined in chapters 6 and 7 through the lenses of four contentious subjects: clerical celibacy, indissolubility, contraception, and reproductive technologies. Although the first three of these have been at issue more in Catholicism than in other Christian denominations,[2] they offer an occasion to look at the emergence in Christianity historically of sexual disciplines which resisted the sexual enforcement of status hierarchies but which tended eventually to be co-opted by lines of control in the church. All four issues also permit examination of the moral significance of sexual pleasure, the emergence of intimacy as a Christian sexual ideal, and the importance of procreation in defining the spousal relationship. Chapter 7, on the new birth technologies, will put the conjunction of sex, love of spouses, and parenthood in the context of Christian contributions to public policy debates in Western democratic societies.

CELIBACY

Although, as we have seen, sexual continence has been a Christian ideal since NT times, Roman Catholicism is unusual among the churches today in requiring a vow of permanent celibacy of all candidates for the priesthood. Although the Reformers were later to reject it, the discipline of clerical continence, having gathered momentum since the fourth century, was formally instituted for the whole church in 1123 (at the First Lateran Council). This regulation provided that priests who were already married must live continently with their wives. The Second Lateran Council (1139) went further and precluded ordination for anyone who did not observe strict celibacy, that is, who did not abandon married life entirely. The requirement of celibacy was reversed by the Reformers on the grounds both that marriage was instituted by God as most people's natural "estate," and that the rarity of a genuine celibate vocation had led to all kinds of abuse and vice among the supposedly virginal clergy.

The earliest legislation concerning celibacy dates to the Council of Elvira (*c.* 306), a local Spanish council, which decreed that bishops, priests, and deacons abstain from sexual relations with their wives; the Council of Arles concurred (314), and the practice was reaffirmed by Ambrose and Jerome. The ecumenical Council of Nicaea (325) decreed that men could not marry after they were ordained to the diaconate, though those who already had wives could still proceed through the levels of ordination to priesthood, remaining married but continent thereafter. The same practice was established by the Eastern Council of Ancyra (358), whose ruling was adopted as legislation for the Roman Empire (420). A similar practice continues today in the Orthodox churches. Married men can be ordained to the diaconate and priesthood, though bishops are chosen only from among celibates.[3]

In modern times, the Second Vatican Council of the Roman Catholic Church supported celibacy in its decree on priestly ministry (*Presbyterorum Ordinis*, 1965), and the 1967 encyclical *Sacerdotalis Celibatus* (1967) confirmed that the discipline would continue. The 1983 Code of Canon law states, "Clerics are obliged to observe perfect and perpetual continence for the sake of the kingdom of heaven and therefore are obliged to observe celibacy, which is a special gift of God, by which sacred ministers can adhere more easily to Christ with an undivided heart and can more freely dedicate themselves to the service of God and humankind" (Can. 277).

The currents of renewal in the church which led to and flowed from Vatican II included reconsideration among laity and theologians alike of almost all traditional Catholic sexual teachings, and clerical celibacy was no exception. Arguments in favor of change included the shortage of priests and consequent sacramental and eucharistic deprivation of the faithful; the centrality of marriage and fatherhood to male status in many countries of the world; a renewed appreciation of the goodness of sexuality and of marriage as a vocation in the church, with consequences for the "superiority" of virginity; the pastoral assets of a married clergy which could identify with the daily lives of their congregations; and the essential separability of celibacy and priestly ministry, as attested both in the New Testament (1 Tim. 3:2, 12; Tit. 1:6) and at least sporadically in church practice up to the Middle Ages. But perhaps the greatest focus was the personal plight of men who had complied with the celibacy requirement in order to enter the priesthood, yet had suffered as a result not only sexual frustration but deep loneliness. In the wake of the Council many have left the active ministry and married, but still yearn for a life in which one vocation does not have to be sacrificed for the other. Compounding the problem is the perception that many youthful candidates for the priesthood had in the past been ill-prepared for the demands and costs of sexual renunciation, and, indeed, had been trained to repress, rather than to live constructively with, their sexual drives and needs for intimacy.

The psychosexual well-being of individuals and the importance of freedom to choose celibacy as an "option" for priests thus moved to center stage in much of the debate about celibacy following Vatican II. Many felt that celibacy as a charism could only be appropriated in freedom, not legally imposed.[4] Arguments against mandatory celibacy frequently stressed the negative attitudes toward sex (and women) out of which it had seemed to emerge and which it continued to perpetuate. Although official documents spoke of celibacy for the sake of the kingdom, church practice seemed to many to amount to juridical control over the rank-and-file of priests and a sign of Christian misogynism and depreciation of sex.

Conversely, those who wanted to reconstrue celibacy positively, and who aimed at least to make the discipline not only bearable, but even attractive to priests and religious, focused on the goodness of sexuality, and the possibility of healthy psychosexual development even in the celibate state. Introducing his influential book, Donald Goergen avows, "*The Sexual Celibate* is based upon the growing conviction that friendship is not detrimental but central to celibate living, that celibate persons are also sexual persons, and that celibate life is a profound and rewarding way of living."[5] The eschatological witness of celibate life, as an embodiment of the radical nature of Christian love, and its availability for community service, did not drop out of sight, even among supporters of optional celibacy for priests.[6] But, especially with the continued decline of numbers of priests in those same cultures in which sex as embodying intimacy and love is prized, celibacy is more and more regarded in restrictive terms and suspected to be the bodily symbol of a repressive and highly controlling ecclesiastical hierarchy.

The truth behind this perception, as well as the possible renewal of celibacy's witness to the church, can be better appreciated in light of the ambivalent relation of celibacy to the ideals of early Christianity, as celibacy was gradually established to be the officially "higher vocation" in the mind of the church.

Peter Brown reviews the first centuries of Christian history in light of his thesis that Christian celibacy is a bodily symbol of resistance to the pagan state and family. Because young people, especially women, were still married off early by their parents in the first generations after Christ, virginity was not a decision that was likely to be undertaken as a life-long vocation. Brown surmises that Christian continence originated as a practice within marriage, and that the audience of moral exhortation regarding it was those whose spouses had died.[7] Widows were apparently more numerous in the early Christian communities than widowers, since women married much older men, and since the church discouraged women bereaved even in their twenties from re-entering the marriage market. Later New Testament materials reflect a special office of widows in the community (1 Tim. 2:11–15). Widows, many quite wealthy, thus made up an important and potentially influential constituency, and were seen as fulfilling an established and recognized role, often including patronage.

Following the example of the Hebrew prophets, sexual abstinence was associated with receptivity to the Spirit of God and to prophecy; and with martyrdom, which celibacy democratized as an analogous participation. By at least the second century, monastic communities began to withdraw into the hills and deserts to pray, to seek communion with God outside the social norms of home and family. Communities of consecrated women not only cultivated spirituality, but carried out a subtle revolt against cultural definitions of their roles in marriage and household.[8] Membership in the churches was, at the beginning of the third century, still dominated by married householders; continence served as an equalizing factor between men and women and between ordained ministers and laity. In particular, it allowed communities which had offended social mores by including women in religious leadership roles, and which constantly fell under pagan accusation of bizarre, demonic, or lascivious sexual behavior, to present male and female working relationships as above reproach. In this way then, celibacy in the early years narrowed the gap between priestly and lay status and facilitated the inclusion of women.[9]

Praise of virginity was not without converse effects on attitudes toward marriage and sex. Brown believes that sexual abstinence symbolizes for Origen (in the second century) a loosening of the bonds of kinship, and a freedom of the soul;[10] but even if so, this was certainly achieved at the price of a denigration of sex, marriage, and parenthood, and even the body, and amounted to the re-creation of a spiritual elite to which only the few could belong. For Tertullian sex was demeaning and impure. He insisted on strict control of the body, denounced sex as spiritually ennervating, and believed that it should be completely renounced after the death of a first spouse. Referring to women as "the Devil's gateway," Tertullian demanded that the holy observe continence in marriage, and maintain strictly the order of the patriarchal household. Both men and women could attain sanctity, however, by giving up sex.[11] In the third century, virginity or choice of the unmarried state by young men and women was acceptable and common. Yet the late second-century author Clement of Alexandria defended the married laity against "the rise of a dangerous mystique of continence"[12] by writing approvingly of sex in marriage, as long as it was ordered by the Stoic values of moderation, reason, and procreation. Moreover, Clement maintained that women and men were of the same moral nature, and were to be encouraged to similar virtues.[13]

By the beginning of the fourth century, celibacy as both a symbol of elitism and an instrument of control had made irreversible inroads. The "Desert Fathers" of the fourth century bore witness to the coming age by giving up the sort of immortality that could be achieved through offspring. The evil of sex was not for them a special focus; a strict asceticism about food was an even more important form of bodily control signifying their dedication to a new life. But by the time the synods of the early 300s began to legislate what was already no doubt well represented in practice, Christians thought in terms of "two ways" of life, highly differentiated both in terms of content and of value. In such a framework, virginity as a special vocation does not contribute much to solidarity among disciples. As Brown quotes Eusebius' account, those who forego marriage are "beyond common human living ... Like some celestial beings, these gaze down upon human life."[14] It was the triumph of this point of view that seems to have backed the installation of clerical celibacy after 300.[15] The hardening compulsoriness of celibacy for clergy seemed to go hand-in-hand with a growing negativity about sex as such. It also served to protect clergy leadership against competition from married benefactors, thus accentuating hierarchies in the community, not overturning them.[16]

John Chrysostom, priest, theologian, and famed preacher of late fourth-century Antioch illustrates that neither the hierarchization of Christian identity, nor the ancillary regulation of celibate clergy, had yet poisoned fatally the transformations that were the Christian body's legitimate children. "His aim was to rob the city of its most tenacious myth – the myth that its citizens have a duty to contribute to the continued glory of their native Antioch by marrying."[17] Chrysostom permits marriage mostly as a compromise with the difficulty of sexual control. Yet he appeals to Christian households to remember the poor, daily collecting savings for them in a box beside the marriage bed. Austerity and almsgiving are a higher calling even than virginity. "For without virginity, indeed, it is possible to see the Kingdom, but without almsgiving this cannot be."[18]

Meanwhile, in the Latin Church, Ambrose and particularly Jerome preserved some of virginity's revolutionary effect by holding it forth to women as an avenue of equality with men. Ambrose insisted on the Christian equality of sexual standards for both men and women in marriage.[19] But he deprecated Roman noble families' pride in their fertility. In fact, he compared a virgin's being offered for marriage to being put up for sale in the slave market.[20] When one young girl sought refuge with the bishop from her family's pressure to marry, Ambrose reflected, "Conquer family-loyalty first, my girl: if you overcome the household, you overcome the world."[21] Upper-class ascetic virgins, of whom Ambrose's elder sister was one, had an impact on the church as both patrons and companions of the clergy and theologians. Through their ecclesial dedication they achieved emancipation from matronly roles within the Roman household.

Like Origen, Jerome thought the sexual body required tight control, but refused to see it as a mirror of spiritual difference between the sexes. Two educated widows, Paula and Marcella, offered Jerome religious and financial support, and became his close colleagues. "Jerome, for all his fashionable misogyny and his sharp sense of sexual danger, would never for a moment have doubted that the minds of Paula or Marcella, and his other female allies and clients, did not have their full share of 'male' bone and muscle."[22]

Paradoxically, it is Augustine, the fourth-century bishop of Hippo in North Africa, to whom is attributed the most lasting influence both in defining Christianity's positive doctrine of marriage, and in surrounding sex with an aura of shame and danger from which celibacy serves as an escape. In Augustine's writing there culminate two tendencies which go back to Paul, and which also had characterized the emergence and interpretation of celibacy as a Christian option in the centuries leading up to Augustine. First, there was the ascetic tradition, always ready to erupt in extremist, gnostic forms, so strong in the first four centuries. Asceticism fed on a suspicion of sexual desire, on a resistance to marriage as a form of social control, and on a positive construal of virginity as offering both spiritual and social benefits. Second, there was a reinterpretation of Christian marriage, which affirmed the marital bond, sex, and family within certain defined structures, and which linked marriage with Christian symbols in a "sacramentalizing" trend. The transformation of marriage will be taken up in the subsequent section, on indissolubility; but it impinges on the discussion of celibacy insofar as approval of marriage as a sphere of sanctification has always furnished an important limit to Christian advocacy of celibacy.

Not only did Augustine stand at a historical point where Christian ambivalence toward sex, and all the social roles which channeled it, was practically unavoidable. His personal experience also positioned him perfectly to reflect and magnify the tension already expressed in the Christian differentiation of celibacy and marriage. Augustine invites biographical references in interpreting his theology, for he himself ties personal history, religious experience, and theological insight closely together in his *Confessions*. While it would be excessive to read Augustine's central theological proposals in light of his sexual history, his own experiences of sex and his relationships with women, as he himself reports them, can legitimately be brought to bear on his ideas about sex and gender.

Two women figured prominently in Augustine's life: his mother, and the woman with whom he lived for fifteen years and had a son. Only his mother, Monica, is mentioned by name and presented by Augustine as someone whose own aspirations, sorrows and loves are worthy in their own right. Augustine's

Confessions are full of Monica's devotion to her son, her incessant prayers for his conversion away from Manicheanism, his long resistance and spiritual return to Catholicism, and his suffering upon her death.

Augustine's concubine was a woman of lower-class status, with whom a full Roman marriage would have been out of the question. As a young professor of rhetoric, from a respectable family but of scant means, Augustine might have been content to continue indefinitely in a "second-class" marriage, as other notable citizens had done.[23] However, his mother eventually intervened to arrange for Augustine a marriage with a young girl who could offer the son improved social standing and the prospect of an inheritance.[24] The concubine was sent away, back from Italy to Africa, though she vowed never to be united with any other man. Augustine kept their son. And, since he had to wait two years until his bride was of marriageable age, he promptly took another mistress, of whom he tells us almost nothing.[25]

Augustine mentions his concubine wholly in terms of his own desires and responses, and of those he focuses on a sexual need so acute and unrelenting that it binds him – according to his own testimony – in a sort of "slavery." Margaret Miles even describes Augustine as a sex addict,[26] although it is difficult to weigh his level of actual compulsiveness against his overwhelming revulsion in the face of sexual drives and reactions, especially in view of the fact that they represented to him a shameful lack of control.[27] Sex was much maligned by the religious sect (Manicheanism) to whose ideals he aspired. He once referred to "the shameful motions of the organs of generation," and went on to opine that in Eden sexual intercourse might fittingly have taken place without any sexual desire whatsoever, but rather by an act of sheer rationality.[28] Although Augustine says that "[t]o love and be loved was sweet to me," still, physical enjoyment of love turned friendship into "the hell of lustfulness."[29] Even though he describes his heart as "torn, wounded, and bleeding" at separation from his lover, he still looks back on their relationship as making him "a slave to lust."[30] He remembers himself as "enslaved with the disease of the flesh," captive to "an insatiable lust."[31] Of his son, who died as a youth, he also writes sparingly, though with emotion.[32] But, as Miles notes, Augustine never portrays his lover in a maternal role, reserving the honorifics of motherhood for Monica.[33]

Another factor in Augustine's view of sexuality must be the complex relations within his household of origin. His pagan father, Patricius, made enormous sacrifices to give his son an education, but was, in the latter's rather arrogant view, shallow in both intellect and paternal ambition.[34] Patricius' death is passed over almost in silence,[35] and in sharp contrast to the emotions lavished by his son on Monica. Augustine describes his parents' marriage – or at least his mother's role in it – in exactly the terms admired by Roman society in his day and in earlier times. His mother was given to a husband as soon as she was of marriageable age, served her husband "as her lord," and never began quarrels about his infidelities or his angry outbursts. She advised her friends to avoid beatings by considering their marriage contracts as "instruments whereby they were made servants." Against adversity and despite seemingly constant ill-treatment, she had honored her parents and mother-in-law, raised her children piously and governed her household well, and in widowhood had earned the Latin encomium *univira*, "wife of one man."[36] When one adds to all this the fact that Augustine's own prospect of marriage began with a political arrangement that promised perfectly to imitate the circumstances of his upbringing, one can hardly blame him for failing to perceive in the marital bond much potential for spiritual companionship and love.

Augustine came to see celibacy as his only hope for an integrated life, a life he heard praised in Ambrose's sermons, and to which he was eventually turned through a vision of Continence as a beckoning and reassuring mother.[37] His hope for friendship and progress in the love of God came to reside in a community of men, of close associates who would undistractedly share a way of life, intense conversation, prayer, and sexual sublimation. It is only male friendship which to Augustine finally seems noble, and he recalls mourning for a dead companion as for "a friendship that had grown sweet to me above all the sweetness of my life."[38] He is inspired to praise his mother as "in a woman's garb, but with masculine faith."[39] Margaret Miles remarks that Augustine "apparently has no fear of the 'glue of love' [IV.4] when it connects his life with that of another man," even though "he cannot imagine loving a woman in a relationship in which each partner supported, encouraged, and provoked the other to self-knowledge and spiritual progress."[40] His spiritual life had to be focused with metaphors of sexual restraint, as well as with its physical reality.

No wonder that the works of this theologian transmit a certain negativity on sex and sexual pleasure. It was not in his emotional and imaginative range to discern in sex any potential for personal or spiritual enrichment. He had few models for mutual respect and devotion in a marriage committed to Christian ideals. He was all too familiar with impermanent, only unintentionally procreative, sexual liaisons which ended badly, and which contributed to the demeaning both of a mistress's humanity, and of a lawful wife's position. Even sex in marriage for the wives of his acquaintance would have been the husband's prerogative and too often brutal or violent.

In the writings of the figure who has been most central to Roman Catholic ethics, we note a shift in perspective. Although, as far as we know, Thomas Aquinas lived an entirely celibate life himself, he was able to see sexual pleasure as a good if properly ordered within marriage; he also saw marriage as a friendship of the most intense sort, a friendship cemented by sexual intimacy. His view of marriage will be taken up further in the next section. No doubt this shift was enabled by the changes in the understanding of marriage which were already taking place in the Middle Ages, though Aquinas still quite definitely places women as the inferior sex. On celibacy, it is enough to say that Aquinas sees virginity as the higher way for a Christian without resorting to any crude denigration of marriage and sex.[41] Aquinas believes that virginity is preferable to marriage, since sex is a hindrance to the contemplative way of life.[42] Like the Fathers, Aquinas does think marriage "holier" if it remains without "carnal intercourse."[43] Virginity fosters a life hospitable to "thinking on the things of God" and thus to "the good of the soul."[44] Because Aquinas links virginity with contemplation, in contrast to an active life (which marriage serves), his theology diminishes the socially radical value of early Christian celibacy. He even characterizes the excellence of virginity as a "private good" in contrast to the common good of marriage.[45] He does, however, retain the equal accessibility of the celibate state to both men and women, and so it continues to serve as a path to spiritual equality in what was still a very gender unequal social world.

Although celibacy was institutionalized by church law in the twelfth century, it has never ceased to be disputed, whether more or less openly and vociferously. First of all, even in the second half of the twelfth century, clerical concubinage was still alive and well.[46] In the thirteenth and fourteenth centuries, some theologians, canonists, and even bishops, called for a repeal of mandatory celibacy; and the fourteenth and fifteenth centuries saw a resurgence of concubinage among the clergy, contributing to Luther's complaints. An extended debate at Trent (1545–63) produced a renewed insistence that priests and vowed religious could not contract valid marriages. This declaration was partly a reaction to the Reformers' challenge to church authority, as well as to the numbers of priests who were abandoning their Roman Catholic status and taking spouses.

The reaffirmation of celibacy was no doubt in some part a protective move on behalf of authority, and an exertion of control over clergy and religious. However, the exclusion for priests of sex, procreation, and even marriages without sex, also served the freedom of the clergy and of the church over against the medieval family. The children of married clergy stood to inherit church property; and not only a priest's own natal family, but also that of his wife (especially the children's maternal uncle) would customarily have taken an active interest in the social, economic, and political future of his offspring.[47]

It must be remembered as well that the association of continence with spiritual commitment still served to offer lay-people, especially women religious but occasionally married couples, the choice of a way of life outside the hierarchies and machinations of the feudal family. Communities of consecrated women had existed since the patristic period. In the "Dark Ages," women found a measure of independence from husband and family by entering convents and monasteries, sometimes after having raised a family. Widows often went to monasteries, and some women even left their spouses to do so. Noble women used their own resources (property received at marriage from their husbands, or inherited at the death of their fathers) to found religious communities, in which their daughters could be educated, and to which they themselves could later retire. Such houses, sometimes with separate accommodations for women and men, could become centers of learning. An example is Whitby, founded in Northumbria in the seventh century by Hild, a noblewoman baptized at the age of fourteen. Convents also served as a refuge for unmarriageable daughters, primarily of wealthy families, since entry required a dowry. This function contributed, predictably enough, to some scandalous violations of vows on the part of nuns who were personally less than fully committed to a religious vocation.[48] In the eleventh and twelfth centuries, a few men of means established religious communities which were open to persons, men and women, of any social standing, including repentant prostitutes.[49]

Continence in marriage, often at the urging of the wife, was another way to attain spiritual equality of men and women, clergy and laity, as well as to escape the heavy social determinations of family and parenthood. Augustine is reported by a fourth-century biographer to have commended a couple, who, at the woman's urging, had achieved self-discipline, replaced physical bonds with spiritual ones, and thus "passed from your own bodies into that of Christ."[50] Tracing the history of marital continence among laypersons in medieval times, Dyan Elliott notes that the great preponderance of women who instigated the practice, gaining not only freedom from standard domestic expectations but also the spiritual upper hand, represented a threat to male authority in the family and in public life. Continent lay married women, in particular, eventually presented a challenge to the spiritual superiority of the clergy. By the sixteenth century, after the appearance of a post-

Reformation reinterpretation of the sanctity of married life, the custom of sexless marriage was in decline.[51]

Controversy about celibacy in the church today is sparked largely by its survival, primarily in Roman Catholicism, as a disciplinary requirement of priests, many of whom acquiesce to rather than embrace it. Vowed but nonordained members of religious orders, not all of which are Roman Catholic, are also obliged to celibacy; however, in such cases, it does not assume the form of so "extrinsic" a requirement as does priestly celibacy, since it is not attached to a state of life from which it is separable in principle, but to which there is no other ecclesially legitimate route of access. Groups of men or women living together in religiously consecrated community by definition choose to give up (or to avoid) marriage; there are other lay orders and even forms of communal life available to married couples. But in the Roman Catholic Church priests can be priests only by accepting celibacy, whether or not they live in community with other men. To choose the priesthood is to be made to choose celibacy. This has given debate about the value of celibacy much wider currency than would otherwise have been the case, and has forced a demand for consensus on the issue.

Sacerdotalis Celibatus (Paul VI's 1967 encyclical on priestly celibacy) praises celibacy without denigrating marriage, though it does see celibacy as manifesting the new reality initiated in Christ "in a clearer and more complete way" (.20). It portrays celibacy as a "support" for "the minister in his exclusive, definitive and total choice of the unique and supreme love of Christ," and in his offices of public worship and service to the Church (.14). It also commends "the free choice of sacred celibacy" as signifying "a love without reservations," and as stimulating "a charity which is open to all." One notes in *Sacerdotalis Celibatus* a tendency to portray celibacy as a heroic vocation in which the priest transcends earthly loves and takes on the likeness of Christ the eternal Priest (.26). The question remains whether the mandatory nature of what is legislated militates against its signification of solidarity in the body of Christ.

Schillebeeckx observes sensibly that as marriage is progressively re-evaluated as a fertile field for the kingdom's servants, religious fervor and enthusiasm which once found their outlet in virginity are able to energize Christian marriage. Of course, the embodiment of Christian ideals in marriage is facilitated today by increasing historical recognition of the equality and reciprocal contributions of all family members. Modern values distance family life more from the economic and political factors which have always determined its inner relations and social functions, and which were so objectionable to members of the early churches. This is not to say marriage and family should or even can be "freed" from their complex lines of connection to all levels of communal life. Individualism in the family is as unbalanced and pernicious as tyrannical social control. But the Christian family today, in nourishing the human capacity for compassion and solidarity, can provide a school for and support to Christian commitment which was once much more easily embodied in a renunciation of kin ties and of the bondedness to social structures represented by marital, procreative sexuality, or by other forms of sexuality (like concubinage, prostitution, and ancient homosexuality) which were just as bound to the enforcement of dominative gender roles.

The worth of celibacy itself, in Christianity today, must also be measured in communitarian terms, not in those either of personal perfectionism or of a new sexualization of the celibate state. Part of the value of celibacy is its witness to a transcendent fulfillment of all human strivings and the relativization of all human loves;[52] part of it is even a testimony that sexuality is not as deep and definitive a component of human identity as it seems for post-Freudian Westerners or was socially for premodern women. But surely another test, even a more important one, is its role in building up discipleship community. Seeing marriage and celibacy as interdependent gifts, William Spohn subjects celibacy to the tests of deeper intimacy and social fruitfulness. Drawing on Paul's corporate imagery, he rejects "an isolated or detached asceticism," in favor of celibacy as a "focused passion for the Kingdom," "ordered to building up the Body of Christ."[53] The test of consecrated celibacy is the concrete capacity of those who live it to magnify in the life of the community those values and relationships which Jesus held up as embodying the kingdom: compassion, mercy, forgiveness, and solidarity with the deprived and the "sinful."

INDISSOLUBILITY

Another distinctive mark of Christian sexual ethics traditionally is its prohibition of divorce. This prohibition has had a long and tortuous career in church history and canon law. Since the Reformation, Protestant churches have, with varying degrees of leniency, permitted marriage to be dissolved in exceptional circumstances. The Anglican Church forbids divorce in theory, but sometimes permits pastorally the remarriage of persons divorced under civil law. But Roman Catholicism forbids the divorce of any two baptized persons whose marriage has been consummated sexually, and – at least in theory – excludes divorced and remarried persons from reception of the Eucharist. Indeed, dissolution of a valid marriage and consequent remarriage is viewed as ontologically impossible. The huge increase in the number of annulments after Vatican II, along with expansion of the grounds on which declarations of nullity may be justified, have led to the perception (sometimes the accusation) that Catholic annulment amounts to a tacit form of divorce.[54]

The suffering of those who have experienced marital breakdown, who have established new relationships, and for whom religious identity is of immense importance, has led to many a call for a removal of the bar to remarriage or a relaxation of the penalties against those who transgress this line. (The prohibition of divorce is maintained more firmly in Roman Catholicism and Anglicanism than in many other communions.) A woman with long experience in ministry to divorced and remarried Catholics opens a collection of essays on the subject by asking, "How can we communicate the message of God's ever-present love to those who feel devastated and powerless in the wake of the loss of a marriage?" "How can we offer a support system in which hurting people can heal, learn from the past and have the hope of one day forming life-nurturing relationships?"[55]

This approach to divorce clearly represents the modern Western valuation of personal fulfillment and emotional welfare in marriage, and sees the alleviation of individuals' pain as a central part of the church's pastoral mission. Laws prohibiting divorce are perceived to injure and alienate those who are "powerless" in the face of church authority. Yet Christianity's stance against divorce was originally a stance against the manipulation of marriage, and of children and women, to serve family interests in power and property. A corollary was that permanency in marriage better served the growth of marital friendship and the nurturance of offspring. To understand the historical significance of the church's stand on indissolubility and divorce, one must return to some of the same considerations about social control of marriage and the family which bear on celibacy in primitive, patristic, and medieval Christianity. It is through the emergence of indissolubility as a mark of sacramental marriage that we may view the deepest transformations of Christian thinking about marriage as a relationship of equal persons who ideally unite their whole lives, and not only their bodies for procreation and their property for the formation of new households.

Virginity in the early church objected to institutions of marriage and kinship which made intimacy, reciprocity, and mutual responsibility for children virtually impossible. Yet, from primitive Christian times, marriage was respected as a realm in which a disciple could give practical expression to faith, and whose internal order could even be transformed by *agape*.[56] In the New Testament and in early teaching like the decrees of Elvira (which warned Christians away from adultery, but permitted men – not women – to remarry after divorcing an adulterous spouse[57]), Christians were instructed to adopt special marital behavior. Gradually marriage was taken over explicitly by the church as an arena of grace in its own right, with the implication that the social meaning of marriage, and not only the personal relationships of Christians within the standing institution, could be changed.

At the beginning of the fourth century, the assumption was that Christians would follow the marriage ceremonies and contracts of their pagan neighbors, according to Roman legislation. Marriage was a secular affair, arranged by families, celebrated in the home, and conformed to pagan traditions, though the baptized were expected to live in marriage, as in all relationships, by faith, hope, and love. In the fourth century, a priest's prayer and blessing begin to be associated with weddings, though not for second marriages. The first evidence of a nuptial mass and the solemnization by a priest of a marriage contracted civilly occurs in the fourth and fifth centuries. There was no obligation to receive such a blessing until the tenth century, around which time the church began to insist that the wedding ceremony be a public affair, in front of the church. The church was also assuming more jurisdictional power over marriage, not in the sense of legislating the contract, but in the sense of settling disputes about its validity, including the determination of impediments to marriage. Complete jurisdiction was to be in the hands of the church by the eleventh and twelfth centuries, and by the thirteenth, a developing theology of marriage's sacramentality had matured.[58]

From the end of the fourth century and on into the next three generations, Western Europe experienced a series of migrations of largely Germanic peoples, which were important to this process of church involvement in marriage and family practices. These migrations gradually displaced Roman institutions and government; by the beginning of the sixth century, the Roman Empire had been divided into a number of different states ruled by peoples with different tribal histories, for example, the Anglo-Saxons in Britain, the Franks in Gaul, and the Visigoths in Spain. The Roman population continued to observe its own customs alongside the newcomers. In a pluralistic situation, the Roman and "barbarian" ways influenced and modified one another, and Christian practices evolved partly as attempts to moderate both.[59] If anything, the Germanic influx accentuated the Greco-Roman proclivity to place authority over marriage in the hands of the kin group, represented by senior male members, and to determine the fate of young people and women in general according to the welfare of the family as a whole.

The law of the Germanic societies hinged on two archaic principles which made the Christianization of their marriage customs especially challenging: collective responsibility of the kindred for the actions of any members, and, derivatively, reciprocal revenge. Peace and security were valued and sought within the group, but the right of violence against outsiders was taken for granted if the interests of the kin group were at stake. For example, Germanic folklaw recognized three ways of contracting a marriage, one of which was by capture (abduction and rape). The less violent alternatives were purchase and consent. The latter was primarily an option when the groom and his family could not or would not come up with the price of a woman, but the woman agreed to marry. In such cases, the husband did not acquire the same legal rights over the wife as if he or his family had purchased her. Concubinage was also very widespread, and involved longstanding unions (often polygynous) without full legal rights.[60] While divorce was almost exclusively a male prerogative, adultery was a crime of which virtually only women were accused.

Even by the time the migrations in Europe began, ancient assumptions had begun to undergo modification. However, the records of a few extreme cases – illustrating the effects of such practices on marriage and on the status of women, even after Christianization – survive to tell us that old attitudes die hard. Gregory of Tours relates a case from the early Middle Ages in which a family was humiliated by a daughter who had been taken as a priest's concubine. Imprisoning the priest, the family redeemed its honor by burning the woman alive. In another instance from the eighth century, a man abducted an engaged girl by force and raped her. The aggrieved fiancé obtained a court judgment by which both the victim and perpetrator were turned over to him. He spared their lives, sent the girl to a convent, then belatedly decided to marry her after all. Also reconsidering his pardon of the rapist, he killed him. As a result, half of his property and all of his bride's were confiscated by the king, who donated it to a monastery; the groom entered the same monastery, and "presumably" the woman had little alternative but to repair likewise to the cloister.[61]

Throughout the Middle Ages, church law attempted, with admittedly uneven results, to curtail sexual violence (for example, marriage by rape), to equalize sexual norms for men and women (no adultery or divorce), and to protect marriage as a personal relationship by making it contingent on the consent of the parties, not family negotiations or male prerogatives alone (Gratian's codification of church law, 1140). The legal definition of the "conjugal debt" as a claim right either party could exact from the other partly equalized the relationship of spouses, and protected their union from outside interference (for example, of parents or feudal lords controlling the movements of serfs).[62] The fact that by the time of Charlemagne (eighth century), the Western family had assumed the form of "a coresidential, primary descent group" also supported these trends, insofar as the quality of emotional relationships among family members had assumed a new domestic priority.[63]

Theologically, Augustine set the stage for the path the church was to follow in this gradual appropriation of marriage as a specifically Christian way of life. He wrote *On the Good of Marriage* in 401 as a rejoinder to the proposal of Jovinian that marriage was equal to virginity. However, he was also anxious to refute the teaching of the Manicheans that all sex and procreation were wrong. Augustine calls the union of "man and wife" "the first natural tie of human society," ideally "a kind of friendly and genuine union of the one ruling and the other obeying." He does not link sex directly to this relationship, for sexual passion seems inimical to the peaceful concord he envisions between spouses. Children "are the only worthy fruit" of sexual intercourse.[64] Although it would be better to refrain from sex entirely, by begetting children, "marital intercourse makes something good out of the evil of lust."[65] Sex outside of marriage is of course a mortal sin; even within marriage, it is a venial sin if sought for the purpose of pleasure. Only children or compliance with an undisciplined spouse who might fall to fornication save sex from sin.[66]

Children are not the only good of *marriage*, however; Augustine's enumeration of its three goods is the backbone of all later Christian teaching (which tended to convert them to "ends"[67]). They are *fides* (sexual fidelity); *proles* (offspring); and *sacramentum* (the indissoluble bond). Although Augustine indicates that even natural marriage should be characterized by permanence, the "sacred bond" takes on a special significance for baptized persons. The bond is a mutual pledge of permanent fidelity. Christians, even if separated from their spouses, should not remarry as long as the spouse lives.[68] The permanence of Christian marriage is comparable to the union of Christ and church (Eph. 5:25), an analogy Augustine develops in *On Marriage and Concupiscence* (418).[69]

For several centuries after Augustine, the church wavered on indissolubility. From the time of the Fathers, adultery had been considered grounds for divorce, though not all presumed a right to remarry. Even when a marriage was unjustly terminated, the "adultery" of a remarriage was forgiveable, and the second marriage was not necessarily considered invalid.[70] Although in the medieval theology of the sacrament, indissolubility came to be understood as an ontological reality that could not be dissolved, for the Fathers and their immediate heirs, the *sacramentum* of marriage was an obligation and task for Christian couples, a duty which they could fail to meet.[71]

As we have seen, divorce in the ancient world was generally to the disadvantage of women as individuals (even when legalized as a woman's "right"), and to the advantage of individual men and of powerful and wealthy families. This situation persisted through the Middle Ages, though early medieval women may have had considerable personal and economic freedom.[72] Marriage in feudal society was a social act which linked one blood line to another, and ensured that the eldest son of the eldest son would inherit the family patrimony. The virginity of women was a "saleable commodity," and their fidelity in marriage was paramount to the secure transmission of family wealth.[73] Women who were barren of male heirs could be divorced, abandoned or replaced by a fertile second wife. The upper classes in Europe also contracted mercenary child marriages – forbidden by the church but not declared invalid. The *Life of St. Hugh of Lincoln* tells of one child who was widowed by two noblemen and married to a third before she was eleven; Richard II of England was engaged to the seven-year-old daughter of the French king in 1395, and married to her the next year.[74]

The machinations required to protect property also had consequences for men, since younger sons were prevented from contracting legal marriages or setting up households. The conventions of courtly love, governing twelfth-century romantic liaisons between knights and married noblewomen, may be explained as a nonprocreative, non-kin-linked alternative both for men who found their marital opportunities to be virtually nonexistent and for women who found that marriage afforded little emotional fulfillment. Georges Duby conjectures that, in a military society, the ritualization of desire in courtly love reinforced "the rules of the ethics of vassalage," binding the knight to the lady's lord, and training the knight in submission, sublimation, and loyalty. Hence, it was at bottom a love between men, and in its own way misogynist.[75]

Three developments of church law in the Middle Ages were instrumental in fighting such abuses, although clearly not with total consensus behind them, nor success in attaining their aims. These remedies concerned the stability and permanence of a monogamous relationship, and centered on consent, indissolubility, and exogamy (enforced by "incest" laws). All of these developments reduced inequalities between rich and poor, and, to a perhaps lesser extent, those between men and women.

Going back to classical Rome, lawyers had debated whether consent or sexual consummation, or both, was necessary to bring marriage into being. From a Christian point of view, to require sexual intercourse threatened the perfection of the marriage of Mary and Joseph. Although Gratian's twelfth-century laws distinguished two stages of matrimony (as initiated by consent and confirmed by sexual union), the theological and canonical tide turned in favor of Peter Lombard's opinion in favor of consent alone. Pope Alexander III, later in the same century, after having wavered between Gratian and Lombard, decreed that the consent of the marrying couple alone made their union valid and binding.[76] A contracted but unconsummated marriage could be dissolved under rare circumstances (such as the taking of religious vows by the bride), and only by special ecclesiastical dispensation. This had important consequences. The necessity and sufficiency of mutual consent to establish a marriage disrupted the authority of parents to trade or sell their offspring, especially those who were under the already-low legal age. The consent requirement also lent support to couples who desired to marry – or who had eloped – without parental consent. Not only did this deter the rich in their pursuit of wealth through arranged marriages, it refocused the meaning of marriage on the personal commitment of young women and men. Families were also less well-positioned to forbid marriage to sons in order to prevent division of the family estate. Indissolubility, realized haltingly over several centuries of developing church law, characterized the marriage of two baptized persons who had given their free and witnessed consent to the union, and only if that consent had been given. As in ancient Greece and Rome however, rapid repeat trading on the marriage-market was more a ploy of the higher classes than of the common people. Phillipe Ariés notes that rural communities no doubt depended on the stability of unions for their own stability and prosperity, and for the reliable continuance of the extensive and delicate negotiations necessary for the exchange of sons and daughters among families.[77]

Certain impediments to marriage – which would make consent ineffective – were also instituted by church law, and among these the one with the most serious consequences was the impediment of close relationship. Elite marriages within close degrees of relationship, between cousins for instance, were common in order to consolidate property, and had become more so after about 1100, with a reorganization of aristocratic inheritance to more strongly favor male lineages than they had even in the previous century.[78] The church unsettled the picture – in which there was less and less financial independence for women – by forbidding marriages within the seventh degree of kinship (eventually reduced to four), including relations by marriage and shared godparenting of a child. Legally mandated exogamy (marrying outside one's own kinship group), replacing endogamy (marrying kin), meant that wealthy households could no longer accummulate as many women or as much property, thus increasing the circulation of both in the less well-to-do population.[79] Perhaps predictably, those used to having their own way in the politics of marriage rebounded quickly by exploiting or creating loopholes in church regulations. Consanguinity at rather distant levels became a belated excuse for some divorces (as when Louis VII of France divorced Eleanor of Aquitaine). Betrothed couples could arrange to become co-godparents in order to break off the arrangements. Church bureaucrats, and even popes, were not above giving dispensations and legitimizing marriages for money, or in cooperation with figures allied with their own political interests.[80]

Accompanying the development of church law enhancing the permanence of Christian marriage, equalizing the obligations of the classes and sexes,[81] and carrying forward the personal meaning and mutuality of marriage by grounding it in consent, was an evolving theology of marriage as a sacrament. The special function of marriage as a sign and mediator of grace rested neither in sex nor in the production of children; both of these had too long been manipulated by worldly "regimes" which undermined the gospel. Moreover, sex itself had been too lately identified by Christian thinkers as an unparalleled occasion of moral disgrace.

Since Augustine, it was the bond between spouses which was the sacramental analogue to redemption in Christ; and so consent was identified as establishing an indissoluble contract which becomes the bearer of sacramentality. Critics today rightly note the extrinsic and juridical nature of the virtual equation of consent with a contract, and the association of consent and indissolubility in canon law.[82] Yet it remains true that in opting for consent over familial financial negotiations or sexual consummation, the church enabled later sacramental theologies to magnify the personal meaning of marriage, gradually replacing contractual language with that of personal covenant. By the thirteenth century, a theology of marriage had emerged which combined the elements of personal commitment and union, sexual intercourse, and the education of children in a fitting social institution, albeit with a continuing gender imbalance. Although the majority saw sex as primarily for reproduction, a minority of thirteenth- and fourteenth-century theologians (like Hugh of St. Victor) stressed mutual love in their model of marriage.

The medieval theologians would have identified those things that make a marriage as the partners' mutual consent, primarily as spiritual communion and a desire for relationship, but open to and presuming sex, formulated legally in respect to both spouses equally as a "right to sexual intercourse."[83] The metaphysical bond of marriage existed from the moment of consent, and was irrevocable. The consent was the sacramental sign; the sacramental reality was the bond established by consent; and the grace caused by the sacrament created the unity and faithfulness represented legally and negatively as indissolubility.[84] The increased investment of the church in defending the goodness of legitimate marriage, and its lessening interest in placing moral capital in the perils of sexual intercourse, was prompted in part by the Catharist and Albigensian heresies. Their dualist and pessimistic views of the body and sex were condemned repeatedly in the twelfth century. Councils in the thirteenth through sixteenth numbered marriage among the seven sacraments. The indissolubility of Christian marriage, as obligatory and binding, was defined at Trent (1545–63).

The accomplishments and continuing ambivalences of the developing theology are well represented in Thomas Aquinas. Confirming the biases of his own culture with the philosophical explanations of Aristotle, Aquinas saw the female sex in pejorative terms, and as destined for a procreative role.[85] He takes a strongly communal view of marriage, subordinates wife to husband, sees the first purpose of sex in terms of the needs of the species, and defines marriage as a social and domestic partnership, rather than as a personally rewarding, mutual affective union.[86] Aquinas essentially follows Augustine and the *Sentences* of Peter Lombard in offering three purposes of marriage, among which he designates procreation as primary. The indissolubility of marriage, a natural property, is more directed to the proper education of children; to the need of the family for certain paternity; to harmonious familial relations; and to the fulfillment of the social obligations of the couple; than it is to their mutual self-dedication in love. However, the Christian couple's mutual fidelity is a sign to the church of Christ's presence.[87] And Aquinas shows some appreciation for the importance of mutuality in marriage when he objects that a husband's freedom to take many wives, or to send away an older wife who was no longer fertile or beautiful, would reduce wives to a state of servile inequality.[88]

Aquinas describes the love between husband and wife as the greatest sort of friendship, and as characterized by the highest intensity of all loves, because of their union "in the flesh."[89] Although Aquinas retains the Augustinian teaching that sex for pleasure's sake is a sin, he does not see the enjoyment of pleasure itself as wrong, as long as it is properly contained within the marital and procreative union. Aquinas has achieved a link between sexual intimacy, even sexual pleasure, and the intense love of spouses; his definition of marriage as a sacramental vehicle of Christ's presence in the church is not achieved over against or apart from sexual love and sexual pleasure.

For contemporary Christians, as for most members of modern society, the highest meaning of marriage, and its only really indispensable one, is love. In Catholic sacramental theology, the love union of the partners is associated with marriage's sacramentality, and mutually pleasurable sex and children are expressive and derivative of this union. In the words of Walter Kasper, "The love that exists between man and wife is ... an epiphany of the love and faithfulness of God that was given once and for all time in Jesus Christ and is made present in the Church."[90] This reinterpretation undoubtedly owes much to Enlightenment and Romantic ideals of personal freedom and fulfillment outside the constraints of institutions. Also contributory are the Reformation affirmation of the equality of all persons in the sight of God; the presence of God in ordinary human vocations, including marriage; the strengthening of the idea that marriage is a social tie of which a key good is companionship; and the concomitant beginning of a deemphasis both on procreation and on juridical control over marriage.

Contemporary Roman Catholic thought about marriage has been shaped markedly by personalist philosophies growing out of the phenomenology of Edmund Husserl, Max Scheler, and Maurice Merleau-Ponty, and represented in relation to marriage by Dietrich von Hildebrand and Herbert Doms.[91] Personalism is a characteristically modern phenomenon in that it stresses the priority and the experience of the human subject. Intersubjective values become pre-eminently important in moral thinking. In the nineteenth and early twentieth centuries, Catholic moral theology had narrowed sexual morality to the act of sexual intercourse, especially its setting and structure, rather than considering the quality of the relationship in which sex occurred. Sex belonged in marriage; its form had to follow the requirements of conception. Marriage was in principle established by consent, and the conditions of consent could be juridically ascertained. Unconsummated marriages were in practice dissolvable, which led to theological and canonical inconsistencies, but to no great additional difficulty in the determination of the fact of a marriage. The universal moral relevance of the procreative end of sex was captured in crude if convoluted propositional form by any number of seminary manuals: all intentional acts resulting in "venereal pleasure" outside of marriage were illicit. And in marriage, all acts were required to follow the structure necessary to procreation. The "secondary ends" of marriage, mutual help and the avoidance of sexual sin, did not figure significantly when compared to procreation. Pregnancy could be avoided only by refraining from procreative acts; neither incomplete sexual acts (for example, withdrawal) nor artificial contraceptives were allowed.

Thus the moral theologians adopted the legalist approach of the canon lawyer, who determines validity and invalidity of unions; and of the confessor, who investigates degrees of sin and assigns penance. Moral casuistry did not adduce the quality of the couple's relationship as a measure of the morality of their sexual union. One moralist (who objected to the "personalist" reinterpretations) insisted that "[e]ven a marriage in which there is no mutual help, no life in common, hatred instead of love, and complete separation, both bodily and spiritually, remains a true marriage in the sense that the essence of marriage is still there."[92] To be fair, this man expressed some misgivings about such a conclusion, owning that it might seem an "affront" to the common sense of married people. It was a sign of the times that the latter consideration had no bearing at all on his final determination.

The casuistic approach took sex and marriage seriously as realms of moral striving and of social importance, about which the church was obliged to give guidance; but it was grievously inadequate to the human experiences of sex, marriage, parent-hood, and family. In favor of the security of an instantaneous ontological change at the moment of consent, it abandoned the Fathers' vision of indissolubility as a "guiding ideal" realized only over the lifetime of a marriage.[93] It perpetuated enigmas such as the readiness of the church to dissolve unconsummated marriages (now even on the grounds of psychological noncon-summation), all the while maintaining that consent alone estab-lishes the sacramental bond forever (compare new Cans. 1057 and 1055.2 with 1142).

It failed especially in identifying and nurturing the positive values that give these relationships their personal texture and might encourage moral excellence.

Whatever the medieval redefinition of marriage as a personal union of spouses had gained in human terms, or in terms of Christian compassion and upbuilding, had been submerged. The prevailing rigorist and "scientific" moral approach was sometimes "pastoral" about human failure, but created immense anxiety and guilt among the faithful and did little to encourage genuine sexual virtue. And yet, the personalist proposal that it is the actual love relationship of partners that constitutes marriage was already eroding the idea that an act of consent creates an ontological bond which cannot disappear, no matter what the real circumstances of the relationship which it supposedly grounds.

Another menace to the received definition of indissolubility was the move away from sexual acts as a tangible test of both the validity of the contract and the morality of married life. The 1917 Code of Canon Law had defined marriage as a contract in which spouses exchange the right over one another's bodies with a view to the acts apt for procreation (*ius in corpus*). As long as consent is given, the contract comes into being, the rights persist, and the specific bodily means of fulfilling the right can be used to supervise the couple. The actualization of the virtues of marital love are irrelevant to marriage's sacramental meaning.[94]

The 1983 Code replaces the definition of marriage as a contract to exchange sex acts with a combination of covenant and contract language, and indicates that that to which the partners consent is the partnership of the whole of life (*communio*).[95] This has so far meant no specific changes in magisterial teaching on sexual morality. Standard conclusions about sacramental marriage, indissolubility, and divorce, once derived from the notion of marriage as a contract, remain in place alongside the less congenial covenant and partnership language.

It is ironic that, despite the initial flood of objections and even incredulity directed at the personalists from the deputies of the magisterium, certain of the new recommendations were eventually to find their way into papal encyclicals, canon law, and other official teaching. Even while upholding the ban on contraception, Pius XI in 1930 (*Casti connubii*) already began to speak of marriage in terms of the fundamentality of the mutual love of spouses. Since Vatican II (*Gaudium et spes*, 1965) and the encyclical *Humanae vitae* (1968) the language of primary and secondary ends has been sidelined. And in the 1980s, John Paul II built an entire theology of sex and marriage around the concept that sex in marriage is first and foremost a total self-gift of spouses. Both Paul VI and John Paul II use personalist depictions of marital love to explain the immorality of artificial birth control. But the foundations of the edifice of tradition have been shaken.

The Christian normalization of permanency and sexual

fidelity in marriage has, over the centuries, tended to equalize the relations of wife and husband, and to decrease the usefulness of marriage as a tool to secure political and economic goods. With these developments has come a proportionate rise in the companionate value of marriage. Especially since the Enlightenment, the distinction between passionate and romantic love outside marriage and loyal, domestic, procreative love in marriage has gradually diminished.[96] We (modern Westerners) expect from marriage and from our spouses a high degree of sexual and emotional fulfillment, as well as continuing to rely on marriage to supply household and family security. While the affective expectations of marriage present rich opportunities to overcome gender disparities, and to accomplish the sort of genuine friendship which supports and unites spouses in hardship and success, it also places new burdens and stresses on the marital relationship and on the family.

Divorce is no easy answer to difficulty, for it exacts a high psychological price from all involved, and usually places women and children at a consequent economic disadvantage.[97] Privatized sexual and marital decision-making, so often focused on the self-fulfillment of those individuals whose personal, economic, or social assets position them well to "trade up" in sexual partners, or to abandon the disappointments, sacrifices, and difficulties of an ongoing commitment to spouse and children, is a "liberal" version of the patriarchal socializations of sex against which Christianity originally reacted. Yet the painful exclusion of divorced and remarried persons who seek to mend their lives and make amends with the Christian community is neither a productive nor a compassionate method of countering marital breakdown. It offers no compelling alternate vision which can heal the ills of consumer sex and fragmented family ties.

The indissolubility of a personal, sexual union once served as an embodied sign of social solidarity, even if union in the Body of Christ has never been fully realized by any historical community. Indissolubility, as a canonical requirement of or limit on marital behavior, has since the Middle Ages become more and more marginal to, and even destructive of, a sense of communal

transformation of spouses and families in Christ. New interpretations of marital love, consummated in pleasurable sexual
intimacy; and of family, where shared parental love complements the love of woman and man, promise to renew Christianity's witness against the cynical, oppressive, and degrading
transience too often seen in sexual relationships in modern
societies. But this promise will not be realized if the agenda of
renewal holds as its centerpiece the old machinery of constraint
and condemnation; nor if it persists in continuing subtly to
define women's identity in sexual terms.

At the bottom of some of the lingering paradoxes in
Christian teaching on marriage may be the Augustinian
anxiety that, while marriage is good, sex is dubious if not evil.
A woman will wonder to what extent it is a male experience of
sexuality, especially an experience of males struggling toward
continence while shaping a normative theory and theology of
sex, that has fostered this particular ambivalence. Male sexual
drives are more genitally focused and urgent than those of
most women; male sexual response may seem to have an
autonomy and uncontrollability that accentuates sex's danger
and easily represents all that is obsessive and addictive in
human moral fault.[98] Marriage and family, as structured
trainings and channelings of wild impulse, may appear to men,
especially celibate men, as safe moral havens, as the counter-
balancing sublimation of sexual gratification into socially constructive human relationships.

For women, on the other hand, sexual drives assume less
importance on the landscape of identity. Although sexual
pleasure may be a good and a goal, uncontrollability is rarely
an issue.[99] Women's sexual dilemma focuses more on maternity
– on the immediate and highly consequential potential of
sexual acts to result in pregnancy and motherhood, and all that
these realities socially entail. For women, it is precisely the
social institutions that men find so consoling which, structured
as a "male" solution, present personal and social perils for
women. For men, sex is the locus of moral danger. For women,
marriage and family are dangerous, at least as traditionally
practiced. Women seek not so much a structuring of unruly

sexual passion, as a mutually responsible and intimate human relationship in sex, including an experience of maternity that flows from and represents such reciprocity.

Male theologians early on praised virginity as a relief from the degradations of sex itself, as well as from women's ubiquitous subjection to husbands. For Christian women, sex was mostly an extrinsic demand to which one was subjected, requiring reluctant compliance, just as one was subjected to domestic structures dominated by, and at the service of, a "lord" and "master." The history of Christian teaching on marriage reveals the gradual ascendency of the marital relationship as a covenant of spouses. Much of the ambiguity that remains is a symptom of the lasting influence of the perspective on sexual danger that has given form to most of the tradition.[100]

PROCREATION AND RELATIONSHIP IN TENSION: THE BIRTH-CONTROL DEBATE

The issue of birth control, especially artificial contraception, has been a nexus of the difficulties in reinterpreting procreation as "parenthood": a social relationship over time in which the emotional bonding of parents and child is as important as the physical realities of conception, birth, and kinship and the socioeconomic functions of the intergenerational family. Traditionally, birth control was forbidden both because procreation was seen as a duty to the family and species, not as a means of parental fulfillment, and because procreation was considered to be the ultimate purpose and sole real justification of sex. The protection of procreation as a divinely ordained reason for sex also counteracted religions and philosophies which saw the material world, the body, sex, or marriage as evil.[101]

In the early modern period, Catholic moral theology developed a rational, scientific casuistry, focused on clearly defined *acts*, isolable for analysis in terms of their empirical or material structure. The intentions behind the acts were also considered morally relevant, but the moralist's incisive logic and razor-thin distinctions were exercised nonetheless on fairly narrow slices of human sexual experience, from which the ambiguities and shadings of human emotions and relationships had been trimmed.

As the certainty and objectivity of the Enlightenment epistemologies have come under fire, the methods and conclusions of recent centuries of moral teaching have been re-established increasingly on church authority. A major consideration in the 1968 reassertion of Catholicism's condemnation of birth control – which many wanted withdrawn precisely in view of the total relation of spouses and the welfare of families – was consistency in authoritative church teaching. Thus have the stakes been raised.

Since the advent of personalism, relationship has become paramount in sexual ethics, even in Catholic theory. In accepting that couples could engage in sex acts while intentionally avoiding procreation, *Humanae vitae* envisioned a meaning of sex that was nonprocreative, that expressed the mutual commitment of the couple. Sex took on more meaning as part of the couple's intimate, loving relationship – but relationship remains disconcertingly hard to quantify. Current teaching and its backing theologies use the physical procreative structure of each sex act to test the personal intimacy of the union the acts express. The teachings are still put forward as genuine representations of human sexual experience. But the more relational and personal meanings of sex are not commensurate with a criterion of biological structure, and the insistence on interpreting experience this way seems more motivated by a desire to redeem the past than by a readiness to look carefully at what sex really means for couples today. The new values of interpersonal communion and sexual intimacy which receive such high magisterial praise, are already from the outset expected to carry the weight of the moral prescriptions whose originating "scientific" methodologies have fallen into disrepute.

A corollary problem is that "procreation" is often read in excessively individualist terms. The magisterium practically reduces it to a requirement of *sex acts*; the magisterium's critics usually move procreation out to the relation of the *couple* (and immediate family). But the meaning of parenthood, cross-culturally, historically, and experientially, is more *social* than either alternative. This at least was captured by Aquinas' (and the older tradition's) view that procreation is a service to the human race. The "procreative purpose" of sex cannot be adequately grasped, explained, or protected by the narrow access road of individual acts of sexual intercourse; to see parenthood as an undertaking of couples is an improvement, but does not go far enough. Parenthood makes sex (the couple's sexual relation) fully accountable for, and contributory to, human well-being and interdependence in communities beyond the couple. Although sexual couples can and should contribute to society and church in many ways, their union in parenthood is a specifically *sexual* mode of social participation. Not only the unity of love and procreation, but also the social implications of sex and its reproductive potential are at stake in the debate on contraception. Moreover, if woman and men are to be equal partners in the conjugal relationship, their reproductive, familial, and social contributions must be seen in genuinely equal terms, and their control over family size must be shared.[102] This is poignantly evident in debates over population control in relatively poor countries where women are among the most disadvantaged. (We shall return to this question at the end of the chapter.)

DEVELOPMENT OF CHURCH TEACHING

In *Casti connubii* (*On Christian Marriage*, 1930), Pius XI calls marriage a "sacred partnership" (.9), of which children are the greatest blessing and fruit (.11, .12). The encyclical ranks procreation and fidelity as primary and secondary ends of sex and marriage (.17, .19, .54).[103] Any sex act which "is deliberately frustrated in its natural power to generate life is an offence against the law of God and nature" (.56). Procreation is completed in the education of offspring, in which parents give one another "mutual help" (.16). But the structure of the family, divinely instituted, is patriarchal: "This order includes both the primacy of the husband with regard to the wife and children [and] the ready subjection of the wife and her willing obedience" (.26). To say that the subjection of the wife is offensive to human dignity, or that rights of husband and wife are equal, is "a crime." A woman should devote her attention to children, husband, and family, and should not take up business or politics, or even be at liberty to "administer her own affairs" (.74).

On the other hand, the personalist philosophical trends which diminish procreation and enhance spousal reciprocity have already had a destabilizing effect on this procreation-centered hierarchy: "the love of husband and wife ... holds pride of place in Christian marriage" (.23). "This mutual inward moulding of husband and wife ... can in a very real sense be said to be the chief reason and purpose of matrimony" (.24). After the next half century, mutual love becomes dominant in Christian approaches to sex; in Roman Catholicism, it remains in uneasy alliance with the privileged role of procreation in defining sexual morality. The high praise accorded to marital love, coupled with an insistence that it be measured by its physical "openness" to conception, is symptomatic of this tension.[104]

Pope John Paul II is particulary energetic in pursuit of personalist as well as biblical themes, using the metaphor "language of the body," to play out sexuality's intersubjectivity.[105] The pope suggests that Adam's exclamation "This at last is bone of my bone and flesh of my flesh" (Gen. 2:23) recognizes the woman's human identity, realized bodily as "femininity" and in "the reciprocity and communion of persons" which sexual difference makes possible.[106] Moreover, the "finality" of "the life of the spouses-parents" is to make their "humanity" "subject, in a way" to "the blessing of fertility, namely, 'procreation,'" (Gen 1:28).[107] Leaving aside the question whether or how these theological interpretations are linked to the original meanings of the biblical texts, one can still appreciate John Paul II's attempt to engage Catholic sexual morality with Scripture and to explore basic male-female relationships and their potential for mutual self-donation.

In *Familiaris Consortio* (Apostolic Exhortation *On the Family*, 1981), the pope elaborates sex as a language of totality.

Adherence to *Humanae vitae*'s use of "each" sex act as final measure of the interpersonal and parental commitment of spouses is still demanded.[108] Every act of sexual intercourse is invested with the full weight of the couple's love and relationship, and that weight is pinned, not on the emotional or pleasurable aspects of the act, but on its procreativity, reduced to pristine biological format. "The total physical self-giving would be a lie if it were not the sign and fruit of a total personal self-giving" (.11). "When couples, by means of recourse to contraception, separate these two meanings [unitive and procreative] ... they ... degrade human sexuality and with it themselves and their married partner by altering its value of 'total' self-giving. Thus the innate language that expresses the total reciprocal self-giving of husband and wife is overlaid, through contraception, by an objectively contradictory language, namely, that of not giving oneself totally to the other" (.32).

On what basis is it affirmed that marital *experience* requires procreation as the completion of conjugal love (especially if tied to each sex act)?[109] The idea that each act is a total self-gift depends upon a very romanticized depiction of sex, and even of marital love. Certainly there will be times when an act of sexual sharing is hampered or disturbed by factors, intrinsically or extrinsically generated, which impinge, either temporarily or permanently, on the couple's relationship. They are stressed by economic difficulties, an ongoing disagreement about a family matter, blind spots in seeing one another's emotional needs, a crying child, lack of sleep, or an important project due at work. But even more than that, in the *most* ideal of circumstances, human beings rarely if ever accomplish "total self-gift." And the level of self-gift we do accomplish is rarely required to manifest itself, all or nothing, in a single action, much less in every one of a series of actions that we perform regularly. Would we subject the self-offering of the priest in the Eucharist to such a standard (under pain of mortal sin), even though the priest is supposedly standing in for Christ himself?

Couples need encouragement and support in nurturing a sex

life which is indeed faithful to their full relationship, especially
its interpersonal dimensions. Parenthood may well be a normative part of that relationship, and a part of which sex remains
always a symbol and a bodily connection, even when sex acts
are not individually fertile. A "positive refusal to be open to
life" would certainly be wrong. But that refusal of or openness
to "life" can be adequately tested in the way proposed, seems
to me not only a preposterous but a harmful and even
oppressive suggestion. This high and narrow standard militates
against success in meeting the more practical demands of
sexual, marital, and family life. When aligned with an "authoritative" overemphasis on procreation, an unreal idealization of
sex acts can demean married persons' positive experiences of
sexuality by labeling any so-called "compromise" of the ideal as
dishonest, contradictory, false, and selfish.

As Rosemary Reuther observed early on in this debate, it is
important to understand that, while the celibate cultivates
sexual self-control and asceticism, that ethic should not dominate the sexuality of wives and husbands. Ruether insists
rightly that a married person "has sublimated the sexual drive
into a relationship with another person," the demands of which
are "real and meaningful demands."[110] Yet one often finds
couples who deviate from magisterial norms accused of a "lack
of self-mastery."[111] The reality is that the sexual union of
spouses needs at least as much to be encouraged, occasioned,
and sustained, as to be mastered, limited, and scheduled.

Another critical issue is the assumptions about women which
lie behind *Familiaris Consortio*'s delineation of the mutuality of
sex. The pope deplores "machismo" as humiliating to women
(.25), and declares that "the equal dignity and responsibility of
men and women fully justifies women's access to public functions." However, the value of women's "maternal and family
role" is supposed to exceed that of "all other public roles and
all other professions;" women should not renounce their "femininity" or imitate masculine roles (.23). Apparently the full
interpersonal and sexual reciprocity of women and men does
not imply equality in all spheres of familial and social life.
Therefore control of reproduction adequate to permit women

as well as men to mesh family life with their contributions in other spheres is not a priority.

Indeed, the ideals of unity and mutual self-donation are presented with little attention to the social conditions which would make true reciprocity in sexuality, marriage, and parenthood a genuine possibility. The "mutual self-gift" language must be placed against the backdrop of gender roles, especially the pre-eminence of motherhood for women, which clearly color the picture John Paul II paints of sexual fulfillment in marriage.[112] One commends the pope for speaking out against injustice to women,[113] and giving attention to biblical evidence for the equality of women and for the sinfulness of their subordination to men.[114] Yet the practical consequences of biblical and personalist themes are far from receiving full recognition. One is struck by the coalescence of a sexual ethics of procreation and union represented in each and every sexual act, and a social context in which motherhood must constitute the primary identity of women.

In 1962, one author, in admittedly strong but not unrepresentative language, advanced the view that contraception is a bodily sign of "monstrous selfishness,"[115] and that it amounts to an unconscionable reversal of sex roles. "The woman who uses a diaphragm has closed herself to her husband. She has accepted his affection but not his substance. She permits him entrance but does not suffer him to be master." Thus sex as the "sign and symbol of wifely submission, of patriarchal authority, is made over covertly to serve the purposes of a weakly uxorious male and a domineeringly feminist wife."[116] One would expect that such florid language, enjoining in no uncertain terms the subordination of women and the equation of masculine identity with ejaculation of semen, would be unparalleled in theological writing over three decades later. Yet this essay was selected for publication in a major collection defending *Humanae vitae*, which appeared in 1993.[117] It seems not unreasonable to suppose therefore that fear of women's social equality with men and a tenacious grip on subordinating practices lie not far below the surface of readings of women's "dignity" which equate it with maternity and limit reliable control of pregnancy. Defenses of the magisterial view of sex rarely, if ever, explicitly envision a marital and familial situation in which both husband and wife serve in professions outside the home, and share equally in domestic responsibilities and rewards.

And yet the defenders of official Catholic teaching are not wrong in their uneasiness about the prevalence of social attitudes toward sex which, in divorcing sex from procreation, also seem to divorce it from commitment and responsibility.[118] Paul VI predicted "a general lowering of morality," and increasing disrespect for women as consequences of the contraceptive revolution (*Humanae Vitae*, .17). The status of women worldwide has certainly improved since 1968, partly due to increased access to education, health care, and family planning measures. Yet, at the same time, continuing permissiveness toward men's sexual behavior, combined with a greater social expectation that women will trade sex for relationship even without commitment, and the effective cultural dissociation of sex from responsibility for procreation, has contributed to widespread use of abortion as a means of birth control, and to the destabilization of families in industrialized nations. A result is that the psychological and economic needs of both women and children are often miserably neglected. Even progressive Catholics are likely to agree that "widespread unchastity has corrosive effects," and that a "contraceptive ethic" is rightly condemned, "if by that is meant a hedonistically inspired rejection of the deep and truly natural connection between making love and making babies."[119] I would only note that "permissiveness" and "hedonism" as cultural norms and realities are still gender-unequal.

The connection between sex, love, and babies cannot be apprehended, much less credibly advocated, in any individualist or act-oriented concept of sex, becoming a parent, or making a commitment. A strength of Catholic tradition is its strongly social vision of these realities.[120] They now require re-visioning toward a personalized and gender-equal paradigm, which recognizes the biographical and diachronic context of sexual and parental meaning and hence of sexual morality. To rehabilitate the parental significance of sexuality within such a paradigm, it may be necessary to give up specifying those purposes which fulfill sexual activity in the immediate experi- ence of participants – where, in the event, procreation is rarely the dominant conscious aim – and to reposition reproduction in the social context which has for so long been so important in constituting its human meaning. The parenthood of the indivi- dual should be placed in the context of relationship to one's co- parent; conceiving, birthing, and parenting a child should be placed within the family, both nuclear and extended; and the family must be seen, neither as a "haven" from the world, nor as a nexus of social control, but as a school for critical contribution to the common good. To place parenthood in social context would also mean, from a Christian standpoint, to ask how Christian values transform the family, and shape the family's contribution to society.

FAMILY AS DOMESTIC CHURCH

One resource of renewal for a Christian theology of the family is the metaphor of "domestic church," harking back to writings of the Fathers. Currently enjoying a resurgence in Roman Catholic writings, this metaphor may be of general use in meshing social context with personal vocation and fulfillment in marriage and family. Indeed, an exclusively Roman Catholic exposition of this new theology might suffer from the gender imbalance in ecclesial roles (the exclusion of women from priestly ordination) which makes "church" an unhappy model for the Christian family and an inadequate foundation for the family's social mission. But important assets of this metaphor as developed in Catholicism to date are its vision of the family's transformative commitment to society, and its presupposition that the family as a community of social service can by virtue of that very function be a locus of its members' happiness and fulfillment.

The phrase "the domestic church," goes back to Irenaeus and Augustine; and other patristic writers also referred to religious devotion in the home.[121] "Domestic Church" appears in the documents of Vatican II (*Lumen gentium*, 11). In *On the*

Family (.21, .49), it is linked to the reciprocal roles of men and women in the family, to the indissolubility and sacramentality of marriage, as well as to the nurture and education of children, and the contributions of families to church and society. "The Christian family constitutes a specific revelation and realization of ecclesial communion, and for this reason too it can and should be called 'the domestic church'"(.21). The purpose of this community, however, is not to enclose its members or Christian values for safety in a hostile world. The family should serve, in the words of *Gaudium et spes* (.52), as "a school of deeper humanity." "This happens where there is care and love for the little ones, the sick, the aged; where there is mutual service every day; when there is a sharing of goods, of joys and of sorrows" (*Familiaris Consortio*, .21).

In John Paul II's 1994 *Letter to Families*, in honor of the United Nations' Year of the Family, the family is defined as a community with a social vocation. The letter makes repeated use of the phrase "domestic church" (.3, .15, .16, .19), and defines the family as "a firmly grounded social reality," and "an institution fundamental to the life of every society" (.17). Contraception (.12), broken families (.13), and abortion (.13, .21) are mentioned more with an eye to social dangers than to condemnation of individuals. Probably the major shortcomings of the letter are that the family's social mission is still focused on overcoming practices which contradict the magisterium's sexual teaching, rather than on social and economic injustices; and that the letter is not much attuned to the shapes and circumstances of families around the globe. The author seems much more to address dangers that are perceived to exist in consumerist societies where the standard family form is nuclear, with some intergenerational extension, and where various new technologies of birth control and reproduction are commanding social acceptance and medical and funding support. Not much encouragement and counsel are provided in this letter even to families in the assumed cultural setting who for a variety of reasons do not fit the standard model. However, given the model that the letter assumes, the family is expected to be socially engaged, and especially to focus on the humanization and "civilization" of relationships in the larger communities in which the family participates.[122]

The Christian family's "true vocation" is "the transformation of the earth and the renewal of the world, of creation and of all humanity" (.18; cf. .15). The interior solidarity of the family flows outward in a "civilization of love" for humanity and the common good, in country, state, and world (.15). Civilizing love, gift of self, and the social role of the family are directly linked to Jesus' commands to provide food, drink, clothing, and welcome to the needy (Matt. 25: 34–36); and to his warning of judgment on those who turn the needy away (Matt. 25: 41–43). These commands are given application in terms of problems besetting families and family members, however, not directly in terms of the family's contribution to wider justice concerns. Christlike action is exemplified in welcome to the unborn child; adopting abandoned or orphaned children and raising them as one's own; helping pregnant women under pressure; and assisting large families and families in difficulty. Judgment falls on families, social institutions, governments, and international organizations which cannot identify with the vulnerable and rejected, exemplified in the conceived "child" or the abandoned husband or wife (.22). Moreover, "[m]otherhood, because of all the hard work it entails, should be recognized as giving the right to financial benefits at least equal to those of other kinds of work undertaken in order to support the family during such a delicate phase of its life" (.17).

New attention to the family as a theological and ethical *topos* in Roman Catholic teaching and theology thus represents a social and relational appreciation of marriage, now informed by more egalitarian and personalist insights. It engages not only the spouses' personal commitment, but also the parental, intergenerational, and communal relationships out of which it flows and which it in turn augments. Whether Roman Catholic rhetoric about family as domestic church will succeed in rising above well-meaning but ineffectual piety will depend on overcoming Catholicism's recent history of approaching both sex and marriage with a regulatory mentality, infected by fear and ignorance of the sexual lives of its audience. It will also depend

on whether, in practice, it can escape being dogged by the
sexism that shadows official presentations, with their expectations about women's roles.[123] Local episcopacies have often
been more responsive to the social causes and symptoms of
sexism, like domestic violence;[124] realities of family life in the
more prosperous countries, like nontraditional families, economic pressures on the family, and gender stereotyping and
working parents;[125] and the effects of economic deprivation
and political repression on the family in the Third World.[126]

The family as a bounded kinship group is ever an occasion of
temptation to sublimate self-interest into dedication to one's
mate, offspring, or kinship group, using these objects of devotion to justify callousness toward outsiders. The Christian
meaning of parenthood takes biological kinship as a base, but
not as a limit. Children fulfill a couple and link their sexuality
and commitment to intergenerational embodiment of human
bondedness and community. The community which is family
can be a place in which to nurture spiritual ideals, and to
transmit a sense of the "unconditional love" which Christ
promises the church. The Christian family may be seen as a
biologically-based sphere of special affections, "a school of
virtue" in which we learn what love means.[127] But the specifically Christian meaning of family does not stop with biology,
mutual love, or even religious practices and cultivation of
spirituality within the family.

If the family is truly a community of disciples, then it reflects
the transforming power of kingdom life. It educates in solidarity
and compassion for those excluded from the social, material,
psychological and spiritual conditions of human flourishing.
The specifically Christian contribution of the family is sublimation of kinship loyalty into identity with all those who suffer or
are in need, as "God's children" or our "brothers and sisters in
Christ." "As the gospel parables indicate, the church of God is
to be a leaven in society, deeply transforming the world, God's
instrument in the completion of God's kingdom or reign. If this
is how we understand church, then to invite families to see
themselves as domestic church will help families move more
fully into the world rather than retreat from it."[128]

POPULATION, BIRTH CONTROL, AND GENDER

Birth control is a social as well as a personal and marital problem. The issue of population control demonstrates quite clearly the inadequacy of act-oriented moral analysis to address the transformative effect Christianity should have on social practices in which sexual behavior and gender roles are entwined with inequities of political and economic power. This was evident during the September, 1994 United Nations International Conference on Population and Development, which met in Cairo. Two earlier UN population conferences met in Bucharest in 1974 and in Mexico City in 1984, but the Cairo conference much more explicitly set population in the context of worldwide distribution of resources. The primary thrust of the draft document was development, especially health care and the education of women.

The Vatican affirmed these social objectives, and did not make condemnation of artificial means of birth control an agenda item. Yet Vatican representatives clashed with other delegates, especially from the US, over the inclusion of abortion as part of health services. The final conference document (a 113–page "Program of Action") was changed to exclude abortion as a means of family planning. Any suggestion that legal abortion should be a legal right for women was eliminated in favor of a statement that simply prescribed that where abortion is in fact legal, it should be safe. But church representatives still approved only the sections on development. Several Third World delegates, mostly from Muslim countries and from Latin America, sided with Vatican concerns.

Three aspects of this incident have particular bearing on the church's vision of sex and gender, and on its role as a public moral voice. First, both the Vatican and its "liberal" opponents contributed to polarization of the debate in terms of issues which they see both as sexual and as symbolic of their general social commitments. Both employed the rhetoric of power struggle in depicting their interaction on population issues, rather than that of cooperation toward consensus. One reporter for the *New York Times* saw the Vatican representatives, described as "the legalistic warriors of the Roman Catholic Church," as "unable to prevent" the mention of legal abortion, and pronounced that they had capitulated in "a total denial of Roman Catholic doctrine."[129] This characterization of the Vatican's situation was not only inaccurate but inflammatory and prejudicial. On the other side, Archbishop Renato R. Martino, head of the Vatican delegation, referred to the changed abortion wording as "a great victory," while a fellow delegate relished it as "a great gain, a great success" that "made the feminists angry."[130]

Second, both the Vatican and its counterparts in fact modified their positions in order to produce more mutually agreeable wording. So, despite the verbal and political polarization, practical engagement "around the table" did result in movement. As the Catholic News Service reported, the "verbal battles overshadowed the fact that 90 percent of the 'Program of Action' has drawn widespread support – including the Vatican's – for its promotion of women's health, improved education, reduction of child and maternal mortality, and greater international economic balance."[131]

Some of the most effective promoters of women's health and women's agency in family planning are women in poor countries themselves. Just before the Cairo conference convened, ten developing nations with successful family-planning programs announced a cooperative partnership formed to share experience with other Third World countries. All emphasize the role of women as agents of change, and most rely on the leadership of local religious leaders, whether Christian, Muslim, or Buddhist.[132] Bangladesh, still one of the poorest countries, has achieved a cut in birth-rate among rural, illiterate women by the use of female health workers, who sometimes must brave the insults and criticism of fellow Muslims who link women's control over fertility with women's abandonment of traditional wifely and maternal roles, and with sexual permissiveness in general. Zimbabwe similarly has managed a steady decline in population growth through the work of over 800 women who are bicycle-riding "community based distributors," and a government-sponsored male awareness campaign.

Many population experts concur in seeing the reduction of infant mortality and women's literacy as the key factors in reducing population growth, and these are usually associated with economic development. What the Vatican fails to appreciate, however, is that abortion functions for many as a symbol of women's rights; to effectively promote other means of limiting family size, the Vatican must also demonstrate strong, practical support for women. Archbishop Renato R. Martino, head of the Varican delegation, in fact drew attention on the third day of the Cairo conference to the fact that Catholic agencies and donors worldwide support a range of health and education services, "with special attention to women and children, especially the poor."[133] However, undisguised hostility toward "feminists," and greater apparent expenditures of energy and activism on abortion than on maximizing opportunities for women, undercut the Catholic Church's social commitment. Chief Bisi Oguuley of the Country Women Association of Nigeria expressed the fundamental problems of justice which were almost lost in the Cairo duel: "What is more clearly seen in Africa is hunger, poor health, even the lack of the recognition that women are people. Our program is: 'Allow people to count, do not count people.'"[134]

The lesson to be drawn is that the moral significance of sex's procreative power can be adequately captured neither with a criterion of biological structure, nor with a personalist one which does not extend much further than the spousal relationship. The social conditions in which marriage, family, and gender relations are realized are an inalienable dimension of sexual morality, including the proper use of procreativity. The welfare and flourishing of spouses, families, and communities may require the limitation of births, but the question of fertility and its limits must be addressed in light of economic and political justice, including justice for women. Considerations of personal, marital, familial, and social justice will be more important in determining times and means of fertility regulation than a truncated version of their human context, as a reproductive structure. By the same token, calls for the global slowdown of population growth, urging contraceptive availability, must be assessed in light of the fairness of geopolitical resource distribution and in terms of the interdependence of family size and other social factors in disadvantaged populations.

CONCLUSIONS

Procreation is an important meaning of human sexuality, as Catholic representatives rightly perceive, and its value should be institutionalized in family forms which are stable and beneficent toward children. Abortion as a "means of birth control" is a threat to social support of pregnancy, birth, and childrearing in the family. And when promoted individualistically as a "woman's right," it also detracts from public awareness of the much broader and deeper economic and political supports needed to ensure equality and full moral agency for women. However, Catholicism has not gone nearly as far in implementing responsibility for women cross-culturally as it has in establishing itself as a foe of what to many Western or educated women has become the banner of their liberation from patriarchal gender stereotypes and dependence on men for economic survival. Many Third World countries would align themselves against the individualist "rights" rhetoric with which Western feminists can seem to denigrate the importance of motherhood for women in traditional societies, where kin and community are much more definitive of any person's identity than individual achievement. Unfortunately, women's community-oriented roles are still very often placed at relatively low levels of the family and community hierarchy, and this is a social problem in which "official" Roman Catholicism has as yet a seemingly slim interest at the concrete level.

Since at least the 1960s, contraception has functioned as a status-marker in the church, defining "orthodoxies" on both sides, and fueling division, attack, and self-satisfied defense. Abortion is an issue on which most Catholics are in much more general agreement with one another, and are sympathetic to Catholicism's positive valuation of unborn life, if not always to the absoluteness of the prohibitions their church derives from it. Yet abortion has become another weapon of division, now between the church and the larger public order which it ought to influence constructively by building reasonable consensus about the values of sex, commitment, and parenthood. Although Christianity, including Catholicism, is gradually coming to recognize the value and equality of women, and interprets marriage and the family in "personalist," nonhierarchical terms, it still has not registered the range of ecclesial, familial, and social change which women's equality requires. Catholicism's inability to recognize and come to terms with the reasons why so many Western women advocate "abortion rights" is emblematic of this failure.

The failure is played out tragically when a Christian church addresses women in dreadful situations of poverty, violence, and devaluation by investing most of its public capital in the anti-abortion campaign and in scoring political victories over "feminists." The "language" of the sexual body for women in acutely deprived circumstances is not romantic mutuality, spiritual union, or a celebration of women's reproductively oriented, nurturing psychology. It is submission, exhaustion, poor health, a continual struggle to provide materially for one's young, and the probability of early death. The personalist potentials of sex and marriage are in fact being destroyed for poor women because the biological meaning of sex as reproduction is culturally not only primary, but often a means of constraint and even oppression, even as, through motherhood, it can be poor women's only source of social prestige and personal joy.

The Christian social message of reciprocity and inclusion must begin by transforming the family – and women's sexual roles as mothers and wives – if it is to be a genuine school of Christian values, and if it is to redefine biological connection in Christian terms. The role of Christian disciples, and of the Christian family as a kinship group whose interests and actions are transformed by Christian values, is to work to overcome every inequity of race, class, or gender. The way to this end is not condemnation of the sexual sinfulness of those who are already on society's bottom rung, or who are already devalued even by their own family members and religious communities.

Jesus never addressed his warnings of perdition to the prostitutes and tax collectors, but to their "righteous" oppressors.
The Christian way of participation in public, intercultural
efforts toward social change is to constantly refocus attention
on those who are most excluded from the process, gradually
enabling their greater contribution to the common good, and
their equal share in the benefits flowing from it.

CHAPTER 7

The new birth technologies and public moral argument

I have argued that modern Westerners prize the intersubjective meanings of sexual and parental relations, while their socio-economic conditions play a shadow role. Social critics, Marxist and feminist, have attributed family and gender to economic origins; but such criticism generally has enhanced, rather than undermined, our perception that intentionality and choice should govern these institutions, shaping them toward greater personal equality and emotional reward. Reproduction, in turn, has become a personal option gauged to the relational needs of sexual partners. The bodily aspects of parenthood disappear to the moral backstage, while the affective and intentional ones part the curtains to a standing ovation.

This dynamic is being played out in full dress in the social and legal installation of reproductive technologies in Europe and North America, especially in the widespread acceptance of donor arrangements. The function of reproductive embodiment in establishing enduring human relationships is much reduced: conception, birth, and social parenthood may be undertaken without sex between the biological parents of a child; neither gamete donors nor recipients deem an adult's genetic tie to offspring to require social recognition; the connection among genetic, gestational, and social motherhood has been weakened; and neither a genetic co-parenting relation shared with one's mate and social co-parent, nor an affective relation to one's genetic co-parent, are any longer considered determinative for reproductive decisions.

These social realities and the ideology of choice and consent which supports them make a "statement" about the cultural primacy of the voluntary and intersubjective meanings of sex, marriage, and parenthood. Decisions about whether and how to combine the intentional meanings with biological ones are left up to individuals, and are protected by policies of informed consent. They also tend to be governed in practice by the scientific model of rationality, on which the justifiability of acts and practices is measured by their efficiency in gaining the ends autonomously chosen. To have "one's own" child is an aspiration toward which social expectations and their own sense of identity compel many. Diagnostic and therapeutic measures hold out hope to the infertile, even if only at the current average 10–15 per cent success rate of IVF. Yet sustained, critical analysis of the final values or ends for which reproductive clients act, or of means proportionate to those ends, is hard to come by.

Autonomy is an unquestioned value, even as other values, such as community and kinship, are relativized to the pragmatic good or bad consequences in which their recognition or suppression is predicted to result. For instance, third-party gamete donorship is evaluated in terms of the informed consent (autonomy) of the adults concerned, and of lack of demonstrable potential harm to the child or the marriage of its social parents. But concerns about the intrinsic value of the embodied nature of the parent–child relationship (an issue from the standpoint of the donor as well as of the receiving couple and child), or of the unity of marriage as extending to reproductive exclusivity, are dismissed as insubstantial (or religiously sectarian), as long as the criteria of low risk and informed consent have been met. Autonomy, on the other hand, is assumed to be absolute, and is not made subject to proofs of the harm in which proposed limitations would result. Autonomy in reproductive matters is simply taken for granted in cultures where political, legal, and moral traditions of liberty shape public consciousness.

In the absence of a critical discernment and balancing of autonomy and other values, a vacuum is created where the still strong forces of patriarchy and market economics can move in to govern "autonomous" reproductive choice. The most obvious example is contracts between poorer women and wealthier individuals or couples who seek to bear "their own" children. The clients seeking these technologies often see biological paternity or the experience of pregnancy and childbirth as crucial to personal identity, and seek to achieve it by trading on the available market, little regarding whether their choices are subject to pressures from culturally transmitted values whose consistency with human flourishing, the common good, and their own good further scrutiny could challenge.

Certainly, the desire for a child, especially for a child who embodies physically the love and commitment of its parents and the future of their families, is not only "natural" but good and "humane." To share the parenthood of such a child expresses the embodied relation of a couple and fulfills them emotionally and socially. The ethical questions regard the priority such a desire should have on the landscape of identity, and the means which are legitimate to realize it. The desired end and the means must be carefully balanced. When the end the means makes available is a biological or genetic relation to one rearing parent only, and the means is the reproductive partnership of that parent with a third party, the costs are high for a greatly reduced gain.

In sum, the practices of donor insemination, in vitro fertilization with donor gametes, and surrogacy, depend on several assumptions: that choice is a universal and nearly absolute value; that individuals may and should choose whether and how to recognize other moral values, such as a biological relation to a co-parent or a child; that trading with someone who is uninterested in these values is legitimately instrumental to the agent's choice of a genetic or gestational relation to a child, whether or not one also chooses a social relation with one's biological co-parent; and that a biological asymmetry of social parents' relation to child will normally make no difference in family ecology. The end result socially and morally is a dearth of resistance to patriarchal socializations of embodiment, including men's need for guarantees of biological paternity; women's social- and self-definition through motherhood; the sale of gametes, embryos, and, in

surrogacy, children; as well as of the "services" of economically disadvantaged women.

Needed to redress this situation is a re-evaluation of intersubjectivity and biology as together normative for sex, marriage, parenthood and family, a re-evaluation in which biology
is a subordinate, but important and protected, meaning of these
social relations. The challenge is to reinstate full sexual-repro-
ductive embodiment as part of the positive ideal of human
sexuality, in a context of gender equality. The reality of public
discourse on reproductive technologies, however, illustrates
that the embodied relationality of sex and parenthood is almost
entirely subjected to the primacy of choice, and that even when
honest concerns about the social repercussions of new techniques are voiced, analysis often seems impotent in showing
persuasively how they bear upon the common good.

Three documents, all published within a decade of the first
successful in vitro fertilization, which resulted in the birth of
Louise Brown in England in 1978, illustrate forcefully both the
state of public debate and the limitations thus far of Roman
Catholic attempts to influence it. The UK's Warnock Report
(1984), the Vatican's Instruction, *On Human Life* (*Donum vitae*,
1987), and the USA's Office of Technology Assessment report,
Infertility (1988) address similar questions from very different
cultural vantage points.[1] The key moral issues, at least from the
perspective of the present discussion, are twofold: the use of
artificial means, such as artificial insemination and in vitro
fertilization, to achieve conception without sexual intercourse;
and the use of donors to enable infertile couples to bear and
raise children who are genetically related to one rearing parent
as well as to the donor. (All three documents also give
substantial consideration to the status of embryos, and to the
moral limits of their use in therapy and research.)

While both the Warnock Report and *Infertility* approve
homologous and heterologous measures, the Vatican accepts
neither. For the Vatican, sex, love, and procreation are bound
together in each and every act of intercourse or of conception;
no intentional disruption of their unity is morally allowed.
Although it affirms the consistency of this conclusion with

church tradition, it also assumes its arguments to be generally persuasive, and appeals to governments to enact them as law.

The Warnock Commission, indeed acting on behalf of a government, and writing before the Vatican's intervention, begins with an expression of confidence in the possibility of reasonable moral argument about the public good ("Foreword," 1.). Allowing that reason and "sentiment" are not opposed, it also cautions that "matters of ultimate value are not susceptible of proof" (2.). It recognizes that reproductive technologies raise questions both about "family values" and individual rights (3.), about both consequences and the "nature of the proposed activities themselves" (4.). Accordingly it lines up on every issue all the arguments and counterarguments. Yet it seems rather arbitrarily and without much analysis to conclude on the permissive side of most of them. Choice and risk are prominent in the Commission's approach, despite the somewhat more complex analysis projected in the beginning.

The OTA report, by contrast, more strongly and overtly endorses individual reproductive choice. Following four years after Warnock and one year after *Donum vitae*, it could stand as an example of what the Vatican feared, and what Warnock's reticence in setting limits on choice encouraged. In practice, the conclusions of the British and American groups are not all that different. But Warnock's mood of caution has given way to advocacy. Above all, we find in the three documents quite varied conceptions of what constitutes suitable matter and content for public moral argument. The Vatican confidently supposes that appeals to "human dignity" can settle matters of intrinsic morality and shape a consensus about limits on research and therapies which it thinks transgress the human meanings of sex, marriage, and parenthood. The Warnock Commission initially steers away from utilitarianism, and acknowledges that some means to ends may be morally objectionable in themselves. In the end, though, it has difficulty establishing how and when to let those objections be determinative, and falls back on consequentialist considerations. The central premise of the OTA report is the right of individuals to procreative liberty; it is not intrinsic morality but contemplation of practical harm that governs its review of restrictions. Far from cautious, the tone is more defensive of medical progress against the anxieties of religious bodies which present no rational arguments.

For religious ethicists, the interplay of these three voices suggests the importance of presenting religiously-based commitments in terms intelligible to other morally serious persons and communities. Specifically, the higher level of reservation many religious ethicists have about heterologous (donor) techniques needs to be better clarified. From opposite ends of the spectrum, the Vatican, the UK and the US analyses neglect adequate moral differentiation among methods and types of therapy. However, heterologous and homologous methods can be recognized as quite different morally if sexual and parental embodiment are brought into mutual connection, and if subjectivity and embodiment are maintained in a relationship which is constant, albeit weighted in favor of subjectivity.

The Warnock Committee was established under the Department of Health and Social Security by the British parliament in 1982, and rendered its report six years later. It was composed of fifteen members, who represented medical, legal, social service, theological, and pastoral professions. The Commission, chaired by Dame Mary Warnock, received advisory submissions from numerous consultative bodies as well. Unlike the OTA, the Commission was willing to assert as a general proposition that children should ideally be born into loving, stable, heterosexual, two-parent families (2.9, 2.11).

Yet not every couple who aspires to this ideal is successful, which results in "stress" (2.2), and even mental disorder (2.4), owing to the disappointment of expectations and a certain measure of social exclusion. The Report alludes to "a powerful urge to perpetuate their genes through a new generation," an urge which cannot always "be assuaged by adoption" (2.2). It thus approves both artificial conception in marriage, like AIH (4.4); and methods which employ donor sperm or ova (4.16, 6.6: the gestating mother should be legally recognized as the legal parent of the child), and possibly even embryo donation ("the least satisfactory form of donation," 7.4). It recommends, however, that professional surrogacy operations be illegal, and that private surrogacy contracts be rendered unenforceable (8.18, 8.19).

In considering donor methods, the Commission gives credence to the idea that "the introduction of a third party into what ought to be an exclusive relationship" is widely thought to be "morally wrong in itself" (4.10, on AID; 8.10, on surrogacy). However, in the case of AID, no clear and immediate threat to the marriage can be predicted (4.11), and ill effects on the children so born cannot be verified (4.12). Hence, no legal barrier is warranted. Egg donation is approved on the same basis (6.6). Noting that many people do not share the beliefs of those who object to AID, the Commission supports the legal recognition and regulation of this means to the goal of pregnancy (4.16). The Warnock Commission's arbitration of competing arguments is rarely explicated at any length, and often seems to rely on de facto social acceptance or lack thereof. This is strikingly represented in its handling of IVF. A simple statement of the fact that the technique offers some couples their only chance for a child is quickly followed by the bald conclusion that "IVF is an acceptable means of treating infertility" (5.10).

Surrogacy, the one reproductive measure which is excluded outright, is acknowledged to be some couples' [men's] last hope for a genetically related child (8.13). Yet it is described as a legally "risky" business (8.6), which could lead to instrumentalization of women and their bodies (8.10), and is degrading to the child (8.11). The negative considerations decide the issue, apparently because in this case "the weight of public opinion is against the practice," an opinion which is said to rest primarily on the belief, already discounted by the Commission in the case of AIH and egg donation, that "to introduce a third party into the process of procreation which should be confined to the loving partnership between two people, is an attack on the value of the marital relationship" (8.10).

Four years later, the Congregation for the Doctrine of the Faith of the Roman Catholic Church released its analysis of the moral and social implications of reproductive technologies:

Instruction on Respect for Human Life in Its Origin and on the Dignity of Procreation: Replies to Certain Questions of the Day. The authors' names were undisclosed, although the foreword to the document claimed "wide consultation." The following year, the Office of Technology Assessment of the US Congress released a report – lengthy, authored by project staff with the assistance of an advisory panel of experts, and entitled fully *Infertility: Medical and Social Choices*. If the Warnock Commission's work can be conceived as a sort of theoretical and political midpoint, the two later documents are the easily contrasted poles of a spectrum.

The Vatican *Instruction* (*Donum vitae*) focuses on the rights and welfare of embryos, and on the integral connection of sex, marital commitment, and parenthood, following through on the norm proposed in the "birth control encyclical," *Humanae vitae*. The more recent document insists not only that conception should not take place outside marriage, but, even in marriage, should take place only through an act of sexual intercourse. Even if loss or destruction of superfluous embryos can be avoided, techniques of laboratory conception are prohibited, whether they involve the gametes of a married couple or introduce those of a donor. Couples have a duty not only to respect the lives of embryos, but to respect and preserve the nature of marriage and family as grounded in the psychospiritual and procreative partnership of one woman and one man. The result is a strongly negative reading of the new reproductive technologies as endangering human welfare and rights, rather than as positively enhancing the liberty of infertile couples to build families by offering ways to overcome physical obstacles.

In sharp contrast, OTA's *Infertility* focuses on the freedoms, interests, and rights of would-be parents, and sees the role of government primarily in terms of quality control, and the possible enforcement of reproductive contracts. Donor and surrogate methods raise questions about the conditions necessary for a successful process of parent–child bonding, but are not necessarily excluded. *Infertility* offers extensive information on the medical, legal, and financial aspects of reproductive technologies.

Despite difference – even opposition – in content, the documents do share some similarities. These similarities indicate continuing features of the debate about reproductive technologies. Like the Warnock Report, the Vatican, and US documents attempt to draw together moral notions which will appeal to the relatively prosperous and educated Western audience which is willing and able to use the technologies in question. Relatively homogeneous in its cultural, educational, and economic characteristics, this audience may still be religiously and morally diverse. But, compared to Warnock, the latter two documents use the mechanism of "rights" language much more centrally to establish common ground, to advance moral claims, and to build consensus. For the Vatican, the appeal to rights functions as a plank in its platform of universal moral values and norms. For the North Americans, rights language implies the immunity of individuals from unwarranted government interference in reproduction. This is also the prevalent connotation of "rights" generally in Western democratic countries. The authors of these documents seem to assume that their arguments about rights are self-evident, are grounded in values so basic and indisputable, that the only prerequisite to agreement is elucidation and restatement. As in the reproductive technologies debate overall, the meaning of a "right," its status as a moral claim, and its affiliation with other particular cultural values, are not directly spelled out.

According to the Vatican, among the "fundamental rights" to be recognized by civil law in any decent society are: "*a*) every human being's right to life and physical integrity from the moment of conception until death; *b*) the rights of the family and of marriage as an institution and, in this area, the child's right to be conceived, brought into the world and brought up by his parents" (Part III). OTA asserts, "A fundamental aspect of much modern moral thinking is the significance of free and autonomous choices ... When applied to an evaluation of techniques for preventing and treating infertility, the result is an emphasis on the moral significance of couples and individuals freely choosing to act in accordance with their own values" (205).

As these statements mutually attest, the presumption of self-evidence in either case was premature. The US government document reflects the liberal and democratic traditions of autonomy and freedom in the quest for happiness as the individual defines it; of tolerance of multiple, co-existing moral and religious definitions of the good and happy life; and of government's primary role in protecting such freedoms, mediating conflicts with the aim of maximizing the liberty of every individual and group. Particular freedoms should be restricted only in view of this larger aim, and only so far as permitted by the social consensus reflected in prevailing legislation and judicial interpretations of law and the Constitution. Since free choice is the dominant value in human relationships, the parameters of marriage, the family and even the parent–child relationship tend to be defined around freely chosen and nonpermanent alliances, rather than around the traditionally important aspect of biological kinship.

Infertility proposes as crucial six ethical issues: the right to reproduce, the moral status of an embryo, bonding between parent and child, research with patients, truth-telling and confidentiality, and responsibilities of one generation to another (11, 203). The backing of the liberal tradition is evident in this framing of the issues at several levels. Jeffrey Stout's definition of a "liberal society," though not sufficient, is to the point: "any society whose members show considerable diversity in religious or philosophical outlook and whose institutions tolerate such diversity by ascribing certain rights to citizens."[2] But in the US constitutional tradition, at least, diversity is not just a reality which is tolerated and coped with through rights language; diversity and rights are both derivatives of more basic values which shape the national character (or tradition), for example, individualism, freedom, privacy, pragmatism, and tolerance. As a government product addressed specifically to the question of public policy in a culture not only pluralist but aggressively "liberal" in its value orientations, the OTA report focuses on the freedom of adults to take effective steps to achieve their own procreative goals, with minimal interference, and with safeguards to ensure that the decisions of some individuals will not impinge unfairly on parallel freedoms of others, now or in the future. Liberty rights are given priority over welfare rights, and rights to use the new technologies are generally defined in terms of liberty not welfare (204–07). The report appeals repeatedly to social consensus, waiving any attempt to ground its conclusions in some higher order or universally valid value structure, though it frequently rehearses, with a tone of neutrality, a variety of religious stances which are represented within North American culture, and which do claim such grounding.

In addition to the basic right of infertile couples to seek remedies for childlessness, the report treats unmarried (including homosexual) persons' efforts to procreate under the heading "Individual Rights and Freedom to Procreate." It avoids questions of intrinsic morality by reviewing constitutional and judicial support (220–21), i.e., by framing the problem in terms of *de facto* consensus. Moral limits to treatment are examined in a section called "Knowing When to Stop" – suggesting that such limits are contingent on the physical, financial, and psychological welfare of those who choose to undertake them, and that therapists should maximize capacity for well-informed choice about use by encouraging clients themselves to gain perspective on infertility therapies in light of likely benefit and in relation to their other goals. Other limits, such as prohibition of selective abortion or genetic manipulation to predetermine a child's characteristics, are again addressed under constitutional and legal precedents, not in terms of normative moral standards as such, or of the embryo's or child's rights (222–23). Two major issues discussed in the chapter on ethics are the rights of clients as research subjects, and truth-telling and confidentiality. These concerns also help define the ethical aspects of infertility treatments in terms of the autonomy and privacy of those who seek them, of their freedom to choose a course of action in accord with their own goals.

One place at which more traditional concerns about the integrity of the family might have found a point of entry is the potential for the procreative cooperation of three or more adults. As *Infertility* puts it, "it is possible for a child to have a

total of five 'parents' – three types of mothers (genetic, gestational, and rearing) and two types of fathers (genetic and
rearing)." The authors find the language of rights again helpful:
"which of these parents has the right to form a parent–child
bond?" (210). The report just barely raises the possibility that
inadequate conditions for bonding may do damage to the
growth of the child and to the conditions necessary for the
parents to nurture it. However, traditionally *physical* relations of
kinship are mediated by the free-choice interpersonal language
of "bonding," so that the creation of kinship and family
relationships is translated into a matter of autonomous decision.

Much of OTA's attention is devoted to surrogate motherhood, framed not under ethical but under "Legal Considerations" (267–90). A "central issue" posed "is whether a contract
can determine custody and parental rights when the surrogate
mother refuses to relinquish either." Courts thus far have given
surrogate mothers the same rights to their children as other
genetic mothers, so that in the event of a custody dispute
between the genetic parents, "both would stand on equal
footing and the best interests of the child would dictate the
court's decision" (279). Decisions that surrogate contracts are
voidable obviously cut against any view that family relationships rest wholly on freely given commitments, but, unlike the
Warnock report, this one shies away from any normative
inferences from the consensus on this matter that court opinions
may represent. It concludes simply that, without a Supreme
Court decision or federal legislation, "State courts and legisla-
tors are likely to continue to come to different conclusions
about whether these arrangements can or should be enforced,
regulated, or banned" (288).

Revealing of a possible tension between the liberal assumptions of *Infertility* and its incipient recognition of social conditions that qualify liberty, and of the embodied and kinship
aspects of familial relationships, is an appendix titled "Feminist
Views on Reproductive Technologies." In the initial definition
of feminism, the variety of philosophical approaches to feminism is downplayed in favor of those that stress autonomy and

free choice as chief human characteristics, and hence the ones around which egalitarian political objectives ought to rally. Feminists are said to value *"human relationships,* rather than ownership or traditional or legal kinship" – as though to recognize a moral value of blood kinship as a ground of interpersonal relationships would be tantamount to granting men "ownership rights" over women and children. Moreover, women are granted "full rights of *bodily autonomy,*" including full control of fetuses "through birth" – implying that unborn individuals have little if any independent moral status, and that women can effectively be granted a right of ownership over them (326).

On the other hand, it is recognized that many feminists reject a "dualism" of mind and body that suggests that embryos or women are "commodities" to be bought or rented; that social encouragement of women to use their bodies "autonomously" as sources of income is likely to lead "to exploitation of poor or Third World women"; and that the "ties of pregnancy, childbirth, or childrearing" have intrinsic moral significance (327). But overall, the overriding commitment of the OTA report to individual procreative self-determination causes other moral claims to be muted. One is amazed to read, for instance, in a passing remark in the concluding paragraphs of the section on "Ethical Considerations" only that there is culturally "a strong moral sentiment" that women should not be exploited – not that exploitation is inherently a bad thing, should be abjured by any decent society, or has against it strong and convincing moral arguments.

But what *Infertility* lacks by way of unequivocal moral commitment, the *Instruction* more than adequately compensates. It is grounded in an Aristotelian and Thomistic view of "human nature" which sees the exercise of freedom in relation to the common good, and which emphasizes duties equally with rights. And it is much less hesitant than was the British study group to draw specific conclusions about what the common good, duty, and human reproductive welfare demand. Consistently with the recent tradition of moral theology, the moral norm in sexual and medical matters is often tied closely to the physiological outcomes or "purposes" of bodily capacities, allowing procreation through natural sex acts to become a controlling value. The document is replete with absolutes and negatives. The Vatican proposes that a moral evaluation of science and technology requires reference to "the service of the human person, of his inalienable rights and his true and integral good according to the design and will of God" (Introduction, 1.), and to "the dignity of the human person" (Introduction, 3.). Because transmission of life in the human species is the act of a conscious and personal being, its morality "derives from the special nature of the human person." This nature conforms to the "all-holy laws of God: immutable and inviolable laws which must be recognized and observed" (Introduction, 4.).[3]

Human nature is spelled out in its practical implications for several aspects of reproductive technology. Although the Vatican grounds human nature ultimately in the divine creation, it does not see disclosure of the natural law as contingent on revelation. A basic premise of the Catholic natural law tradition is that the natural law is not only objective and universal, but is in principle knowable to all reasonable persons. This premise warrants church involvement in public policy debates, and operates most explicitly in the section of the *Instruction* on "Moral and Civil Law." "The intervention of the public authority must be inspired by the rational principles which regulate the relationships between civil law and moral law. The task of the civil law is to ensure the common good of people through the recognition of and defense of fundamental rights and through the promotion of peace and of public morality" (III.). *Donum Vitae*'s conclusions about what reasonable argument tells us of reproductive technologies and the human and common good, however, are opposite on virtually every point to those of the UK and USA study groups.

The tension between the philosophical standard which the Vatican ostensibly affirms, and the function of church authority in determining conclusions, appears across the spectrum of issues that the document addresses. The Vatican's statement of the "reasons" favoring a negative judgment on homologous and heterologous conception presupposes several understandings of human nature in the spheres of childhood, marriage, and parenthood. A child has a "right" to a "filial relationship" with his or her genetic parents. Spouses have a "common vocation" to "fatherhood and motherhood." The "unity and integrity" of procreation within marriage exclude donor gametes. It is against nature to separate genetic parenthood, gestational parenthood, and social parenthood. Use of donors violates "the family," and is thus dangerous to a just social life.[4] A derivative statement on surrogate mothers focuses on the nature of women as wives and mothers, and presumes essentially the same views of procreative sex within marriage, and of the nature of the family as a biogenetic as well as psychosocial unit, as do the conclusions about donor techniques in general (III.A.3).

Heterologous methods are wrong because they separate procreative cooperation of biological mother and father from the psychosocial and physical partnership of marriage. Homologous methods, while "not marked by all that ethical negativity found in extra-conjugal procreation" (II.B.4), are wrong because they violate the nature of conjugal sexuality. Resembling recent papal writings, *Donum Vitae* speaks of marital sexuality in idealized terms, as a physical and spiritual "self-gift," requiring "openness" to children for its completion. Sexual acts not exhibiting such openness are claimed to be violations of the nature of marital love, whether they are instances of sex artificially made nonprocreative, or procreation artificially accomplished without sex.

There are two problematic dimensions of these fundamental arguments as arguments about basic human values and human rights. First, does *Donum Vitae* adequately assess those characteristics which give marriage, sex, and parenthood their special identity? If so, on what is the assessment based? Can the grounds of the assessment be clarified in sufficiently reasonable and publicly accessible terms? Second, do the terms of the evaluations allow for sufficient moral sensitivity to situations in which the attainment of a reasonably defined ideal is obstructed by practical circumstances? What might such sensitivity require in the cases at hand?

The Vatican condemns any technique which achieves conception outside of sexual intercourse, even if the gametes of a married couple are used to conceive a child which they see as the fruit of their love and the realization of their cherished parental aspirations. "Fertilization achieved outside the bodies of the couple remains by this very fact deprived of the meanings and the values which are expressed in the language of the body and in the union of the human person."[5] *Humanae Vitae* is revisited, with its personalist language, in the proposal that three variables are inseparable in each act, whether of sex or conception: sexual intercourse, love, and procreation. Parallel questions present themselves: Do infertile would-be parents experience laboratory conception as a violation of their sexually expressed love relationship, or as an assisted fulfillment of it? If there are limits to be set on the use of such technologies, does the "each and every act" standard capture them appropriately? Is there a significant moral difference between methods using donors, and those used by spouses alone (which *Donum Vitae* denies)? If so, in what does it consist?

If we were to recognize, as recent papal writings and *Donum Vitae* itself almost imply, that love is the moral *condition* of sexual and procreative acts, then the one inviolable value in the marital-sexual-parental scenario would be the love union of the couple, understood to extend to their domestic, social, and parental partnership. Donor methods would be morally more dubious because they involve a third party in the procreative effort of a marriage. Moreover, they induce the donor dualistically to separate his or her physical partnership in the creation of a child from any psychological and social relationship to that child. (Donorship is different from adoption in that the former involves the premeditated conception of a child *for the purpose of* giving it away.)

In failing to make any significant distinction between homologous and heterologous methods of conception, the magisterial teaching document misses another opportunity to offer prudent and reliable guidance to Catholics and others in a culture which makes any conjunction among sex, commitment, and procreation virtually dependent on free choice. The Vatican fails to elucidate what reasonable relationship might actually be affirmed between love and procreation, once the act-focus is overcome. This shortcoming feeds into the revisionist personalists' difficulty in incorporating the physical experiences of sex and parenthood into their normative interpersonal meaning.

One illustration is an essay of Louis Janssens, who, having established a "personalist foundation" for sexual responsibility and recognized the corporeality and sociality of the person, still can only lift up the personal *relationship* of the infertile couple – its strength and balance – as the final criterion for the acceptance of artificial insemination by donor.[6] The value of corporeality is ambiguous if the level of its practical authority is undefined. If the "prophetic" message of today's church is to be that sexual expression should arise from personal commitment which – barring extraordinary circumstances – is open to and responsible for children, it will have to find a language to ground the meanings of sex and parenthood convincingly in the personal relation of partners. Certainly the sexual–marital partnership is neither defined morally by nor fully recapitulated in any one sexual act. Hence, the tie of love, sex, and procreation must be construed *primarily* in view of the couple's total partnership, including not only its embodied, but also its personal and social dimensions.

In summary, the three documents on infertility therapy take different approaches to moral analysis, which are in many ways representative of the ongoing debate. The Warnock Report alludes perhaps most explicitly to the fact that the public's common moral "sentiment" is both a moral barometer and an audience for moral argument. Progress in moral insight and in policy can be gained by including and weighing together competing moral perspectives, rather than by magnifying one to marginalize or eliminate others in the public realm. But its resort to consequences when the job of negotiating value conflicts seems insuperable typifies a common truncation of the consensus-making process.

OTA emphasizes that neither reproduction nor infertility are matters of mere biology, that human freedom works appropriately within these realms, and that medical interventions which transform the usual reproductive patterns can give alternatives when "nature" offers obstacles. But autonomy is given a precedence among the other values of parenthood and family which is never fully defended. The Vatican highlights the importance of locating reproductive decisions within their physical and social context, giving particular attention to the physical sexual acts through which love is expressed and procreation achieved, to the effects of adults' decisions on children, and on the institutions of marriage and family which give parenthood and childhood social status and protection. But it does not adequately clarify why these values lead to the exact limits the church wants to set, particularly on homologous methods.

No one document is fully responsive to the concerns represented by the others. The authors of each would no doubt regard the others as limited and intransigent. In particular, all documents have difficulty both in making sensible moral distinctions, and in finding ways to encourage some practices and discourage others, even if not with the rather blunt tool of outright illegality. Separated by more than disparate conclusions, they operate out of quite different assumptions about individual and community, and about the relation of reproductive embodiment to freedom.

Do these discrepancies signify intractable cleavages in the moral vision of late twentieth-century Western society? Do they incapacitate moral discourse as far as an outcome of policy consensus is concerned? The intelligibility of public discourse among moral traditions is an important prerequisite of well-considered social practice in any pluralist society, and certainly for any practice or cooperative undertaking that is international and intercultural in character. The particularism of religious traditions, dismissed as tribal and sectarian by critics in secular culture, can be played off against the emergent postmodern insight that "secular reason" is a phony. Jean-François Lyotard mocks the "Enlightenment narrative" of "a possible unanimity between two rational minds."[7] Although the relativity of all narratives may not be the only other alternative, we may still agree that all ethical analysis begins in, and is indebted to, some concrete moral tradition, religiously identified or not, explicitly recognized or not, and whether moving under the aegis of church authority, humanistic universalism, or Kantian rationality.

The point is not reason's demise or incapacitation, but its reinvigoration in a historically conscious era. The question is not how to bracket explicitly religious (or tradition-based) language and concerns, but how to forge them into a "reasonable" consensus among members of overlapping religious and moral communities facing urgent and shared practical concerns. Policy debates about health care issues provide a window onto the meanings rationality may have once we have given up the Kantian and Cartesian ideal of clear and distinct ideas about universal or a priori moral obligations.

Why not see the unavailability of, in Jeffrey Stout's memorable phrase, a "privileged vantage point above the fray,"[8] as, not a liability, but an integral condition of human knowing, and one which does not necessarily preclude the raising of truth questions? Richard Bernstein urges us to exorcise the seductive polarity of Descartes' drastic alternatives. "*Either* there is some support for our being, a fixed foundation for our knowledge, *or* we cannot escape the forces of darkness that envelop us with madness, with moral and intellectual chaos."[9] The bioethics policy equivalent of this dilemma, of course, is the demand *either* that arguments be wholly "neutralized," *or* that they be excluded from the public forum as the tip of religio-moral fanaticism erupting in the body politic.

Certain theologians, by emphasizing the nature of theology as an internal communal language, a symbol system with reference only to the shared but limited universe of a religious tradition (for example, George Lindbeck's "cultural-linguistic" model of theology), may seem to play into the hands of the narrow, Enlightenment definition of rationality which rules religion out of court. But the defense of an *historical* reasonableness, recognizing the inevitable contextuality of all moral argument (not just religious moral argument), is not a patently absurd project.

David Tracy, as we have already noted, establishes theology's public credibility on a communicative power, which is potentially universal, but which does not reside in some culture-free vocabulary, foundations, or essence. The thesis that religious traditions can communicate on a broadly human and cross-traditional level via the perennial appeal of religious and cultural "classics" does not require any abstract "reason" or "nature" beyond culture, but does presuppose that there *reliably* will be elements of consistency and recognition resounding in human experience throughout cultures. On a view such as that of Tracy, Nussbaum, or moral theologians revising Roman Catholic resources, human reason, as a deliberative and evaluative power, can work within, between, and among cultures, looking for common ground and moving inductively but defensibly toward moral and social consensus.

Theological language ought to provide a critique of the Enlightenment ideal of so-called "secular" rationality, without abandoning engagement with the moral quandaries and the modes of discourse of liberal culture, or trust in the feasibility of rapprochement. Theological ethics can help move the understanding of rationality commonly presupposed in bioethics policy from an ideal of a tradition-free "public realm" and a transcendent reason, to an ideal of critical conversation within and among communities on the basis of shared (and to that extent, "public") values.

Although they are certainly not alone among Christian authors desiring to further public discourse,[10] Roman Catholic authors typically do so by developing the "natural law" conviction that human beings share certain basic tendencies and values (physical, intellectual, and social), which provide the substructure of a universal ethics. For instance, Bryan Hehir, who is the pastor of a large Catholic parish, a professor at the Center for International Affairs at Harvard University, and an influential consultant on social ethics to the US Catholic bishops, sees Catholic tradition as proposing a positive view of the state in society, conferring on it "a broad social mandate" in achieving the common good. The foundation of a natural law jurisprudence is a conception of a higher moral law by which positive law can be tested. Despite critiques aimed at the potential erosion of the specifically religious message of ecclesial bodies, the church, according to Hehir, continues to maintain that "the search for civil consensus is a valid and necessary ecclesial task, and that the Church's case can be made at the bar of reason."[11] His confidence in the potential for rational discourse on the most inflamed topics leads Hehir to affirm the church's public advocacy even in such highly contested areas as abortion and health care policy.[12] As has been noted earlier, a historical liability of the natural law tradition has been insufficient attentiveness to the actual religious and cultural assumptions which have been operative in delineations of the "natural" norm.

Placing the emphasis somewht more on the historical context of moral advocacy, Edward Vacek argues that Aquinas allowed for more change and flexibility in interpretations of natural law than the recent tradition has been willing to recognize.[13] The viability of this tradition lies in reliance on a "dialectic of reason and experience" rather than "some special divine revelation," and it results ideally not in an absolutist moral code, but in "various revisable rules."[14] The present charge is to achieve a more holistic approach emphasizing freedom, reason as reasonableness in historical context, and the location of human nature and moral acts within interpersonal and social relationships.

These two are representative of most Roman Catholic authors, insofar as they are committed to the translation of religious values into an inclusive and philosophically hardy moral vocabulary. At the same time, they certainly recognize that, in practice, moral language emerges out of, and speaks to, specific moral and political communities, whose membership may well be forged from a variety of traditions. As David Hollenbach has stated well:

The recovery of openness to the possibility that visions of the good life may not be simply personal preferences but can be subjected to intelligent assessment in a community of genuine discourse is urgently needed to counteract the breakdown of serious political debate and cultural self-criticism in American life today.[15]

The contrast of this approach with the liberal one, agnostic about, and privatizing of, other values than autonomy and avoidance of harm, is brought into full focus by a report of the American Fertility Society on reproductive technologies. The AFS policy report, which ultimately limited consent by few if any criteria other than good medical prognosis and absence of risk, began on a footing not so far from Vacek and Hehir. In laying out the basis for ethical evaluation, the guidelines observe that many factors, such as religious authority, personal experience, immediate utility, vocational commitments, autonomy, and what is legally required, may weigh in in favor of a moral conclusion by a given individual or group. Yet such appeals all come together insofar as they illuminate a more fundamental moral criterion, "the human person integrally and adequately considered." What is necessary to secure the welfare of the human person is not derived from quantitative studies alone, but "calls for an inductive approach, based on experience and reflection." This approach looks toward the "comprehensive impact" of actions on persons, and acknowledges the necessity of sometimes having to live with ambiguity and uncertainty, or to revise past judgments.[16]

The phrase "human person integrally and adequately considered" reveals the hand of committee member Richard A. McCormick, S. J., a Catholic theologian. It is based on *The Pastoral Constitution on the Church in the Modern World* (.51, .59, .61, .64), a document of the Second Vatican Council of the Roman Catholic Church.[17] Note that the criterion of respect for the fullness of the human person is, in the AFS report, not advanced under the aegis of religious authority, but as the expression of a fundamental moral insight shareable even in a pluralistic society. An insight originated within a religious group is not thereby disqualified from the public conversation, in which it may find a more "universal" resonance. A humanistic and not merely tribal basis for debate of the fundamental values at stake in reproductive practices was indicated when the committee as a whole accepted McCormick's basic criterion and inductive approach as part of its general considerations.

Perhaps unsurprisingly, McCormick himself responded to the

AFS guidelines' permission of donor methods with a "Dissent on the use of third parties," in which he concluded that the use of donors "is not for the good of persons integrally and adequately considered. It involves risks to basic dimensions of our flourishing," such as the unity of marriage.[18] This is especially true when the institutionalization of donorship is considered. The point is not that McCormick's analysis of human flourishing in the area of reproduction is necessarily correct, but that his objections and possible counter-objections are publicly discussable.

The fact that McCormick is a Roman Catholic may account for some of his moral sensibilities, but it will not relativize his conclusions to that tradition, if they are not presented on the basis of religious authority alone. The same will be true of other contenders in the policy arena, all of whom will necessarily come from some background or perspective. Considerations which arise from the particular standpoint of any theologian, lawyer, medical practitioner, or philosopher will never be "neutral" or "free" of shaping moral influences. This does not prevent their appropriately being tested in the public forum on the basis of their ability to persuade and their confirmation by the moral experience of others. This is how social consensus is built. Liberals may still have something to teach Catholicism about equal worth, human rights, and the exercise of liberty; but they are still inadequately prepared "to enter into a serious discussion of what constitutes the human good," much less of "collective responsibility for social outcomes" and "the common good."[19]

The perspective on reproductive technologies presented here places infertility therapy as a matter of social as well as of sexual ethics. It is feminist and nonindividualist. It is "objectivist" in the moderate sense of affirming the possibility and importance of a public conversation about the human goods involved in reproductive and family policies. Because of moral pluralism in our culture, our respect for differences, and our valuing of tolerance, we who speak from North Atlantic Western societies, especially the United States, tend to approach disagreements over moral practices in terms of procedural solutions rather than substantive ones. That is, we reconcile opposing view-points by such guarantees as free speech, equal access, and informed consent. We avoid substantive discussions of the content of speech, the priority of the various goods to which we want access, or the value of the relations which individuals freely choose to enter. Procedural solutions are not, however, adequate to the human moral reality, nor to the human need to build communities of civil discourse and practical cooperation where the concrete problems of living together can be resolved.

Procedures which support the equality and self-determination of every individual are no doubt extremely important. Nazi medicine and Nuremburg teach us of the indispensability of informed consent in medicine and research. But informed consent is not enough as an ethic. What are the goods (or evils) to which we give consent – what sorts of goods ought a good society present as most worthy of choice and realization? Gamete donation is not adequately understood in terms of free individual decisions to employ "remedies" which those involved expect to provide the most beneficial consequences. While our general cultural tendency – popular, medical, legal, and philosophical – is to approach the new reproductive technologies with a moral vocabulary of procreative choice and privacy, there is more to the human reality of parenthood than autonomy.

Neglected areas of moral concern are: the nature of human parenthood as ideally grounded in biological kinship relations as well as in chosen social commitments; the contextualization of choice by inevitable and universal aspects of "the human condition" (for example, health and illness; aging, diminishment of some of our youthful powers, death; our interdependence within communities and families); the relation of individual choices to the common good, especially when choices become social practices; and the moral role of policy in cultures in which legality is often equated with unobjectionability.

I believe it would be well to ask some second questions about any society which sets up large, profitable, and science-driven programs in which donors and recipients are encouraged to dissociate genetic from social parenthood, biological partnership in conceiving from social partnership in rearing, and to see medicine and technology as "desperate" but inevitable and "necessary" solutions to problems which have social as well as medical origins. A fundamental concern is the degree of pressure on clients, especially women, to "choose" this means of resolving infertility.

GAMETE DONATION, CHOICE, AND A LARGER HORIZON OF VALUES

Gamete donation programs are typically offered as an available elective therapy for individuals or couples who can afford to choose them. Applicants are screened for medical suitability and are offered counseling to ensure that the consent they give to the procedure is based on a full understanding of the facts – medical, psychological, and social. Donors are actively recruited for such programs, and are similarly screened on the basis of medical criteria; psychological counseling is much more frequently offered for female than for male donors. Although some programs have age-based cut-offs (which are primarily for medical rather than for social reasons, and are applied earlier and more strictly to donors than recipients), few if any other limits are finally placed on the free choice of participants. The American Fertility Society, in an appendix to its 1993 report on gamete donation, offers to provide sample consent forms.[20] A 1991 overview of ovum donation programs in the US found that "Most programs had no specific stated exclusion criteria for recipients," other than their willingness to bring a donor into the program.[21]

In early 1994, extensive media coverage was given to an English woman who chose to give birth to twins at 59, and to a 63-year-old Italian woman who was three months pregnant.[22] A practitioner at one clinic which was reported to have been among the first to implant ova in post-menopausal women commented to the press, "They have a purpose again."[23] Such a rationale raises questions about the social as well as the medical meanings of infertility, and about our ability to confront or find significance in the human life-cycle, ageing, and mortality. Does a woman's purpose consist in having children – does the specialist's "again" mean that older women lose purpose unless they can recover their fertility? A deeper consideration of the social values at play might reveal the collusion of gender stereotypes and market forces in producing a clientele for the technological recombination of parent–child relationships. "An enormous industry has grown up in recent years to postpone or prevent menopause through hormone replacement therapy; now reproductive life can also be pro- longed ... There are questions of what we value in women."[24] The fact that older men beget children says more about the state of gender relations than it does about the suitability of persons at the far end of the life-cycle to become parents of infants. These men invariably have young wives to mother their children – and usually a divorced wife their own age.

Questions about the fundamental human values which come into play in sexuality, parenthood, and gender relations receive little sustained attention in public and policy discussions of gamete donation, except for freedom of choice. Medical practi- tioners, lawyers, policy makers, and much of the North Amer- ican public, tend to be pragmatic, individualist, and expectant that technology will resolve human difficulties. In the common view, the only real limit to free consent is the possibility that individuals' choices will bring significant measurable harm to themselves or others. The reproductive technology guidelines of the American Fertility Society Ethics Committee identifies the "common thread running through ... possible constraints on the moral right to reproduce" as "a concern about harm." Absent harm, couples have "a liberty right to reproduce," including the enlistment of third parties.[25] Charles Taylor has noted that instrumental reason operates on a delusory model of the detached human subject, which, even when predicting costs and benefits, is hardly free from its "messy embedding in our bodily constitution, our dialogical situation, our emotions, and our traditional life forms."[26] Technological instruments in the hands of a disembodied reason tend, thinks Taylor, to slide toward dominance and hence to subvert the very goal (benefi- cence) toward which they were originally directed.

Attacking the liberal model of unlimited procreative liberty on feminist grounds, Maura Ryan (a Roman Catholic) raises objections about this model's tendency to treat children as property to which adults have rights; to define the family in terms of contractual rights, while neglecting the relevance of the kinship bond to parents' unconditional love of children who are not "chosen"; and to displace the moral evaluation of means to one's reproductive ends.[27] "The common expression, 'This child has a face only a mother could love' speaks, of course, to the fact that a parent's bond to her child transcends all cultural standards of beauty, etc., but also alludes to a deeply entrenched understanding of the 'givenness' and duration of parental responsibilities."[28] Similarly, Sidney Callahan faults practices whereby a gamete donor "does not assume personal responsibility for his or her momentous personal action engendering new life," but contracts "to abdicate present and future personal responsibility."[29] Insofar as adoption is "after the fact' crisis management," it is dissimilar.[30] From a feminist viewpoint, the contractual model of procreative liberty assumes that family bonds are governed by rights and ownership, an assumption that can prove as dangerous for children as it has been oppressive historically for women.

FEMINIST CRITIQUES OF "CHOICE" IN REPRODUCTION

The radical feminist critique allows us to look below the surface of free and informed consent, and to recognize that powerful social forces always shape choice and define the options that we are able to discern as available to us. A morality of private choice is ultimately self-delusory. As Foucault has urged us to recognize, our freedom can be co-opted by "discourses" of power and knowledge, pre-eminently medical discourses, which structure our perceptions of ourselves and our world.

An ethicist, who with his wife endured a taxing series of infertility therapies while considering donor insemination, verifies that "the tyranny of available technologies" constitutes "a form of coercion."[31] After each unsuccessful attempt, the patient asks, How can I not try the next technique? Moreover, the pressure to advance carries with it relational problems for the couple, insofar as one who refuses to go any further may be blamed for denying the spouse the opportunity to procreate.

The trajectory toward the use of reproductive technologies is often given momentum by a rhetoric of "desperation" surrounding the couples and their need to bear a child. One IVF client, who quite understandably wanted to help assuage her parents' grief over the recent death of her brother, is portrayed as giving the goal of a birth nearly ultimate importance. The woman is repeatedly characterized as desperate. We hear of prayers for the baby she "so desperately desired," she tells us how she "so desperately wanted to give my parents a grandchild," and we learn that during a phone-line wait for the doctor, she "despaired."[32] In an essay entitled "Deconstructing 'Desperateness,'" anthropologist Sarah Franklin recounts headlined and emotionally overloaded stories of infertility from the British press. She concludes that the media are contributing to a mythology in which parenthood is a precondition of adulthood and social approval, and in which the only real solution to childlessness lies in the capabilities of medical science.[33] The story of the desperate infertile couple is

both an adventure story and a romance, in which a successful "fight against the odds" may end in "a dream come true." It is an epic story of medical heroism in the face of human suffering and the forward march of scientific progress. It is a story of winners and losers, of happy endings for some and hopelessness for others.[34]

The personal consequences of living this story cry out in the words of one woman who was obviously not only at the point of desperation, but also emotionally dependent on the medical profession. "After more than four years of infertility, I am pregnant ... The last three months have been a black hole of terror. The overwhelming fatigue and constant nausea were bad enough, but the fear of miscarriage nearly drove me crazy ... I live from one obstetrical appointment to the next."[35]

Even those who win the happy endings do so at an enormous emotional and financial cost. Many of the veterans speak of profound personal humiliation, as the intimacy of one's sexual and procreative capacities is invaded, one's person is objectified into a set of body parts and reproductive processes, and one's success or failure as a person is equated with the capacity to conceive. Gena Corea makes a disconcerting comparison of artificial insemination, IVF, embryo transfer, and sex determination in cows and in women. One veterinarian who worked for a company which transferred fertilized eggs from donor to host cattle "gently soothed a cow while he was hurting her, saying, 'I'm sorry, honey.'" One of the farmers with whom this man worked described the operation as "making babies." He herded cows into confining equipment by shouting, hitting them on the side, twisting their tails, and finally urging, "What's the matter with you woman? Step up!"[36]

Janice Raymond finds a disturbing sexualization of the technically desexualized procedures of reproductive medicine, which compounds the experience of the woman as object and victim. Even if sexual banter and phallic references among physicians are more rare than some critics report, teams which prod and inspect a prone woman, feet in stirrups, genitals exposed, all the while discussing ways in which she can be made pregnant, reduce her to a state of sexual humiliation. Raymond recounts attending a world IVF conference on reproductive technologies in Paris in 1991, at which part of the entertainment for the "appreciative male medical audience" was a cancan in which women's bodies were exposed in a display of thrusting pelvises and buttocks.[37]

In such an atmosphere, it is difficult to dismiss the argument that infertility medicine is inherently coercive, especially for women. One may hope that, as more women enter this specialty, its dehumanizing effects on women will be diluted. I believe that specialists who practice infertility therapies usually do so with honorable intentions and a Hippocratic commitment to relieve human suffering and "do no harm." But a liberal philosophy and politics of choice does not adequately address the fact that women are presented from birth with images of mothering as crucial to their identity, with pregnancy and childbearing as the culmination both of their sexuality and of their relationships of intimacy, and of fertility as a sign of youthfulness, desirability, and worth. Men are taught to see virility and sexual potency as confirmed in the ability to "father" a child (i.e., to inseminate a woman), and both men and women are led to see the sexual and reproductive services of women as men's natural right and due. As recently as 1994, I attended a seminar at the National Institutes of Health in Washington, DC, at which a renowned infertility specialist from a stellar institute in a northeastern state outlined the latest techniques. One slide was entitled, "Assessment of Ovarian Competence," which the physician explained as "a *woman's* ability to respond to ovarian stimulation." To competence, he contrasted "ovarian [a woman's] failure." (When "male factor infertility" was remedied by in vitro fertilization, however, the process was called "assisted fertility," and although the problem was characterized as "male," it was never attributed to "the man.")

No wonder the "desperation" that surrounds failure to realize the socially requisite roles of wife and mother, and the insidious power of a highly technological medical establishment which holds out promise of a reversal of fortune.[38] The fault lies not with the doctors only, however. Not only practitioners but their petitioners, as well as a larger public whose attitudes laissez faire policy represents, have a responsibility to consider carefully the human values at stake in family and parenthood, as well as our trust that technology will provide a way around intractable human difficulties.

THE ADOPTION OPTION

The desire to conceive and birth a child "naturally" is not only understandable and appropriate, but is prevalent cross-culturally, both among married couples and many singles. The disappointment of this desire is a heavy burden, and it is valid to attempt to relieve that burden by remedying possible physiologic causes. The moral question concerns the proper limits of recourse to medical therapy. That question must be answered partly in terms of nonmedical alternatives.

One social answer to infertility is adoption. Adoption allows an infertile couple to nurture a child without requiring a reproductive alliance of one member of the couple with a third party. Adoption preserves a symmetrical relation of parents to child. It allows them to accept the limits of their fertility (and perhaps age), while recognizing that other, creative ways of satisfying their generative impulses and their desire to share the rewards of childrearing can be found. This is not to say that the need to parent is itself so strong that infertile persons cannot deal with this limitation through nonparental forms of relationship, service, and fulfillment. But, given the availability and need of parentless children worldwide, adoption is a viable way to channel one's parental aspirations.

I have a personal investment in adoption because three of my five children are adopted from Thailand, and adoption has been a tremendously rewarding experience for our family. The adoption of a child in need of loving parents can be an opportunity for adults who strongly desire a child to transform their own needs and frustrations into compassion and care for another. Parties to adoption can recognize that the sundering of the biological and social relationships of birth parents to children often arises from social injustices, and that the causes behind the availability of children for adoption should be addressed in their own right. Moreover, adopted children, adoptive parents, and birth parents will all need to come to terms with their "loss" of a unified bio-social child–parent relation. Regret can be expressed for this loss, a subsequent necessity which the birth parents did not plan as a reason for conceiving the child. Yet adoption can transform a reproductive "failure" on the one side, and a disrupted birthing situation on the other, into a constructive reconformation of family relationships. The matching of adults' needs and childrens' needs is an equation in which a double negative can become a positive accomplishment.

Elizabeth Bartholet, an advocate for adoption as a resolution of infertility, makes the case that adoption laws, health insurance policies, and the medicalized infertility scenario conspire to make it easier for parents to seek high-tech therapies than to parent already-existing children. Bartholet writes of her own experiences with fertility specialists. Those who are financially able are led ineluctably "down the treatment path," by a doctor whose advice "is inevitably biased toward the treatment option." Few doctors see it as "their job to explore with patients why they are considering medical treatment, whether continued treatment efforts are worth it, or when enough is enough."[39]

Bartholet also addresses the argument that adoption is exploitative, since it takes advantage of the misfortune of birth parents, contributes to its social causes, and even constitutes a form of "trafficking" in babies.[40] Kidnappings may occasionally occur, as does coercion of birth parents – especially impoverished birth mothers – and improper payments either to parents or to intermediaries are not as rare as one might wish. Moreover, it is true that the demand of relatively well-off Western couples for healthy white infants indicates that need fulfillment (a need for a specified kind of "acceptable" child) often dominates in the adoption situation over outreach to homeless children. Abuses and distortions of the adoption relationship must be identified and abolished, not tolerated.

Nevertheless, adopted children are not most accurately seen as "products" who are "marketed" to the middle class, or "exported" from Third World countries. As Bartholet insists, mistreatment of children and oppression of birth parents must be kept in perspective. Even if all abuses were eliminated, and even if longstanding and worldwide injustices, such as poverty and the subordination of women, began to be substantially addressed, it is difficult to imagine that the numbers of children in need of families would be drastically reduced in the near future. Moreover, in many cultures, biological kinship is seen as so indispensable to a parental attitude toward children, that adoption of those who are not related by blood is virtually inconceivable. Adopted "slum children" are suspected of having "bad blood" and their true origin is often hidden in secrecy. (This extreme is the opposite of the voluntaristic view of parenthood that we find in North America.) "International adoption clearly represents an extraordinarily positive option for the homeless children of the world, compared to all other realistic options."[41] To denigrate legitimately formed adoptive families in order to promote a view either for or against reproductive technologies,[42] to give a focus to poorer countries' well-founded resentment of Western colonialism, or to compensate for the indignity many of these countries experience in not being able to care for their own children, is to reduce needy children who deserve families to pawns in political battles.

To counter charges of adoption racketeering and exploitation, it should also be recognized that many international adoption agencies (and the parents who have adopted through them) make contributions, both financial and social, to improve the situation of children in their birth countries. These include social services for families who are under duress and in danger of disruption; education for children of poor families, including girls; financial support for birth mothers who desire to keep their children; foster family programs; educational and social programs for institutionalized children; care for handicapped children and a chance to be adopted (almost nil in-country for most); advocacy for in-country adoption; and the reuniting of birth families where possible. These organizations typically provide counseling and support for adoptive families, including programs which reinforce and support the ethnic and racial identity of adopted children. While problems and difficulties undoubtedly exist in the practice of adoption, and while it will not be a satisfying solution for all couples experiencing infertility, it is one viable avenue to relieve the suffering that infertility unquestionably can bring.

POLICY AND MORALITY

It is a truism that most North Americans tend to equate law with morality. The legalization or legal facilitation of any activity is likely to short-circuit further public discussion (and personal consideration) of whether that activity is worthwhile or objectionable in itself or in certain circumstances. Conversely, illegality makes a negative moral statement in the minds of many. Contrast public attitudes to abortion and to the use of marijuana, in view of the fact that the former is, from almost any credible standpoint, a more serious moral decision.

Institutionalized gamete donation, especially when or if it is facilitated by policies which provide it financial support, or specify and protect the rights of the parties to it, makes a public statement. The message is that the separation of biological from social parenthood, and the equation of family relations with voluntarily assumed contracts, are morally unproblematic. Ovum donation reinforces the view that women must become pregnant in order to be fulfilled as women, and that this goal is important enough to justify extreme measures, including subjecting oneself to serious emotional and physical stress, and having one's spouse conceive with a third party. Gamete donation as a personal "choice" also conveys the priority of privacy and liberty over sociality and the common good, and the validity of personal risk and harm as compasses of moral reasoning. It reinforces our expectation that technology will resolve complex human problems, and reposes in the medical profession a confidence and a set of expectations that it neither should want nor receive.

Institutionalized gamete donation is thus morally questionable as a social practice for a number of reasons that go far beyond the concerns we might have in an isolated case. However well-established sperm donation has already become, we need to take another look at what it represents, and the arrival of ovum donation gives us that opportunity. This is not a matter of some marginal "religious" objection, but of our ability to think and act morally as a society and to use reason in a "transformative" as well as in an instrumental way.[43] We need to consider, not just protections of the decision-making process and efficient means to freely elected ends, but the substantive values whose realization we encourage by means of the policies we set.

Outlawing and attempting to eradicate well-entrenched practices is not the only way to advance their moral reconsideration; nor is it usually the most prudent and effective way. Laws and policies usually do not command compliance unless they are met by at least an approximate social consensus in their favor. But policy can have a role in shaping consensus if it proceeds by relatively moderate measures, and if it encourages and comes out of broad and civil public discussion. Policy-making bodies can express the importance of ongoing moral scrutiny of gamete donation in a variety of ways. Some examples of restraints on the practice (here more suggestions than proposals) are refusing to let donors totally off the hook and out of the picture, for example, by making identifying information available to the adult child; declining to make gamete donation a research funding priority; denying insurance coverage to these technologies; setting an age limit for recipients as well as donors; and discouraging or denying ovum donation to single women.

Positively, policy could support other options, especially adoption, and could encourage more thoughtful and extended counseling about alternatives. Counseling should be offered by persons with no vested interest in the success of gamete donation as a socially approved and supported practice. This might include the opportunity to share experiences with other individuals or couples who had taken a variety of routes in coping with infertility. Counseling and opportunities for reconsideration should continue throughout the infertility treatment process.

We should not overlook another morally important dimension of reproductive technologies: their expense and availability. Despite its implicit valuing of duty to others and to the common good, the Vatican exhortation, partly by appropriating modern "rights" language, focuses quite individualistically on the couple, their marital relationship, and the rights of the embryo they create, attending to few of the broader economic and social justice concerns. *Infertility* makes it quite clear that infertility therapy is expensive. Infertility expenditures for 1987 in the US were estimated to total one billion dollars. Not surprisingly, such treatment is sought by the more affluent, even though infertility is most likely to strike blacks and couples in which the wife has less than a high school education (51). The potential exploitation of the reproductive services of poorer women by more wealthy couples has been mentioned. More comprehensive and difficult allocation questions should also be addressed. Within the full realm of medical care, is it prudent and just to devote significant resources to infertility therapy, given other health needs, and given the possibly greater long-run effectiveness of funding research to discover the causes and aid the prevention of infertility?

CONCLUSIONS

A Christian perspective on reproductive technologies can appreciate the human and moral importance of biological kinship, without either absolutizing it or making its level of importance to social parenthood totally dependent on individual choice. The "need" to have a biologically related child is natural, and its fulfillment is worth pursuit and the support of modern medical technology. Pressures on couples, and especially women, to see biological parenthood as essential to adult identity needs to be re-examined, however. In addition, the natural convergence in human experience of biological kinship and social family should be consulted as a source of moral insight, and of the goods that a society should encourage.

The basic difference between homologous and heterologous techniques is that the latter sever key physical relationships from one another and from the interpersonal relationships of which they are the complementary dimension, thus denying them any significant moral weight. One should neither overstate the case, nor minimize the plight of childless couples who very likely have tried assiduously to achieve a shared biological relation to a child before turning to donorship. This relationship is undoubtedly valued by them.

However, the decisive moral question is what constitutes adequate recognition of the value of *shared* biological parenthood in reproductive ventures. While in homologous techniques this relationship is concretely and enduringly realized, in heterologous methods it is not. Further, the asymmetry between the two "social" or "rearing" parents, for only one of whom the interpersonal parental relation is undergirded by a biological one, creates an imbalance in their relationships to each other and to their child. For a married couple who limits recourse to homologous methods, their marital, sexual, and parental commitment to one another supercedes any reproductive cooperation which one partner might undertake with an outsider. At one and the same time, they testify that their unity as spouses is more important than realizing the physical reproductive potential of one without the other; that there is a natural unity of the intentional and physical dimensions of spousehood and parenthood which should not be broken deliberately.

Turning to the child, the physical and psycho-social dimensions of its relation to its parents are ideally related; to make them independent of one another would again be dualistic. *Donum vitae* speaks in a rather rhetorical and idealized way of the "right" of the child to be raised by its biological parents, and the language reveals more assertion than argument. But there is truth in the insight that corporeal kinship bonds are important to our identities as human beings. Consider the cross-cultural phenomenon of identifying individuals by reference to their kinship affiliations. Witness the frequent and consuming interest of parents and children or siblings separated at birth in questing to discover identities and achieve reunion. Witness the legal and social assumption that every effort should be made to rest custody of a child with his or her parents or other relatives, even in cases of significant psycho-social disadvantage. Explore the reasons why persons feel a special social commitment, however grudgingly acknowledged, to persons related to them by birth – certainly parents and children, but also siblings, cousins, and distant relations.

From this point of view, donor methods may satisfy the "needs" of the contracting parties, but they do so at the cost of denying the significance of important dimensions of the relationships they create. While adults may use the arrangement to bring to fruition their own hopes, they create a birth-situation in which the child's "natural" relation of offspring to parent is impaired. If the state of "childhood" implies vulnerability and dependency on the protection of adults, then those adults responsible for the existence of a child have a duty to ensure as far as possible that the basic components of his or her identity and welfare as a human person not be sacrificed to the adults' ends. Thus being raised in a context of mutual support and love by one's biological parents is a valuable component of the welfare of a child.

Parent–childhood is an embodied as well as a freely chosen relationship, and it is best carried out as an extension of the mutual spouse–parental relationship (also embodied as well as freely embraced) with which procreative sexual intercourse ideally connects it. The physical or embodied aspects of marriage and parenthood are not as important morally as those which are psychospiritual and social, which is why sexual intercourse is not a morally necessary means of conception, and why it is morally commendable in many circumstances to parent genetically unrelated children. However, it is crucial to recognize the unity of both aspects of the person and of morality by giving even the subsidiary dimension (the physical) some significant weight and role in decisions about reproductive technologies.

The final question is not so much how to judge, condemn, or control individual couples who are so "desperate" for a child that they find the new birth technologies virtually irresistable. It is how to open public discussion to values of parenthood which extend beyond freedom to embodiment, and to see use of reproductive technologies in a larger context of technical reason operating toward unexamined ends, of gender hierarchy, and of economic inequity.

Concluding reflections

In the modern period, both Roman Catholic and Protestant ethics have defined sexual morality primarily in terms of commitment and intersubjectivity, a move made possible by the modern recognition of the worth of individuals and the emergent social equality of women. However, a postmodern reticence about moral foundations has made it difficult for many social critics – Christian and otherwise – to argue convincingly that equality, reciprocity, and respect should function as cross-cultural norms. Moreover, liberal assumptions about the priority of freedom have made it equally hard to complement the importance of these values with a more complete consideration of human embodiment, its social dimensions, and its function in defining human goods and suggesting human moral values. The aim of this study has been to propose contributions that a Christian perspective on sex and gender can make to cultural debates about women's equality and sexual meaning, while reinforcing the sort of ethical foundations which are hospitable to moral criticism and consensus-building across moral and cultural traditions.

The Roman Catholic tradition in Christianity has persevered in its commitment to embodiment and sociality as important parameters of sexual meaning, and as defining the institutions (marriage and family) in which women's and men's sexuality and parenthood have been realized historically and cross-culturally. The Roman Catholic commitment to (provisional) objectivity in moral evaluation; and to the ideal unity of sexual expression, sexual pleasure, commitment of partners, and shared parenthood, can contribute to a more complete Christian ethics of sex as an embodied and social reality.

Persistently captive to patriarchal assumptions, however, Catholic teaching about sex and gender has still not effectively surmounted its tendency to define women's nature in terms of reproductive function, to tie sexual meaning to the biological structure of sex acts, or to focus on the morality of individual acts instead of on the personal, familial, and social relationships in which they occur. Its lack of demonstrated commitment to the equality and well-being of women worldwide remains the greatest liability of official Roman Catholicism's message on sex. While most "mainstream" Protestant denominations, especially perhaps in North America, have set a better record on women's equality, the theological and moral foundations of their ethics of sex and gender have tended to center on affirmations of intersubjective values, sometimes combined with communitarian construals of the limits of moral knowledge.

Since the Reformation, it has been Protestant Christianity which has represented the biblical formation of discipleship. However, many thinkers (Protestant and Catholic) have used historical–critical methods to relativize New Testament materials on sex and gender to their original settings, rather quickly substituting for "obsolete" moral prohibitions a modern, liberal set of values focused on consent, tolerance, and freedom. But improved understanding of the differences between the first Christian communities and our own need not lead to the conclusion that their moral outlook on the sexual body is negative, irrelevant, or unmitigatedly oppressive to our own concerns.

Especially when early Christian attitudes toward sex and gender are set against the Greco-Roman family, it is possible to reinterpret them as presenting a *social* sex and gender ethics of compassion, inclusion, and solidarity. The preference for virginity, prohibition of divorce, and exclusion of homosexuality, can be placed within a positive and constructive discipline of resistance to the patriarchal family, the control of reproduction by kin and state, and the subordination of women within the family. In the Christian paradigm, *porneia* includes all dominative sexualities, including gender as a dominating socialization of sex.

Guidance of concrete sexual behavior is not irrelevant to a New Testament social ethic of sex, but must be defined in every place and time in relation to the communal effects of various disciplines of the sexual body. This process is not absolutely open. As did the first Christians, contemporary Christians must and should draw on human and cultural experiences of goods in sex, gender, family, and marriage in order to define concrete moral obligations. The biblical communities, owing their identity to Jesus and his spirit, assume faithful marriage within a family or household, which begins to transform its internal relations toward greater reciprocity, so affecting larger social patterns and expectations. Neither the New Testament nor contemporary Christian ethics demands separation from, or rejection of, human excellence. While excellence or virtue in sexuality, family, and gender relations may have a shared discernible shape among cultures, and while some commonality must be presupposed in order for mutual criticism and improvement to occur, the appreciation of differences among cultures and traditions is crucial to the very process. For instance, "traditional" societies place sex and gender in the context of community, family, and parenthood; "modern" societies respect reciprocity, intimacy, and gender equality. Christian discipleship transforms the human realities of sex and gender by respecting both their embodied and social aspects, and their interpersonal and intentional dimensions. Christian sex and gender ethics, as a transformative ethics of discipleship, builds on but reforms human cultural practices so that they better represent the Christian values of incarnation, community, solidarity, fidelity, compassion, and hope that moral and social change are possible.

Notes

I SEX, GENDER AND THE PROBLEM OF MORAL ARGUMENT

1 *The Postmodern Condition: A Report on Knowledge*, trans. Geoff Bennington and Brian Massumi (England: Manchester University Press, 1984), 82.
2 Judith Butler, *Gender Trouble: Feminism and the Subversion of Identity* (New York and London: Routledge, 1990), 17–18.
3 *Gender Trouble*, 149.
4 John Boswell, *Christianity, Social Tolerance, and Homosexuality: Gay People in Western Europe from the Beginning of the Christian Era to the Fourteenth Century* (Chicago and London: University of Chicago Press, 1980).
5 Among her many works, see *Beyond God the Father: Toward a Philosophy of Women's Liberation* (Boston: Beacon Press, 1973); and *Gyn-ecology: The Metaethics of Radical Feminism* (Boston: Beacon Press, 1978).
6 L. William Countryman, *Dirt, Greed, & Sex: Sexual Ethics in the New Testament and Their Implications for Today* (Philadelphia: Fortress Press, 1988).
7 Recognizing that sexuality must be disciplined as well as freed, Margaret A. Farley notes that, in the present ethical view, sexual desire is no longer suspect, because sex "may enable a concentration of powers so that the deepest and most creative springs of action are tapped close to the center of personal life" ("Sexual Ethics," in Warren T. Reich, ed., *Encyclopedia of Bioethics*, vol. 4 (New York and London: Macmillan, 1978), 1587.
8 James B. Nelson, *Embodiment: An Approach to Sexuality and Christian Theology* (Minneapolis: Augsburg, 1978), 126.
9 Anthony Kosnick, William Carroll, Agnes Cunningham, Ronald Modras, and James Schulte, *Human Sexuality: New Directions in American Catholic Thought*, A Study Commissioned by The Catholic

Theological Society of America (New York/Paramus/Toronto: Paulist Press, 1977), 81, 85.

10 Ibid., 86.

11 *The New Testament and Homosexuality* (Philadelphia: Fortress Press, 1983), 126.

12 *Dirt, Greed, and Sex,* 240–53, 263.

13 Christine Gudorf, *Reconstructing Christian Sexual Ethics: Body, Sex and Pleasure as Grace and Gift* (Cleveland: The Pilgrim Press, 1994), 29, 33.

14 *Familiaris Consortio,* no. 11.

15 See n. 9 above.

16 For an overview of the matter which is readable, critical, and to the point, see Richard A. McCormick, "Humanae Vitae: Twenty-Five years After," *America* 169/2 (1993) 6–12. A recent treatment of the more scholarly side of the controversy is Gareth Moore, O.P., *The Body in Context: Sex and Catholicism* (London: SCM Press LTD, 1992), 156–81. See also Janet E. Smith, *Humanae Vitae: A Generation Later* (Washington, DC: Catholic University of America Press, 1991), which defends the encyclical.

17 This statement is currently more true of the Euro-American population, than of more recent immigrant communities, including African–American, Asian, and even Latino. The latter constitutes a large and growing proportion of lay Roman Catholics in North America.

18 For a compendium of recent thought, see James B. Nelson and Sandra P. Longfellow, eds., *Sexuality and the Sacred: Sources for Theological Reflection* (Westminster/John Knox Press: Louisville KY, 1994).

19 A. E. Harvey, *Promise or Pretence? A Christian's Guide to Sexual Morals* (London: SCM Press, Ltd., 1994), 3–4.

20 Ibid., 115.

21 Ibid., 116. In contrast, the United Church of Canada in 1988 removed a heterosexual orientation from the criteria for ordination.

22 Foucault contrasted the women's movement and "American homosexual movements" on this point. "Well, regarding everything that is currently being said about the liberation of sexuality, what I want to make apparent is precisely that the object 'sexuality' is in reality an instrument formed a long while ago, and one which has constituted a centuries-long apparatus of subjection. The real strength of the women's liberation movements is not that of having laid claim to the specificity of their sexuality and the rights pertaining to it, but that they have actually

departed from the discourse conducted within the apparatuses of sexuality." There has resulted "a veritable movement of de-sexualization, a displacement effected in relation to the sexual centering of the problem, formulating the demand for forms of culture, discourse, language, and so on, which are no longer part of that rigid assignation and pinning-down to their sex" (Colin Gordon, ed., *Michel Foucault, Power/Knowledge: Selected Interviews and Other Writings* [New York: Pantheon Books, 1980], 219–220).

2   FEMINISM AND FOUNDATIONS

1 Gregory Baum, "Modernity: A Sociological Perspective," *Concilium* 1992/6, 3.

2 Marcos J. Villaman, "Church and Inculturation: Modernity and Culture in Latin America," *Journal of Hispanic/Latino Theology* 1/3 (1994) 30–34.

3 The *Critique of Pure Reason* (1781) and *Groundwork of the Metaphysic of Morals* (1785) are among Kant's most important works.

4 A classic theological example is Gene Outka, *Agape: An Ethical Analysis* (New Haven and London: Yale University Press, 1972). See also, Alan Donagan, *The Theory of Morality* (University of Chicago Press, 1977). A Thomist influenced by the Kantian stress on a good will as moral criterion is James F. Keenan, S.J., *Goodness and Rightness in Thomas Aquinas's Summa Theologiae* (Washington, DC: Georgetown University Press, 1992).

5 Thomas Kuhn originally introduced the concept of "paradigm shift" into the history and philosphy of science in *The Structure of Scientific Revolutions* (Chicago and London: The University of Chicago Press, 1970). For a commentary which draws parallels betwen scientific and religious cognition, see Mary Gerhart and Allan Russell, *Metaphoric Process: The Creation of Scientific and Religious Understanding* (Fort Worth: Texas Christian University Press, 1984).

6 Charles Taylor, *Sources of the Self: The Making of the Modern Identity* (Cambridge MA: Harvard University Press, 1989) 5. See also Charles Taylor, *The Ethics of Authenticity* (Cambridge MA and London: Harvard University Press, 1993), 104.

7 Taylor, *Ethics of Authenticity*, 5. Following Habermas, Taylor calls this means–end reason "instrumental rationality."

8 Taylor notes that "the uneasiness of Enlightenment naturalism with any notion of the good, including its own," helps give credence to proceduralist ethics (*Sources of the Self*, 503).

9 See Baum, "Modernity."

10 James B. Miller, "The Emerging Postmodern World," in Fre-

derick B. Burnham, ed., *Postmodern Theology: Christian Faith in a Pluralist World* (New York: Harper & Row, 1989), 8, 13.

11 David Harvey, *The Condition of Postmodernity: An Enquiry into the Origins of Cultural Change* (Oxford and Cambridge MA: Basil Blackwell, 1989) 7–9.

12 Ibid., 4–8.

13 Susan Moller Okin, *Justice, Gender, and the Family* (San Francisco: HarperCollins, 1989).

14 On this point, also see Harvey, *Condition of Postmodernity*, 116–17. "The rhetoric of postmodernism is dangerous for it avoids confronting the realities of political economy and the circumstances of global power" (117).

15 James Miller, *The Passion of Michel Foucault* (Simon and Schuster: New York, 1992) details Foucault's pursuit of "limit experiences" by experimentation with gay sado-masochism, which very likely contributed to his death from AIDS in 1984.

16 See especially Michel Foucault, *The History of Sexuality, Volume I: An Introduction*, trans. Robert Hurley (New York: Random House, 1978); *Madness and Civilization*, trans. Richard Howard (New York: Random House, 1965); *Discipline and Punish: The Birth of the Prison*, trans. Alan Sheridan (New York: Pantheon Books, 1977).

17 Acknowledging that this move is in a way "only a game," Foucault tells a perplexed interviewer that "We have had sexuality since the eighteenth century, and sex since the nineteenth." Contrary to most people's impressions, sex is not "an instance having its own laws and constraints, on the basis of which the masculine and feminine sexes are defined," but "something which on the contrary is produced by the apparatus of sexuality." "What the discourse of sexuality was initially applied to wasn't sex but the body, the sexual organs, pleasures, kinship relations, interpersonal relations, and so forth" (Colin Gordin, ed., *Michel Foucault: Power/ Knowledge, Selected Interviews and Other Writings 1972–77* [New York: Pantheon Books, 1980] 210–211).

18 Michel Foucault, *The History of Sexuality: An Introduction*, trans. Robert Hurley (New York: Random House, 1978). The discourse of sexuality focuses the self-affirmation of the bourgeoisie on the body, via a "technology of sex," and an ever heightening process of medical and psychoanalytic inspection, introspection, and ultimately control. "We are often reminded of the countless procedures which Christianity once employed to make us detest the body, but let us ponder all the ruses that were employed for centuries to make us love sex, to make the knowledge of it desirable and everything said about it precious ... The irony of

this deployment is in having us believe that our 'liberation' is in the balance" (Ibid., 159).

19 Sexual desire was a drive requiring integration into a full life, just as the appetite to eat and drink. The fulfillment of sexual desire was not evaluated so much by the sex of the partners, as by the activity or passivity of their roles. For a free, adult male, master of his own life, only the active role was honorable.

20 Alison M. Jaggar, *Feminist Politics and Human Nature* (The Harvester Press: Brighton, Sussex, 1983) 132; see also 76.

21 Rather obliquely, Foucault defines power as "the multiplicity of force relations immanent in the sphere in which they operate and which constitute their own organization," forces which emanate from below rather than from a distinct ruling class, and which engender states of power which "are always local and unstable" (*History of Sexuality I*, 92–93).

22 Ibid., 123–24.

23 Bernauer is the author of a major critical work on Foucault, *Foucault's Force of Flight* (Atlantic Highlands, NJ: Humanities Press International, 1990), and has shared his insights on the philosopher in many conversations with me and with my graduate classes. In Bernauer's view, Foucault's ethical concerns were not nihilist, but empathetic with human suffering.

24 James W. Bernauer, "Michel Foucault's Ecstatic Thinking," in James Bernauer and David Rasmussen, eds., *The Final Foucault* (Cambridge, MA: MIT Press, 1988), 71.

25 "The single experience which was always at the source of his thought was the reality of imprisonment, the incarceration of human beings within modern systems of thought and practice which had become so intimately a part of them that they no longer experienced these systems as a series of confinements but embraced them as the very structure of being human" (ibid., 44).

26 *Herculine Barbin, Being the Recently Discovered Memoirs of a Nineteenth-Century French Hermaphrodite*, introduction by Michel Foucault; trans. Richard McDougall (Brighton, England: Harvester Press, 1980).

27 Charles Taylor, "Foucault on Freedom and Truth," in David Couzens Hoy, ed., *Foucault: A Critical Reader* (London: Basil Blackwell, 1986), 69.

28 Mark Kline Taylor, *Remembering Esperanza: A Cultural-Political Theology for North American Praxis* (Maryknoll NY: Orbis Books, 1990), 37.

29 Ibid., 37.

30 Foucault's program finds substantial support among philosophical

feminists, many of whom attack both gender and heterosexuality as dominatively "constructed." Some central examples are Jane Flax, *Psychoanalysis, Feminism and Postmodernism in the Contemporary West* (Berkeley CA: University of California Press, 1990); Judith Butler, *Gender Trouble: Feminism and the Subversion of Identity* (New York and London: Routledge, 1990); Judith Butler, *Bodies That Matter: On the Discursive Limits of "Sex"* (New York and London: Routledge, 1993); Linda Singer, *Erotic Welfare: Sexual Theory and Politics in the Age of Epidemic* (New York and London: Routledge, 1993), edited and introduced by Judith Butler and Maureen MacGrogan; Jana Sawicki, *Disciplining Foucault: Feminism, Power, and the Body* (New York and London: Routledge, 1991); Iris Marion Young, "The Ideal of Community and the Politics of Difference," *Social Theory and Practice*, 12/1 (Spring, 1986); Susan Bordo, *Unbearable Weight: Feminism, Western Culture, and the Body* (Berkeley, Los Angeles, London: University of California Press, 1993); and Catharine MacKinnon, *Toward a Feminist Theory of the State* (Cambridge MA: Harvard University Press, 1989).

31 Sheila Greave Devaney, "Problems with Feminist Theory: Historicity and the Search for Sure Foundations," in Paula M. Cooey, Sharon A. Farmer, and Mary Ellen Ross, eds., *Embodied Love: Sensuality and Relationship as Feminist Values* (San Francisco: Harper & Row, 1987) 92. In a more recent article, Greave Devaney allows that simply to deconstruct the past is not enough. She calls for a "pragmatic historicism" or "constructive historicism" in which symbol systems are "reconstructed," in order that we might gain orientation in life and better confront the specific issues, crises, and transitions that face our era" ("A Historicist Model for Theology," in Jeffrey Carlson and Robert A. Ludwig eds., *Jesus and Faith: A Conversation on the Work of John Dominic Crossan* [Maryknoll NY: Orbis, 1994], 44–560). This leaves us with essentially the same question that we posed to Foucault: What should that orientation look like? What are the criteria of the "better"?

32 Ibid., 90. Rebecca Chopp has similarly faulted Rosemary Ruether for her "abstract" notion of "full humanity," because it seems to postulate "a metahistorical structure" which is "merely realized in historical experience," and to suppose that "we can grasp something indpependent of our concrete situation" ("Seeing and Naming the World Anew: The Works of Rosemary Radford Ruether," *Religious Studies Review* 15 (1989), 10.

33 "Problems," 93

34 *Disciplining Foucault*, 10. Dawn Currie and Valerie Raoul give a

representative statement of this problem in the "Foreword" to their edited book, *The Anatomy of Gender: Women's Struggle for the Body* (Ottawa, Canada: Carleton University Press, 1992), ix.

35 Barbara H. Andolsen, *Daughters of Jefferson, Daughters of Bootblacks: Racism and American Feminism* (Macon, Georgia: Mercer University Press, 1986).

36 Maria Lugones and Elizabeth Spelman, "Have We Got a Theory for You! Feminist Theory, Cultural Imperialism and the Demand for 'The Woman's Voice,'" in Janet Kourany, James P. Sterba, and Rosemarie Tong, eds., *Feminist Philosophies: Problems, Theories, and Applications* (Englewood Cliffs, NJ: Prentice Hall, 1992), 384.

37 Ada María Isasi-Díaz, *En la Lucha: A Hispanic Women's Liberation Theology* (Minneapolis: Fortress, 1993), 190–93.

38 Kwok Pui-Lan, "The Future of Feminist Theology: An Asian Perspective," in Ursula King, ed., *Feminist Theology from the Third World: A Reader* (London and Maryknoll NY: SPCK and Orbis, 1994), 67.

39 Overlapping gender and class, race is an important axis of domination worldwide, and deserves more sustained attention than I am able to give it. Slavery, colonialism, and neo-colonialism have generally been perpetrated by whites from North Atlantic cultures against other peoples of the world who are racially dissimilar. These experiences have left their mark not only on colonized and enslaved peoples, but on the mentalities and cultures of their oppressors. For a feminist analysis of colonialism, see María Pilar Aquino, *Our Cry for Life: Feminist Theology from Latin America* (Maryknoll NY: Orbis Books, 1993), 13–18, 43–48.

40 A remark tossed off by Richard Rorty in an essay in which he attacks culturally transcendent universals is a beautiful example of this: "My own hunch, or at least hope, is that our culture is gradually coming to be structured around the idea of freedom – of leaving people alone to dream and think and live as they please, so long as they do not hurt other people – and that this idea provides as viscous a social glue as that of unconditional validity" ("Truth and Freedom: A Reply to Thomas McCarthy," in Gene Outka and John P. Reeder, Jr. eds., *Prospects for a Common Morality* [Princeton University Press, 1993] 281).

41 Judith Butler, *Gender Trouble: Feminism and the Subversion of Identity* (New York and London: Routledge, 1990), x–xi. Butler shows how Monique Wittig and Luce Irigaray agree that gender is a male-serving social construct, but differ in their explanation. For Wittig, only women are gendered, while the masculine functions as the supposedly universal. For Irigaray, the masculine is the single sex,

while women are produced as the "other." See Monique Wittig, "The Mark of Gender," *Feminist Issues* 5/2 (1985); and Luce Irigaray, *The Sex Which is Not One*, trans. Catherine Porter with Carolyn Burke (Ithaca: Cornell University Press, 1985). She also faults Julia Kristeva for positing a "maternal body" prior to discourse (*Desire in Language, A Semiotic Approach to Literature and Art*, ed. Leon S. Roudiez, trans. Thomas Gorz, Alice Jardine, and Leon S. Roudiez [New York: Columbia University Press, 1980].

42 In "Feminist Discourse, Moral Values and the Law – A Conversation," The 1984 James McCormick Mitchell Lecture, *Buffalo Law Review*, 34/1 (Winter, 1985), 27; as quoted by Seyla Benhabib, *Situating the Self: Gender, Community and Postmodernism in Contemporary Ethics* (New York and London: Routledge, 1992), 202. Moreover, while MacKinnon pushes aside the question of a nature of sex, she at times verges on presupposing a violent, dominating, male sexuality, to be countered with a commitment to sexual equality and self-determination for women.

43 *Disciplining Foucault*, 8.

44 Catharine A. MacKinnon, "Crimes of War, Crimes of Peace," in Stephen Shute and Susan Hurley, eds., *On Human Rights: The Oxford Amnesty Lectures 1993* (NY: HarperCollins, 1993), 83–109.

45 Sawicki, *Disciplining Foucault*, 48.

46 Trinh, T. Minh-ha, "Difference: A Special Third World Women Issue," *Feminist Review* 25 (1987) 18.

47 Gareth Moore , O.P., cites Pat Califia on s/m as rebellion against the status quo: "'I like s/m because it is not lady-like. It is a kind of sex that really violates all the things I was taught about being a nice little girl and keeping my dress clean ... .s/m is ... a deliberate, premeditated, erotic blasphemy ... a form of sexual extremism and sexual dissent ... We select the most frightening, disgusting, or unacceptable activities and transmute them into pleasure" (*The Body in Context: Sex and Catholicism* [London: SCM Press Ltd, 1992], 103–04).

48 Jane Roland Martin, "Methodological Essentialism, False Difference, and Other Dangerous Traps," *Signs: Journal of Women in Culture and Society* 19/3 (1994) 630–31.

49 Ibid., 646.

50 Bordo, *Unbearable Weight*, 223. See also Thomas R. Kopfensteiner, "Globalization and the Autonomy of Moral Reasoning: An Essay in Fundamental Moral Theology," *Theological Studies* 54/3 (1995) 490–92.

51 Martha C. Nussbaum, "Human Functioning and Social Justice: In Defense of Aristotelian Essentialism," *Political Theory* 210/2

(1992), 203. See also Nussbaum's "Feminists and Philosophy," *New York Review* (October 20, 1994) 59–61.

52 "Final Document: Intercontinental Women's Conference," in Virginia Fabella, M.M. and Mercy Amba Oduyoye, *With Passion and Compassion: Third World Women Doing Theology* (Maryknoll NY: Orbis Books, 1989) 184; my italics.

53 As an example, see Hans Küng and Karl-Josef Kuschel, *A Global Ethic: The Declaration of the Parliament of the World's Religions* (London: SCM Press LTD, 1993), the result of a September, 1993, conference in Chicago, at which forty-five religions were represented. For a commentary, see Hans Küng, "World Peace – World Religions – World Ethic," in Hans Küng and Jürgen Moltmann, *Islam: A Challenge for Christianity, Concilium* 1994/3 (Maryknoll NY: Orbis Books, 1993) 127–39. For a "global ethic" to have validity and effectiveness, of course, it must be genuinely the product of intercultural participation, and must never be simplistically employed to impose one conception of rights and justice on culturally varied situations.

54 International Film Bureau, Inc., 1991.

55 Rama Mehta, *Inside the Haveli* (New Delhi: Arnold Heineman, 1977). I originally found note of this book and of "No Longer Silent" in Martha Nussbaum's works.

56 Hilary Putnam, *Realism with a Human Face* (Cambridge MA and London: Harvard University Press, 1990) 129.

57 Charles Taylor's historical account of the modern self and its values, in *Sources of the Self*, attends to consciousness of value within a particular cultural tradition; bearers of that tradition will presumably come to recognize that it is richer, and their concurrence in it more complete, than they had realized when viewing the priority of certain values in isolation. Taylor implies objectivity for the moral insights he advocates; and he certainly rejects relativism. Like Taylor and Foucault, feminist critics often use the technique of historical argument, an effective way to give a normative agenda a "soft" foundation when an anti-foundationalist mood prevails. History can be used affirmatively, as when an author demonstrates continuity with an ideal or authoritative past, or "reclaims" a past as shaping "our" identity. Critical uses of history include uncovering the origins of a current normative practice, in order to suggest either that "things were not always this way," or that change produced the present and can produce a still different future. Other authors contrast the present with the past, as if to show that the past or something like it today is an alternative which is "better" than current practice. This move is

especially effective if the past is usually seen in an oversimplified or unitary way and even as "worse" or "lower" than what has not been achieved. These sorts of historical comparisons, however, depend for their moral efficacy on a set of assumptions about the bad, good, and better. They therefore serve primarily as instruments of persuasion within cultures in which some moral beliefs are already shared, not as avenues of approach to those who stand outside the tradition in question.

58 In the wake of the June, 1994, murder of Nicole Brown Simpson, ex-wife of US football star O. J. Simpson, and the arrest of her former husband, publicity surrounding family violence, and calls to domestic abuse hot-lines, saw a sharp increase in the United States, where, according to some reports, a woman is beaten every 25 or so seconds. This incident, and the fact that Ms. Simpson had previously called upon police protection against physical abuse by her spouse, reveal the alarming extent to which domestic violence occurs regularly, but is not taken seriously even in "modern" societies, by either the public or by many law-enforcement agencies. In some other countries of the world, a man's use of physical violence to control his wife's activity is not even legally proscribed.

59 For example, John E. Thiel criticizes "epistemological universality" as "founded on abstract unities or universals transcending space and time." "Foundationalist epistemologies ... posit some first principle that serves as a 'foundation' for the entire edifice of knowledge," according to critics such as Willard Van Orman Quine, Richard Rorty, and Donald Davidson ("Pluralism in Theological Truth," in Claude Geffré and Werner Jeanrond, eds., *Why Theology?*, *Concilium* 1994/6 [Maryknoll NY: Orbis, 1993], 59, 61).

60 See Kant's *Groundwork of the Metaphysic of Morals*, and *Critique of Practical Reason*; but contrast his *Perpetual Peace* as a piece of concrete moral analysis.

61 There are some exceptions. Tina Allik adopts George Lindbeck's "cultural-linguistic" model to affirm the "radical anthropological implications" of acknowledging "our finitude and our openness and vulnerability to our physical, social, and historical environments" ("Religious Experience, Human Finitude, and the Cultural-Linguistic Model," *Horizons* 20 [1993] 259). She does not develop the implications for specific social justice issues. My concern is that the so-called "radical" anthropology removes any stable, intercultural base on which to identify dehumanization and endorse change.

62 Alasdair MacIntyre, *After Virtue; Whose Justice, Which Rationality?* (University of Notre Dame Press, 1988).

63 George Lindbeck, *The Nature of Doctrine: Religion and Theology in a Postliberal Age* (Philadelphia: Westminster Press, 1984).

64 Robin Gill, *Moral Communities: The Prideaux Lectures for 1992* (University of Exeter Press, 1992).

65 Karl Barth, *Church Dogmatics*, III/4 (Edinburgh: T. & T. Clark,).

66 H. Richard Niebuhr, *The Meaning of Revelation* (London: Collier-Macmillan Ltd., 1941).

67 Stanley Hauerwas, *Vision and Virtue: Essays in Christian Ethical Reflection* (Notre Dame IN: Fides Publishers, Inc., 1974); and *A Community of Character: Toward a Constructive Christian Social Ethic* (Notre Dame and London: University of Notre Dame Press, 1981).

68 John Paul II, *Veritatis Splendor*; included, with commentaries, in John Wilkins, ed., *Understanding Veritatis Splendor* (London: SPCK, 1994); also published as *Considering Veritatis Splendor* (Cleveland: Pilgrim Press, 1994).

69 Ronald F. Thiemann, *Constructing a Public Theology: The Church in a Pluralistic Culture* (Louisville KY: Westminster/John Knox Press, 1991).

70 Susan Moller Okin gives a trenchant critique of Alasdair MacIntyre and Michael Walzer on this score.

> The analysis of MacIntyre's turning for valid notions of justice and rationality to "our" traditions, especially to some of the most misogynist and elitist among them, indicates that reliance on traditions simply cannot be sustained in the face of feminist challenges. Walzer's "shared meanings" method of social criticism, too, has been shown to prejudice the conclusions toward maintaining the power of those who historically have been dominant, and therefore to result in either incoherence or less than radical principles on subjects of central importance such as gender." (*Justice, Gender, and the Family* [San Francisco: HarperCollins, 1989] 72–730).

71 Phyllis Trible, *God and the Rhetoric of Sexuality* (Philadelphia: Fortress Press, 1978).

72 Elisabeth Schüssler Fiorenza, *In Memory of Her: A Feminist Theological Reconstruction of Christian Origins* (New York: Crossroad, 1983).

73 Joan M. Nuth, *Wisdom's Daughter: The Theology of Julian of Norwich* (New York: Crossroad, 1991).

74 Kathryn Tanner, *The Politics of God: Christian Theologies and Social Justice* (Minneapolis: Fortress Press, 1992).

75 Ross Shepard Kraemer, *Her Share of the Blessings: Women's Religions Among Pagans, Jews, and Christians in the Greco-Roman World* (New

York and Oxford: Oxford University Press, 1992); and Aquino, *Our Cry for Life*, 178–81.

76 *In Memory of Her*, 32.

77 Richard Bernstein, *Beyond Objectivism and Relativism* (Philadelphia: University of Pennsylvania Press, 1985) 44, 74.

78 Gadamer inaugurated his hermeneutical project with *Truth and Method*, trans. Garrett Barden and John Cumming (New York: The Seabury Press, 1977). See also Hans-Georg Gadamer, "The Universality of the Hermeneutical Problem," in *The Hermeneutic Tradition: From Ast to Ricoeur*, Gayle L. Ormiston and Alan D. Schrift eds. (Albany: State University of New York Press, 1990), 158.

79 *Beyond Objectivism and Relativism*, 38–40.

80 Hans-Georg Gadamer, "Reply to My Critics," in *The Hermeneutic Tradition*, 287, 288.

81 Jurgen Habermas, "On Hermeneutics' Claim to Universality," in Kurt Mueller-Volmer, ed., *The Hermeneutics Reader: Texts of the German Tradition from the Enlightenment to the Present* (New York: Continuum, 1990), 301–302, 317.

82 See *The Theory of Communicative Practice*, vol. 1: *Reason and the Rationalization of Society*; and vol. 2: *Lifeworld and System, a Critique of Function and System*, trans. Thomas McCarthy (Boston: Beacon Press, 1984, 1987); and *The Philosophical Discourse of Modernity*, trans. Frederick Lawrence (Cambridge MA: MIT Press, 1987).

83 Stephen K. White, *The Recent Work of Jurgen Habermas: Reason, Justice & Modernity* (Cambridge, New York, Port Chester, Melbourne, Sydney: Cambridge University Press, 1988) 49. Similarly, William Rehg sees Habermas as able to incorporate some of the values of tradition-based communitarianism by the fact that his procedures for communication have in view an empathetic concern with the specific needs of other individuals, and a willingness to cooperate toward compromise (*Insight and Solidarity: The Discourse Ethics of Jurgen Habermas* [Berkeley, Los Angeles, London: University of California Press, 1994] 173–75).

84 Habermas appears to acknowledge this in "Reply to My Critics," in J. Thompson and D. Held, eds., *Habermas: Critical Debates* (Cambridge MA: MIT Press, 1982) 253.

85 See Paul Lakeland, "Habermas and the Theologians Again," *Religious Studies Review* 15/2 (1989), 109.

86 *Situating the Self: Gender, Community and Postmodernism in Contemporary Ethics* (New York: Routledge, 1992).

87 Ibid., 213.

88 Ibid., 186.

89 Ibid., 128.

90 See the work of Sharon D. Welch, a feminist theologian, who emphasizes the importance of solidarity at the practical level as a prerequisite of work toward justice across cultural boundaries. She draws particularly on the novels of African-American women as a learning resource for Euro-American feminists (*A Feminist Ethic of Risk* [Minneapolis: Fortress Press, 1990]).

91 Ibid., 10; see also 164–70, 185.

92 Ibid., 30. Respect and reciprocity are the "moral presuppositions of the cultural horizon of modernity." The recognition of "universal human equality" is a "specifically modern achievement," made possible perhaps by the many wars, "struggles," and "political and social revolutions" which lie between us and Aristotle (64, 74).

93 Ibid., 227.

94 Ibid., 74–75, 81.

95 Adapting a communicative ethics approach for a global Christian ethics, Thomas R. Kopfensteiner like Habermas avoids the question of the specificity of ethics, but offers that "the 'reading' of the Scriptures sets into motion a new effective history of freedom which allows Christian moral reasoning to reconcile differences into a higher perspective or more inclusive synthesis ... The qualitative more that the Christian moral reasoning strives for ... is not some unattainable or utopian ideal, but the development of genuine, communicable, and plausible possibilities of action for the community of communication" ("Globalization and the Autonomy of Moral Reasoning," 505–06).

3   PARTICULAR EXPERIENCES, SHARED GOODS

1 St. Thomas Aquinas, *Summa Theologica*, trans. by Fathers of the English Dominican Province (New York: Benziger Brothers, 1948), I–II.91.2.

2 Ibid., I–II.94.2.

3 Ibid., 1.79,11–12; I–II.94.1.

4 A major twentieth-century restatement of natural law is Josef Fuchs, S.J., *Natural Law: A Theological Investigation* (New York: Sheed and Ward, 1965).

5 In the past, this interpretation has been stated rather too strongly, as by A. P. d'Entreves: "If so great a body of wisdom [Greek philosophy and Roman law] had been discovered without supernatural help, if a basis was to be provided for human relations independently of the higher requirements of Christian perfection,

surely there must be knowledge of ethical values which man can attain with the sole help of his reason. There must be a system of natural ethics. Its cornerstone must be natural law" (*Natural Law*, 38). John Mahoney today puts the point in a more subtle form: "Aquinas remained ... convinced that morality is essentially rational conduct, and as such it must be accessible, at least in principle to human reason and wisdom" (*The Making of Moral Theology*, 106). That reason is clouded there is no doubt; hence the reinforcement of the moral law by divine revelation (*ST* 1–11. 91.4; 100). However, reasonable agreement, not only on the virtues, but on the common good, is an essential presupposition of Aquinas' social ethics (see *ST* 1–11.100.1). See Stephen J. Pope, "Knowability of the Natural Law: A Foundation for Ethics of the Common Good," to appear in *Annual Publication of the College Theology Society* 40 (1995).

6 In response to the publication of *Humanae Vitae* in 1968, Alfons Auer of Tubingen proposed an "autonomous" morality, holding that material norms are subject to the criteria of reason and general intelligibility, while Christian identity provides motivation and a transcendent purpose for the fulfillment of such norms. Other German theologians (including Karl Ratzinger) countered with a morality of faith, insisting that morality was not autonomous from revelation or church teaching. For a discussion, see Charles E. Curran, *Toward an American Catholic Moral Theology* (University of Notre Dame Press, 1987), 55–61. An attempt to bring the sides of the discussion together while protecting the reasonableness of moral discernment is Josef Fuchs, S.J., *Personal Responsibility and Christian Morality* (Washington, DC: Georgetown University Press, 1983), 84–111.

7 For a discussion of the "naturalistic fallacy" of which natural law theory is often accused (initially so by G. E. Moore), see Kai Nielsen, "The Myth of Natural Law," in *Law and Philosophy: A Symposium*, ed. S. Hook (New York University Press, 1964), 122–43; Peter Simpson, "St. Thomas on the Naturalistic Fallacy," *The Thomist* 51 (1987) 51–69; and Gerard J. Hughes, S.J., *Authority in Morals: An Essay in Christian Ethics* (Washington, DC: Georgetown University Press, 1978), 32. As Simpson says, "Those who say naturalism is a fallacy tend to limit knowledge to the directly observable or the scientifically verifiable" (57). Hughes adds that, "It must be admitted that the study of human nature, and the attempt to interpret human nature in moral terms, is a difficult enterprise, ill-calculated to produce neat and easy solutions to our moral dilemmas ... Lack of total moral clarity is indeed a

challenge which is at times painful; but I see no reason to suppose that God somehow wishes to rescue us from having to face it" (29).

8 *ST*, I–II.55.3.

9 See Alasdair MacIntyre, *After Virtue* (University of Notre Press, 1981); Gilbert Meilaender, *The Theory and Practice of Virtue* (University of Notre Dame Press, 1984); David Mack Nelson, *The Priority of Prudence: Virtue and Natural Law in Thomas Aquinas and the Implications for Modern Ethics* (University Park: Pennsylvania State University Press, 1992); and James F. Keenan, S.J., "Virtue Ethics: Making a Case As It Comes of Age," *Thought* 67/265 (June, 1992) 115–27. The latter reviews the emergence of virtue ethics over two decades, and appears in an issue devoted entirely to the topic. Keenan also prefers to use the term "rightness" to refer to the moral status of the agent, as choosing conscientiously, and "goodness" to refer to the objective status of the act. See also his *Goodness and Rightness in Thomas Aquinas's Summa Theologiae* (Washington, DC: Georgetown University Press, 1991). I would want to maintain a connection between the moral disposition of the agent and the corollary actions through which virtue is expressed, as generally having a similar and interdependent moral quality (a "right" agent will on the whole be disposed to "good" acts). Aquinas states, "virtue is a habit which is always referred to good" (*ST* I–II.55.4).

10 Henry Davis, S. J., *Moral and Pastoral Theology, Volume II: Precepts* (New York: Sheed and Ward, 1946), 156, 161. For the historical development of Roman Catholic natural law morality, see John Mahoney, *The Making of Moral Theology: A Study of the Roman Catholic Tradition,* (Oxford University Press, 1987).

11 Aristotle, *Nichomachean Ethics*, trans. Martin Ostwald (Indianapolis: The Bobbs-Merrill Co., Inc., 1962) II.2; see also I.3 and II.9.

12 Ibid., I–II.94.4.

13 Aquinas, *ST*, II–II.47.7.

14 Aristotle, *Nichomachean Ethics*, VI.12.

15 Jean Porter, *Moral Action and Christian Ethics* (Melbourne: Cambridge University Press, 1995). See also Albert R. Jonsen and Stephen Toulmin, *The Abuse of Casuistry: A History of Moral Reasoning* (Berkeley CA: University of California Press, 1988); and Richard A. McCormick, "Killing the Patient," 19, and Herbert McCabe, "Manuals and Rule Books," 65, both in John Wilkins, ed., *Understanding Veritatis Splendor* (London: SPCK, 1994).

16 Pope, "Knowability of the Natural Law," first manuscript page.

17 *ST* II–II.46.6.

18 In this he shows the influence of the Roman jurist Ulpian. A. P. d'Entreves (*Natural Law* , 24–25) offers the following citation:

> *Dig.*,I,i,1(*ULPIANUS libro primo institutionum*): ... Natural law is that which nature has taught all animals; this law indeed is not peculiar to the human race, but belongs to all animals ... From this law springs the union of male and female, which we call matrimony, the procreation of children and their education ... The law of nations is that law which mankind observes. It is easy to understand that this law should differ from the natural, inasmuch as the latter belongs to all animals, while the former is peculiar to men.

19 *Ibid.*, II–II.153.2 and 3; 154.1.

20 *Ibid.*, 1.92. Jack A. Bonsor warns that "History is strewn with victims of the 'natural order.' Women, people of color, and homosexuals have been exploited, abused, and treated as chattels because this seemed nature's way," "History, Dogma, and Nature: Further Reflections on Postmodernism and Theology," *Theological Studies* 55 (1994) 309.

21 Jean Porter, *The Recovery of Virtue: The Relevance of Aquinas for Christian Ethics* (Louisville: Westminster/John Knox Press, 1990), 68. See also, Jean Porter, "At the Limits of Liberation: Thomas Aquinas and the Prospects for a Catholic Feminism," *Theology Digest* 41/4 (Winter, 1994) 315–30. Another explicitly feminist attempt to develop such an account is Maureen Kemeza's *The Ironies of History* (New York: Continuum, forthcoming), which employs Aquinas' anthropology as a resource for feminist thought about moral selfhood as "embodied relationality," while using feminist theology to correct misogynist strands on Aquinas' differential development of the meaning of virtue for women and men. Kemeza maintains that feminism, especially Christian feminism, must move beyond a postmodern view of the self as ultimately insubstantial, even soluble, and beyond the premise that, since hostility and conflict characterize human nature and the universe fundamentally, hermeneutical suspicion is everywhere called for. Instead, she argues from a concept of "embodied relationality" that selves are destined for connections, for relationships, for union with other selves, both human and divine. Also of promise for the development of a feminist Thomism is the work in progress of Cristina Traina (of Northwestern University, Chicago, Illinois) on a feminist reappropriation of Thomas Aquinas' ethical realism based on the essential characteristics of human being. See her "Developing an Integral Ethical Method: Feminist Ethics and Natural Law Retrieval," Ph.D. dissertation, University of Chicago, 1992.

22 John Finnis, *Natural Law and Natural Rights* (Oxford: Clarendon Press, 1980), 86–92; and *Fundamentals of Ethics* (Washington, DC: Georgetown University Press, 1983), 50–53. See also Germain Grisez, *Christian Moral Principles*, vol. 1 of *The Way of the Lord Jesus* (Chicago: Franciscan Herald Press, 1983), 124; Germain Grisez, Joseph Boyle, and John Finnis, "Practical Principles, Moral Truth, and Ultimate Ends," *American Journal of Jurisprudence* 32 (1987) 107–08; and Richard A. McCormick, S.J., *Health and Medicine in the Catholic Tradition: Tradition in Transition* (New York: Crossroad, 1984) 37.

23 Richard A. McCormick, S.J., *The Critical Calling: Reflections on Moral Dilemmas Since Vatican II* (Washington D.C.: Georgetown University Press, 1989), 230. The Finnis/Grisez theory of basic goods is given critical discussion by Jean Porter in *The Recovery of Virtue*, 17–21; and by Ralph McInerny, *Ethica Thomistica: The Moral Philosophy of Thomas Aquinas* (Washington, D.C: Catholic University of America Press, 1982), 53–59.

24 See Thomas A. Shannon, "The Communitarian Perspective: Autonomy and the Common Good," in M. A. Grodin, ed., *Meta Medical Ethics* (Nijmegen: Kluwer Academic Publishers, 1995).

25 Robert J. Schreiter, C.P.P.S., *Constructing Local Theologies* (Maryknoll NY: Orbis, 1985) 91.

26 *A Theology of Liberation*, rev. ed. (Maryknoll NY: Orbis, 1988), 6. See also, Roberto Goizueta, "Rediscovering Praxis: The Significance of U.S. Hispanic Experience for Theological Method," in *We Are a People!: Initiatives in Hispanic American Theology* (Minneapolis: Fortress Press, 1993) 53–62. For recent liberation theologies which build on Thomas Aquinas' insights, see Thomas L. Schubeck, S.J., *Liberation Ethics: Sources, Models and Norms* (Minneapolis: Fortress Press, 1993); Antonio Moser and Bernardino Leers, *Moral Theology: Dead Ends and Alternatives* (Maryknoll NY: Orbis, 1990); Stephen J. Pope, *The Evolution of Altruism and the Ordering of Love* (Washington, DC: Georgetown University Press, 1994), as well as "Proper and Improper Partiality and the Preferential Option for the Poor," *Theological Studies* 54/2 (1993) 242–71.

27 María Pilar Aquino, *Our Cry for Life: Feminist Theology from Latin America* (Maryknoll NY: Orbis Books, 1994), 56.

28 Raymond Bonner, "Fear Is Still Pervasive in Rwanda Countryside," *New York Times*, June 29, 1994, A10.

29 Molly O'Neill, "A Day with Dr. Susan M. Love: A Surgeon's War on Breast Cancer," *New York Times*, June 29, 1994, C1, C12.

30 Nielsen cites and accepts Margaret Mead's finding that certain "panhuman" moral norms are accepted in all known societies,

which are the incest taboo (banning mother–son, father–daughter, and sister–brother sex, except in some very clearly defined exceptional situations), the institution of private property, condemnation of unjustified killing, and regulation in some way of sexual relations between spouses. These yield a great variety of mutually conflicting specific practices however. Hence, the natural law "avoids the Charybdis of ethnocentrism, only to fall into the Scylla of ethical relativism" ("Natural Law," 126–27). Nevertheless, he retains some "common-sense core" of natural law – similar to Mead's – as essential to "social living" and "human survival" (136–37). What Nielsen objects to most strongly in natural law are the metaphysical and theological claims which he believes necessary to its defense. His attack on, and his cautious return to, it suggest that his arguments would apply less against a natural law approach backed by a more historical epistemology. This is the direction in which recent moral theology has gone. On historicity and the natural law in Catholic moral theology, see Charles E. Curran, *American Catholic Moral Theology*, 3–51; Curran, *Themes in Fundamental Moral Theology* (Notre Dame and London: University of Notre Dame Press, 1977), 27–80; and Josef Fuchs, S.J., *Personal Responsibility*, 153–84, 210–15; Fuchs, *Christian Ethics in the Secular Arena* (Washington, DC and Dublin: Georgetown University Press and Gill and Macmillan, 1984), 29–51; and Fuchs, "The Absolute in Morality and the Christian Conscience," *Gregorianum* 71 (1990) 697–711.

31 Bernard J. F. Lonergan, S.J., *A Second Collection* (London: Darton, Longman & Todd, 1974), 6.

32 Finnis, *Natural Law*, 30.

33 For other projects reconstructive of moral foundations, see David B. Wong, *Moral Relativity* (Berkeley and Los Angeles: University of California Press, 1984); and Lee H. Yearly, *Mencius and Aquinas: Theories of Virtue and Conceptions of Courage* (Albany: State University of New York Press, 1990); Gene Outka and John P. Reeder, eds., *Prospects for a Common Morality* (Princeton University Press, 1993); and John P. Reeder, Jr., "Three Moral Traditions," *Journal of Religious Ethics* 22 (Spring, 1994) 75–92.

34 Martha C. Nussbaum, "Human Functioning and Social Justice: In Defense of Aristotelian Essentialism," *Political Theory* 20/2 (1992) 205.

35 Martha C. Nussbaum, *Love's Knowledge: Essays on Philosophy and Literature* (New York and Oxford: Oxford University Press, 1990) 37–40.

36 Ibid., 41. For an expansion of such themes, see Sidney Callahan,

In Good Conscience: Reason and Emotion in Moral Decision-Making (San Francisco: HarperSanFrancisco, 1991); Mark Johnson, *The Body in the Mind: The Bodily Basis of Meaning, Imagination, and Reason* (University of Chicago Press, 1988); and Patricia B. Jung, "Sanctification: An Interpretation in Light of Embodiment," *Journal of Religious Ethics* 11 (1983) 75–95. In an article which takes questions of recent interpreters back to Thomistic texts, Brian V. Johnstone, C.S.S.R., argues that there is no dichotomy between the practical and speculative reason, or between reason and will, insofar as we seek in action that which attracts us as good, discerned within a complex of available goods ("The Structures of Practical Reason: Traditional Theories and Contemporary Questions," *The Thomist* 50 [1986] 425). If so, then truth in morality emerges very much from concrete location in which both the affections and the cognitive powers of discernment guide us in the achievement of "true good" for ourselves and others, given the practical circumstances in which we act.

37 According to Nussbaum, the "participants look not for a view that is true by correspondence to some extra-human reality," but "a consistent and sharable answer to the 'how to live' question, one that will capture what is deepest and most basic"(*Love's Knowledge*, 26; cf., 28, 95–96). The same anti-metaphysical point is made in "In Defense of Aristotelian Essentialism," 215; see also 212: "When we get rid of the hope of a transcendent metaphysical grounding for our evaluative judgments – about the human being as about anything else – we are not left with the abyss."

38 Ibid., 46–47.

39 Nussbaum's account of nonrelative virtues may be compared to Charles Taylor's account of practical reason as implying and relying upon the possibility of shared knowledge of nonrelative goods which are "strongly evaluated," not only by ourselves but by those with whom we are attempting to be reasonable. A "strongly evaluated goal is one such that, were we to cease desiring it, we would be shown up as insensitive or brutish or morally perverse" (Taylor, "Explanation and Practical Reason," in Martha Nussbaum and Amartya Sen, eds., *The Quality of Life* (Oxford: Clarendon Press, 1993), 210). Taylor's explanation of the basis of agreement, however, is closer to the communitarians in that he appeals to consensus within a given historical tradition; Nussbaum envisions consensus among traditions as based in "vague" but universal conceptions of human needs and goods.

40 Nussbaum, *Love's Knowledge*, 389.

41 Nussbaum, "Aristotelian Social Democracy," 219–24. Essentially the same list appears in "In Defense of Aristotelian Essentialism," 216–21.

42 Ibid., 225; "In Defense of Aristotelian Essentialism," 222–23.

43 Martha Nussbaum, "Non-Relative Virtues: An Aristotelian Approach," *Midwest Studies in Philosophy* 13 (1988) 44. This essay is included in Nussbaum and Sen, eds., *The Quality of Life*.

44 "In Defense of Aristotelian Essentialism," 223.

45 A quite extensive social science literature on "intercultural communication competence" has grown up around the fact that, given the international character of late twentieth-century business, politics, and education, collaborators of different cultural backgrounds need to communicate and do so with varying degrees of success. This literature assumes communication to be, in principle, possible; its actualization depends upon the sincerity, sensitivity, flexibility, and mutual accommodation of participants. Some of it aims, by the collection and analysis of data from particular interactions, eventually to arrive even at a "culture-general model" for communication success. See Judith N. Martin, "Intercultural Communication Competence: A Review," in Richard L. Wiseman and Jolene Koester, *Intercultural Communication Competence*, International and Intercultural Communication Annual, volume XVII, 1993 (Newbury Park CA, London, New Delhi: Sage Publications, 1993), 23. As a general resource, see also, William B. Gudykunst, ed., *Intercultural Communication Theory: Current Perspectives*, International and Intercultural Communication Annual, volume VII, 1983 (Beverly Hills/London/New Delhi: Sage Publications, 1983).

46 Nussbaum, "Aristotelian Social Democracy," in R. Bruce Douglass, Gerald R. Mara, and Henry S. Richardson eds., *Liberalism and the Good* (NY: Routledge, 1990) 236–37.

47 Ibid., 214–15. Nussbaum takes the example from Marty Chen, *A Quiet Revolution: Women in Transition in Rural Bangladesh* (Cambridge MA: Schenkman Publishing Company, 1983).

48 "In Defense of Aristotelian Essentialism," 217–18.

49 *A Quiet Revolution*, 56.

50 Returning to the example of Bangladesh, the government of that country ordered the arrest of a feminist writer, Taslima Nasrin, on July 4, 1994, after a national newspaper reported that she had recommended that the Koran be "revised thoroughly." Islamic fundamentalists threatened Ms. Nasrin with death for insulting Islam (*New York Times*, July 5, 1994).

51 See Valerie Saiving Goldstein, "The Human Situation: A

Feminine View," *Journal of Religion* (1960); and Judith Plaskow, *Sex, Sin, and Grace: Women's Experience and the Theologies of Reinhold Niebuhr and Paul Tillich* (Lanham MD: University Press of America, 1980).

52 *Hispanic Women: Prophetic Voice in the Church* (Minneapolis: Fortress Press, 1992), xvii.

53 Marianne Katoppo, *Compassionate and Free: An Asian Woman's Theology* (Maryknoll NY: Orbis, 1980); Virginia Fabella and Mercy Amba Oduyoye, eds., *With Passion and Compassion: Third World Women Doing Theology* (Maryknoll NY: Orbis, 1988).

54 Delores S. Williams, "Womanist Theology: Black Women's Voices," in Ursula King, ed., *Feminist Theology from the Third World: A Reader* (London and Maryknoll NY: SPCK/Orbis, 1994), 81–83. Citing the novelist Alice Walker, Williams contrasts womanist to feminist "as purple is to lavender" (81).

55 Farley, "Feminism and Universal Morality," 181–85.

56 *Sexism and God-Talk: Toward a Feminist Theology* (Boston: Beacon Press, 1983), 18, 19. Ruether adds:

> This principle is hardly new. In fact, the correlation of original, authentic human nature (*imago dei*/Christ) and diminished, fallen humanity provided the basic structure of classical Christian theology. The uniqueness of feminist theology is not the critical principle, full humanity, but the fact that women claim this principle for themselves. Women name themselves as subjects of authentic and full humanity (19).

> See also, Ruether, "The Development of My Theology," *Religious Studies Review* 15 (1989) 1–4, where she reiterates this principle and affirms the goal of "a redemptive community that encompasses all people."

57 See Susan A. Ross and Mary Catherine Hilkert, O.P., "Feminist Theology: A Review of the Literature," Theological Studies 56/2 (1995) 327–52; and *Studies in Christian Ethics* 5/1 (1992), the entirety of which is devoted to "Feminism and Christian Ethics."

58 Margaret A. Farley, "Feminism and Universal Morality," in Outka and Reeder, *Prospects*, 178–79.

59 Elizabeth A. Johnson, *She Who Is: The Mystery of God in Feminist Theological Discourse* (New York: Crossroad, 1994) 63.

60 For examples, see Christine Firer Hinze, "Bridge Discourse on Wage Justice: Roman Catholic and Feminist Perspectives on the Family Living Wage," *The Annual of the Society of Christian Ethics* (1991), 109–32; and Sidney Callahan, "The Family: The Challenge of Technological Change," in John A. Coleman, S.J., *One Hundred Years of Catholic Social Thought: Celebration and Challenge* (Maryknoll NY: Orbis, 1991).

61 Christine E. Gudorf, *Body, Sex, and Pleasure: Reconstructing Christian Sexual Ethics* (Cleveland OH: The Pilgrim Press, 1994) 144.

62 King, *Feminist Theology*, 20.

63 Ibid., 17.

64 María Pilar Aquino, "Doing Theology from the Perspective of Latin American Women," in Goizneta ed., *We Are a People!*, 91. The theme of the full humanity of women, as developed from the distinctive and original perspective of Latin American women's theology, is developed quite extensively in *Our Cry for Life*, especially 90–97.

65 Rebecca Chopp, *The Praxis of Suffering: An Interpretation of Liberation and Political Theologies* (Maryknoll NY: Orbis, 1986), 149.

66 In *The Abuse of Casuisty*, Jonsen and Toulmin show that even this casuistry depended heavily on generalization to "patterns" among like cases in actual moral experience.

67 Among them are Josef Fuchs, Bruno Schüller, Louis Janssens, Gerard Hughes, John Mahoney, Richard McCormick, Charles Curran, and Phillip Keane.

68 John Paul II, *Veritatis Splendor* (Vatican City: Libreria Editrice Vaticana, 1993) no. 74.

69 Ibid., nos. 27, 110, 112.

70 A fear characterized by Gerard J. Hughes, S.J., "Natural Law Ethics and Moral Theology," *The Month* 1430/2 (1987) 100. Hughes himself defends natural ethics on an historical interpretation, here as in *Authority in Morals*. "That we cannot agree on questions so important as the beginning of human life, or some issues in sexual ethics, or on the details of a just economic policy, or on the extent to which morality ought to be reflected in the enactments of civil law, should not blind us to the enormous areas of agreement which enable us to live in comparative social harmony" (102).

71 Thomas G. Guarino notes Gadamer's move toward practical reason with alarm, seeing even a "moderate postmodernism" as finally unable to sustain the Catholic "salvation narrative" or "the referential and final nature of truth which seems essential to revelation theology"("Between Foundationalism and Nihilism: Is *Phronesis* the *Via Media* for Theology?," *Theological Studies* 54/1 [1993] 54). See also Guarino, *Revelation and Truth: Unity and Plurality in Contemporary Theology* (Scranton: University of Scranton Press; London and Toronto: Associated University Presses, 1993). Although I do not follow along with Guarino's adoption of what I see as a communitarian, fideist solution to the problem of truth "after" postmodernity, his anaylsis of the challenge of postmo-

dernism is adept and fair, as is his treatment of competing theological positions. Both the article and the book are fine resources on these issues.

72 Joseph A. Di Noia, O.P., bearing a Yale Ph.D. and the influence of George Lindbeck, sees postmodernism as freeing theology from the strictures of modern, rationalist paradigms of knowlege. Postmodern thinkers beneficently "insist on the centrality of tradition and authority in legitimating and supporting truth and rationality," whether in science or in philosophy and religion (J. A. Di Noia, O.P., "American Catholic Theology at Century's End: Postconciliar, Postmodern, Post-Thomistic," *The Thomist* 54/ 3 [1990] 513). Di Noia is for a postmodern theology in which "bodiliness, agency, and community replace subjectivity, consciousness, and the autonomous self" as fundamental categories (514). Fred Lawrence, once a Catholic student of Karl Barth, recognizes the radical historicity of meaning and value. He reads in the Catholic philosopher Bernard Lonergan a reflection of postmodern concerns, such as the centrality of freedom and the displacement of the subject, along with "an utterly transcendent God beyond necessity and contingency" ("The Fragility of Consciousness: Lonergan and the Postmodern Concern for the Other," *Theological Studies* 54/1 [1993] 93).

73 Bonsor, "History, Dogma, and Nature," 311. Believing, however, that the conversation with postmodernism's attempts to come to terms with historicity should proceed, Bonsor warns against too hasty a judgment about its inimical relation to Christian theology.

74 *Analogical Imagination, Christian Theology and the Culture of Pluralism* (NY: Crossroad, 1981) 14, 102, 134. Tracy's move seems useful to Martha Nussbaum, as she grants in "Comparing Virtues," *The Journal of Religious Ethics* 21/2 (1993) 354, 357–58. She warns however, against a "too quick and easy" assumption that those holding strong, fundamentalist religious beliefs will agree that justice and human wellbeing should guide communication to its practical outcome. On Tracy's concept of the classic, see Werner G. Jeanrond, *Text and Interpretation as Categories of Theological Thinking*, trans. Thomas J. Wilson (New York: Crossroad, 1988), 133–44. In Jeanrond's *Theological Hermeneutics: Development and Significance* (New York: Crossroad, 1991), he places Tracy within the development of hermeneutics from Gadamer onward, and sees him as among those who "wish to assess the particular Christian vision for this world in the context of a great conversation with all other groups of human thinkers who care for the people of this world and for the universe in which we live" (163; see also 175).

75 *Ibid.*, 408.
76 David Tracy, *Dialogue with the Other: The Interreligious Dialogue* (Grand Rapids: Eerdmans, 1990), 42.
77 David Tracy, "The Uneasy Alliance Reconceived: Catholic Theological Method, Modernity, and Postmodernity," *Theological Studies* 50 (1989) 562.
78 Ibid., 566–67.
79 Ibid., 568–69. On the standard of "relative adequacy," see also David Tracy, *Pluralism and Ambiguity* (New York: Harper & Row, 1987), 22–23.
80 Guarino, *Revelation and Truth*, 38–39.
81 Werner Jeanrond, Review 1 of *Plurality and Ambiguity*, *Religious Studies Review* 15 (1989) 221. (This piece did not have a *title*; the bibliographical information for the book under review was given at the top of the page, then the reviewers were named and identified).

4 "THE BODY" – IN CONTEXT

1 The obsession is fueled by Foucault, virtually all of whose works centered on the body as a "site" of social manipulation. Yet interest in the body reaches back to at least the early nineteenth century in French philosophy. See Michel Henry, *Philosophy and Phenomenology of the Body* (The Hague: Nijhoff, 1975). The works of anthropologist Mary Douglas (*Purity and Danger: An analysis of concepts of pollution and taboo* [London and Henley: Routledge and Kegan Paul, 1966]; *Natural Symbols: Explorations in Cosmology*, rev. edn. [London: Barrie and Jenkins, 1973]) and of philosopher Merleau-Ponty (*Phenomenology of Perception*, trans. Colin Smith [New York: The Humanities Press, 1962]) have moved the discussion in very different directions. Among theologians and historians of Christianity, Peter Brown's *The Body and Society: Men, Women, and Sexual Renunciation in Early Christianity* (New York: Columbia University Press, 1988) has been widely cited. Feminist works on the body are almost too numerous to list, and many have been or will be mentioned in the present work. See Maureen H. Tilley and Susan A. Ross, *Broken and Whole: Essays on Religion and the Body* (Lanham MD: University Press of America, Inc., 1994). Reviews of recent theological work are James F. Keenan, S. J., "Christian Perspectives on the Human Body," *Theological Studies* 55 (1994) 330–46; and Susan A. Ross and Mary Catherine Hilkert, O. P., "Feminist Theology: A Review of the Literature," *Theological Studies* 56/2 (1995) 330–41. Keenan notes that, while Thomas

Aquinas supports generally the contemporary concern for the unity of body and soul, his interpretation is not entirely "immune from the charges of dualism" (330, n. 2). For Aquinas, the emotions and passions are in the soul, not the body.

2 See, for instance, Charles E. Curran, *Tensions in Moral Theology* (University of Notre Dame Press, 1988), 75–76.

3 See Carolyn Merchant, *The Death of Nature: Women, Ecology,and the Scientific Revolution* (San Francisco; Harper and Row, 1980); and Emily Martin, *The Woman in the Body; A Cultural Analysis of Reproduction* (Boston: Beacon Press, 1987).

4 Mark Johnson, *The Body in the Mind: The Bodily Basis of Meaning, Imagination, and Reason* (University of Chicago Press, 1988).

5 James B. Nelson and Sandra P. Longfellow, "Introduction," in Nelson and Longfellow, eds., *Sexuality and the Sacred: Sources for Theological Reflection* (Louisville KY: Westminster/John Knox Press, 1994), xiv.

6 "On Healing the Nature/History Split," in Barabara Hilkert Andolsen, Christine E. Gudorf, and Marry D. Pellauer, *Women's Consciousness, Women's Conscience: A Reader in Feminist Ethics* (Minneapolis, Chicago, New York: Winston Press, 1985), 97.

7 "Notes on Historical Grounding: Beyond Sexual Essentialism," in Nelson and Long, eds., *Sexuality and the Sacred*, 11.

8 Judith Butler, *Bodies That Matter: On the Discursive Limits of 'Sex'* (New York and London: Routledge, 1993), ix.

9 Antoine Vergote remarks on the human plasticity that derives from our absence of physical adaptation to any one natural environment, a plasticity which permits the mediation of both body and mind by language ("The Body as Understood in Contemporary Thought and Biblical Categories," *Philosophy Today* 35/ No. 1/4 [1991] 99).

10 It may be that some sense of "oneness in plurality" is part of our human condition, and partly responsible for our perennial existential anxiety (Reinhold Niebuhr, *The Nature and Destiny of Man*, vol. 1, Human Nature [New York: Charles Scribner's Sons, 1941, 1964] 1–25). Wayne A. Meeks shows that the mind–body relation was a "problem" in antiquity in the West, and not just from Descartes onward (*The Origins of Christian Morality: The First Two Centuries* [New Haven and London: Yale University Press, 1993] 130–310). Writing of out-of-body experiences, Carol Zaleski concludes that "dualism and somatomorphism [quasi-corporeal representations of the soul] are inescapable laws governing the imaginative construction of the sense of self," and that to eliminate such language "is to cut ourselves off from centuries of

tradition, both doctrinal and aesthetic" ("The Life of the World to Come: Near-Death Experience and Christian Eschatology," The Albert Cardinal Meyer Lectures, 1993, published by Munde-lein Seminary/University of St. Mary of the Lake, Mundelein IL, 38). Nelson and Longfellow observe that selves "experience the ambiguity of both 'having' and 'being' bodies" ("Introduction," xiv). Not all traditions, however, develop the dynamic of body–mind relations into the same "problematic" status that it has assumed in the Euro-American West. Asians traditions tend to see mind and body as less distinct, more in terms of "polarity" than "dualism." Hence, Asian approaches to mind and body tend typically to consist in disciplines or practices of integration, such as yoga (T. P. Kasulis, "Introduction," in T. P. Kasulis, with Roger T. Ames and Wimal Dissanayake eds., *Self as Body in Asian Theory and Practice* [Albany: State University of New York Press] xii–xiii, xviii–xix). Sylvia Marcos demonstrates how in ancient Mesoamerican traditions, the boundaries between the body and the cosmos were much more fluid; the body was not a clearly bounded reality, but a center of currents of movement between the body and the universe, and between men's and women's bodies (Sylvia Marcos, *Embodied Thought: Concept of the Body in Mesoamerica*, forthcoming).

11 This is also not to deny that some individuals bear physical traits associated with both female and male reproduction, for example, hermaphrodites and those with atypical sex chromosomes. My premise is that such individuals are atypical in relation to, rather than definitive of, the general paradigm of human sexual char-acteristics. The lives of such persons raise for me the importance of disallowing identity, personality and social roles to be so formed around sex and gender that persons whose sex is physiolo-gically anomolous have little opportunity for self-respect, social acceptance, and social contribution.

12 Susan Bordo, *Unbearable Weight: Feminism, Western Culture, and the Body* (Berkeley, Los Angeles, London: University of California Press, 1993), 233.

13 Susan Moller Okin, *Justice, Gender, and the Family* (New York: HarperCollins, 1989), 171.

14 Eleanor Maccoby and Carol Jacklin, *The Psychology of Sex Differences* (Stanford University Press, 1974).

15 Nancy Chodorow, *The Reproduction of Mothering: Psychoanalysis and the Sociology of Gender* (Berkeley: University of California Press, 1976); Dorothy Dinnerstein, *The Mermaid and the Minotaur: Sexual Arrangements and Human Malaise* (New York: Harper & Row, 1977).

16 Michelle Rosaldo and Louise Lamphere, *Women, Culture & Society* (Stanford University Press, 1974).

17 Claude Lévi-Strauss sees the subordination of women as beginning with their exchange as reproductive commodities, the first form of trade, which makes civilization possible (*The Elementary Structures of Kinship* [Boston: Beacon Press, 1969]).

18 Friedrich Engels blamed the formation of private property for the subordination of women (*The Origin of the Family, Private Property and the State,* first published in 1884). Gerda Lerner builds on Lévi-Strauss to argue that the development of agriculture increased both group cohesiveness and the demand for labor. The result was that women's reproductive capacity came to be regarded as the property of particular kin groups, who then traded women with other tribes (*The Creation of Patriarchy* [New York and Oxford: Oxford University Press, 1986]).

19 Carol Gilligan, *In a Different Voice: Psychological Theory and Women's Development* (Cambridge MA: Harvard University Press, 1982); Nell Noddings, *Caring: A Feminine Approach to Ethics and Moral Education* (Berkeley: University of California Press, 1984); Adrienne Rich, *Of Woman Born: Motherhood as Experience and Institution* (New York: Norton, 1986), and "Compulsory Heterosexuality," in *The Signs Reader: Women, Gender, and Scholarship* (Chicago and London: The University of Chicago Press, 1983), 139–68, originally published in 1980; Sara Ruddick, *Maternal Thinking: Toward a Politics of Peace* (Boston: Beacon Press, 1989); Mary O'Brien, *The Politics of Reproduction* (Boston: Routledge and Kegan Paul, 1981); Luce Irigaray, *This Sex Which Is Not One*; Mary Daly, *Gyn/ecology: The Metaethics of Radical Feminism* (Boston: Beacon Press, 1990).

20 For an overview, see Rosemarie Tong, *Feminine and Feminist Ethics* (Belmont CA: Wadsworth Publishing Company, 1993), 25–48.

21 Nancy Mairs nicely cartoons male reproductive inadequacy and female disdain in *Ordinary Time: Cycles in Marriage, Faith and Renewal* (Boston: Beacon Press, 1993), 36–41.

22 See Bonnie J. Miller-McLemore, *Also a Mother: Work and Family as a Theological Dilemma* (Nashville: Abingdon, 1994).

23 A classic essay is Helene Cixous, "The Laugh of the Medusa," trans. Keith Cohen and Paula Cohen, in Elizabeth Abel and Emily K. Abel, *Signs Reader,* 279–97. An earlier version appeared as "Le Rire de la Meduse," *L'Arc* (1975) 39–54, and was revised for *Signs* in 1976. See also Julia Kristeva, *Desire in Language: A Semiotic Approach to Literature and Art,* ed. by Leon S. Roudiez, trans. Thomas Gora, Alice Jardine, and Leon S. Roudiez (New York: Columbia University Press, 1980); and Luce Irigaray, *This Sex*

Which Is Not One, trans. Catherine Porter (Ithaca NY: Cornell University Press, 1985). A theological work which incorporates insights of these authors is Rebecca Chopp, *The Power to Speak* (1989). See also Paula M. Cooey, *Religious Imagination and the Body: A Feminist Analysis* (New York and Oxford: Oxford University Press, 1994).

24 The essayist Nancy Mairs (*Voice Lessons: On Becoming a (Woman) Writer* [Boston: Beacon Press, 1994], 49) communicates this insight brilliantly. She struggles to capture what might be meant by "writing the body" and the "feminine text" in theories which pass the terms elusively back and forth between *women's* experience and *any* experience that has been repressed and excluded by language. She also wonders what it could mean concretely to write one's own body in foreign, even antagonistic, language. Finally, she says:

> I just keep inscribing the fathers' words with my woman's fingers and hope that the feminine will bleed through ... I can never write as Authority, as Essayist, as Literary Critic. I can write only from this body as it is now: female, white, well-educated, moderately prosperous, crippled, a Roman Catholic convert, heterosexual ...
>   This is the body who works here.

Mairs also appreciates the "explosions" of patriarchal language attempted by radical feminists such as Monique Wittig and Mary Daly, but becomes impatient with the way their very originality frustrates her desire to "speak plainly" about "particulars" (87).

25 Judith Butler, *Bodies That Matter,* xi. See also Bordo, *Unbearable Weight.* The book focuses on eating disorders. Observing that feminist critiques of gender amount to "an extended argument against the notion that the body is a purely biological or natural form" (33), Bordo still views with some skepticism postmodern attempts to fragment the unity of the body into an endlessly shifting multiplicity of parts (227). "Do we want to delegitimate a priori the exploration of experiential continuity and structural common ground among women?" (225).

26 Butler, *Bodies that Matter,* 10.

27 Bordo, *Unbearable Weight,* 230.

28 Raymond Bonner, "Rwandan Rebels Call Truce, But Refugees Are Still Fleeing," *New York Times,* Tuesday, July 19, 1994, A6.

29 See Christine Gudorf, "Women's Choice for Motherhood: Beginning a Cross-Cultural Approach," in Anne Carr and Elisabeth Schüssler Fiorenza, eds., *Motherhood: Experience, Institution, Theology, Concilium* 1989/6 (Edinburgh: T. & T. Clark, 1989), 55–63.

30 *Of Woman Born,* 22.

31 "I have come to believe that female biology – the diffuse, intense sensuality radiating out from clitoris, breasts, uterus, vagina; the lunar cycles of menstruation; the gestation and fruition of life which can take place in the female body – has far more radical implications than we have yet come to appreciate. Patriarchal thought has limited female biology to its own narrow specifications. The feminist vision has recoiled from female biology for these reasons; it will, I believe, come to view our physicality as a resource, rather than a destiny. In order to live a fully human life we require not only control of our bodies (though control is a prerequisite); we must touch the unity and resonance of our physicality, our bond with the natural order, the corporeal ground of our intelligence" (Ibid., 39).

32 Ibid., 36, 40.

33 Ibid., 33.

34 Mercy Amba Oduyoye, "Poverty and Motherhood," in *Motherhood*, 23.

35 For some of these latter aspects, see also Oduyoye, "Women and Ritual in Africa," in Mercy Amba Oduyoye, and Musimbi R. A. Kanyoro, eds., *The Will to Arise: Women, Tradition, and the Church in Africa* (Maryknoll NY: Orbis, 1992), 9–24. Buchi Emecheta's novels, especially *The Joys of Motherhood* (New York: George Braziller, 1979) eloquently spell out the downside of tribal family systems in Nigeria.

36 Rosemary N. Edet, "Christianity and African Women's Rituals," in *The Will to Arise*, 33, 34.

37 Philippe Ariés, "The Indissoluble Marriage," in Philippe Ariés, ed., *Western Sexuality: Practice and Precept in Past and Present Times*, trans. Anthony Forster (Oxford: Basil Blackwell, 1985), 153.

38 Saint Thomas Aquinas, *Summa Contra Gentiles, Book III: Providence, Part II*, trans. Vernon J. Bourke (Notre Dame and London: University of Notre Dame Press, 1975) chapters 123–24.

39 Paul Ricoeur, "Wonder, Eroticism, and Enigma," *Cross Currents* 14 (1964) 137.

40 Sidney Callahan, "Two by Two: The Case for Monogamy," *Commonweal* 121/13 (1994) 7.

41 Such concerns motivated the project which sponsored the present work. See John Wall, "The New Middle Ground in the Family Debate: A Report on the 1994 Conference of the *Religion, Culture, and Family Project, Criterion* 33/3 (1995) 24–31; and Don and Carol Browning, "Better Family Values," *Christianity Today* 39/2 (1995) 29–31.

42 Donald Symons, *The Evolution of Human Sexuality* (New York and Oxford: Oxford University Press, 1979), 23. See also Robert Wright, *The Moral Animal: Why We Are the Way We Are: The New Science of Evolutionary Psychology* (New York: Pantheon, 1994). Legal

scholar and economic theorist Richard Posner provides an example of the appropriation of sociobiology within an economic theory of life as the pursuit of self-interest (Richard A. Posner, *Sex and Reason* [Cambridge MA and London: Harvard University Press, 1992]). Calling his interpretation a "libertarian" and "economic" theory of sexuality, he treats human bodily relations as economic exchanges. The distinctively human trait which is morally crucial to Posner is liberty, which can set some limits on self-interest, but which also warrants a general policy of noninterference in sexual behavior. Posner's theory exemplifies the pervasive modern trust in "scientific" research as a basis of moral claims, combined with a confidence in the self-evidence of autonomy as barely needing defense. Those who disagree are referred (repeatedly) to chapter 4 of John Stuart Mill's *On Liberty* (for instance, on 203). For a feminist legal critique of Posner, see Mary Becker, "Flirting with Science: Richard Posner on the Bioeconomics of Sexual Man," *Harvard Law Review* 106/2 (December, 1992) 479–503.

43 Symons, *Evolution of Human Sexuality*, 157, 161–62.

44 Ibid., 23.

45 Ibid., 180.

46 Ibid., 301. See Wright, *Moral Animal*, 91, 246–50.

47 Ibid., 300. One gap in Symon's use of the homosexual text case is the possibility that the same chromosomal and hormonal factors that may contribute to homosexual object choice could also cause variation in other behaviors also associated with "male" sexual conduct.

48 Sarah Blaffer Hrdy, "Empathy, Polyandry and the Myth of the Coy Female," in Ruth Bleier, ed., *Feminist Approaches to Science* (New York: Pergamon Press, 1986), 128–29. Natalie Angier, "Feminists and Darwin: Scientists Try Closing the Gap," *New York Times*, June 21, 1994, C1, C13, reports on a June 1994 conference at the University of Georgia, led by Patricia Adair Gowaty. Judith Stamps of the University of California at Davis reported on female birds that cheat on their mates to make inroads into a better territory. Marcy F. Lawton of the University of Alabama in Huntsville reported pinyon jay birds, among whom the males were decidedly nonagressive, while females fought furiously just before breeding readiness. See also a major critical study of sociobiology, Philip Kitcher, *Vaulting Ambition: Sociobiology and the Quest for Human Nature* (Cambridge MA and London: MIT Press, 1985), 193.

49 Mary Midgley, *Beast and Man: The Roots of Human Nature* (Ithaca:

Cornell University Press, 1978), 253, 259, 285, 290. Stephen J. Pope observes that evolutionary theory enables us to understand the context within which virtues such as intimacy, honor, and care emerge, and notes that biologically fostered emotions also need to "be complemented by the full range of virtues appropriate to any human life lived well, for example, prudence, courage, honesty, fidelity, and temperance" (*The Evolution of Altruism and the Ordering of Love* [Washington, DC: Georgetown University Press, 1994] 93).

50 Mary Midgley, *The Ethical Primate. Humans, Freedom and Morality* (London: Routledge, 1994), 131.

51 Wright, *Moral Animal*, 201.

52 Alan P. Bell and Martin S. Weinberg, *Homosexualities: A Study of Diversity Among Men and Women* (New York: Simon and Schuster, 1978), 132, 219–20.

53 Stephen Pope's thesis is that Christian ideals of loving behavior need to take into account (as did Thomas Aquinas) the "natural" order of love and altruism, in which close kin are preferred. An ordering of love and responsibility, rather than undifferentiated love for all, is needed as the basis of Christian ethics (*Evolution of Altruism*).

54 Martha Nussbaum sees compassion and respect as human moral sentiments that underlie the recognition of common experiences and needs ("Human Functioning and Social Justice: In Defense of Aristotelian Essentialism," *Political Theory* 20 [1992] 237–41).

55 Kitchner, *Vaulting Ambition*, 430–32; Midgley, *Ethical Primate*, 163–84.

56 Robert Wright, "Our Cheating Hearts," *Time* 144/5 (August 15, 1994) 52. Similarly, Symons refers to behavior prompted by genetic demands as "the nightmare of the past," ending his book with a utopian hope that it can be overcome (313).

57 On this point, see Steven Pinker's perceptive review of Robert Wright's *The Moral Animal* ("Is There a Gene for Compassion? The new evolutionary psychology could explain why altruists haven't gone the way of the dinosaurs," *New York Times Book Review*, September 25, 1994, 3, 34–35).

58 Aquinas, *ST*, ii–ii.25–26, where he agrees that we ought to love more intensely those who are related to us more closely, especially by ties of blood (*ST*, ii–ii.26.8). See also Pope, *Evolution of Altruism*, 50–76 ("The 'Order of Love' According to Thomas Aquinas").

59 Martha Nussbaum, "Aristotelian Social Democracy," in R. Bruce Douglass, Gerald R. Mara, and Henry S. Richardson, eds., *Liberalism and the Good* (New York: Routledge, 1990), 225–26.

60 See Arlene Swidler, ed., *Homosexuality and World Religions* (Valley Forge PA: Trinity Press International, 1993).

61 See John Boswell's contention that it was: *Christianity, Social Tolerance, and Homosexuality: Gay People in Western Europe from the Beginning of the Christian Era to the Fourteenth Century* (University of Chicago Press, 1980); "Homosexuality and Religious Life: A Historical Approach," in James B. Nelson and Sandra P. Longfellow, *Sexuality and the Sacred: Sources for Theological Reflection* (Louisville KY: Westminster/John Knox Press, 1994), 361–73; *Same-Sex Unions in Premodern Europe* (New York: Villard Books, 1994).

62 See Boswell, above; Lillian Faderman, *Surpassing the Love of Men: Romantic Friendship and Love between Women from the Renaissance to the Present* (New York: William Morrow, 1981); Carroll Smith-Rosenberg, "The Female World of Love and Ritual: Relations Between Women in Nineteenth-Century America," *Signs Reader*, 27–55; and Vern Bullough, "The Kinsey Scale in Historical Perspective," in David P. McWhirter, Stephanie A. Sanders, June Machover Reinisch, *Homosexuality/Heterosexuality: Concepts of Sexual Orientation* (New York and Oxford: Oxford University Press, 1990), 6–7.

63 See Bullough, "Kinsey Scale," 8–11.

64 A. C. Kinsey, W. B. Pomeroy, and C. F. Martin, *Sexual Behavior in the Human Male* (Philadelphia: W. B. Saunders, 1948).

65 Ibid., 11.

66 In McWhirter, et al., *Homosexuality*, see "Part II: Psychobiological Perspective," 41–111, and "Part III: Evolutionary Perspective," 115–74. See also Simon LeVay and Dean M. Hamer, "Evidence for a Biological Influence in Male Homosexuality," and William Byne, "The Biological Evidence Challenged," both in *Scientific American* 270/5 (1994) 43–49 and 50–55, respectively. An overview is Chandler Burr, "Homosexuality and Biology," in Jeffrey S. Siker, ed., *Homosexuality in the Church: Both Sides of the Debate* (Louisville KY: Westminster John Knox Press, 1994).

67 Sociologist David F. Greenberg argues that, although sexual identity may not be absolutely plastic, neither is it so clearly an "innate" essence, completely resistant to social molding. His endorsement of the "social constructionist" analysis is strong: "Where social definitions of appropriate and inappropriate behavior are clear and consistent, with positive sanctions for conformity and negative ones for nonconformity, virtually everyone will conform irrespective of genetic inheritance and, to a considerable extent, irrespective of personal psychodynamics" (*The Construction of Homosexuality* [Chicago and London: University of Chicago Press, 1988], 487).

68 For the "lesbian sex radicals," political lesbianism can even include the deliberate separation of sex from love, although supposedly in a context which maintains "female-oriented values such as equality of power, consensuality, safety, and emotional nurturance" (Margaret Nichols, "Lesbian Relationships: Implications for the Study of Sexuality and Gender," in McWhirter ed., *Homosexuality*, 362).

69 John P. De Cecco, "Sex and More Sex: A Critique of the Kinsey Conception of Human Sexuality," in McWhirter et al., ed., *Homosexuality*, 377 and 375–76, respectively.

70 Yet in "Compulsory Heterosexuality," Rich seems more to see both men and women as originally inclined psychologically toward women to meet their needs for intimacy. For references, see note 19 above.

71 For examples, see Robert Nugent, ed., *A Challenge to Love: Gay and Lesbian Catholics in the Church* (New York: Crossroad, 1983); Mary Hunt, *Fierce Tenderness: A Feminist Theology of Friendship* (New York: Crossroad, 1991); Robert Nugent and Jeannine Gramick, *Building Bridges: Gay and Lesbian Reality and the Catholic Church* (Mystic CT: Twenty-Third Publications, 1992); and Patricia Beattie Jung and Ralph Smith, *Heterosexism: An Ethical Challenge* (Albany: State University of New York Press, 1993); and Siker, ed., *Homosexuality in the Church*, especially essays by John J. McNeill, James B. Nelson, and Chandler Burr.

72 Congregation for the Doctrine of the Faith, *Declaration On Certain Questions Concering Sexual Ethics*, 1975. Later documents, however, reveal ambivalence on this score. For instance, the CDF's "Letter to the Bishops of the Catholic Church on the Pastoral Care of Homosexual Persons" (1986) describes the homosexual orientation as "ordered toward an intrinsic moral evil," "an objective disorder" (no. 3), and "a disordered sexual inclination which is essentially self-indulgent" (no. 7).

73 One anthropologist, David Schneider, reports that when he worked on the island of Yap (West Caroline Islands) in the 1940s, he was assured that coitus had nothing to do with the birth of children. Rather, when a man's ancestral spirits are pleased with the conduct of his wife, they reward her with pregnancy. Twenty years later, a colleague was given different information: coitus is necessary to conception, on the analogy of planting a seed in a garden (David M. Schneider, *A Critique of the Study of Kinship* [Ann Arbor: University of Michigan Press, 1984], 28).

74 Bronislaw Malinowski, *The Family Among the Australian Aborigines* (University of London Press, 1913).

75 Ibid., vii.

76 *Critique of Kinship*, 171.

77 Ibid., 173–75.

78 Robin Fox, *Kinship and Marriage: An Anthropological Perspective* (Harmmondsworth, Middlesex, England; Ringwood, Victoria, Australia; Baltimore MD, USA: Penguin Books, 1967), 13–14.

79 Jane Collier, Michelle A. Rosaldo, and Sylvia Yanagisako, "Is There a Family? New Anthropological Views," in Barrie Thorne and Marilyn Yalom eds., *Rethinking the Family: Some Feminist Questions* (New York and London: Longman, Inc., 1984), 25–39.

80 Jack Goody observes that virtually all societies vest the rights over the sexual services of a woman in one man; "in patrilineal societies the rights over a woman that are transferred at marriage include rights to her reproductive capacities as well as rights to her sexual services, whereas in matrilineal societies it is only the latter that are transferred" (*Comparative Studies in Kinship* [Stanford CA: Stanford University Press, 1969) 26.

81 Rayna Rapp illustrates the notion of fictive kinship by citing studies of the African American family, in which friends are sometimes turned into functional family members ("Family and Class in Contemporary America: Notes Toward an Understanding of Ideology," in Thorne and Yalom eds., *Rethinking the Family*, 178).

82 Sidney Callahan, "The Family: The Challenge of Technological Change," in John A. Coleman, S. J., ed., *One Hundred Years of Catholic Social Thought: Celebration and Challenge* (Maryknoll, NY: Orbis, 1991), 174.

83 Not all inequalities in the family are immoral, of course. Obviously, children are dependent on adults. The proper balance of authority and dependence between young adult children and parents, and between mature adults and elders is a matter for practical discernment, and is evaluated differently by cultures. Differences in real needs and capacities ground morally valid inequalities of social relationship. The feminist critique of gender inequalities in the family is based on the argument that such inequalities are premised on fallacious conceptions of the unequal capacities of men and women.

AN INTERLUDE AND A PROPOSAL

1 Robert Wright, *The Moral Animal: The New Science of Evolutionary Psychology* (New York: Pantheon Books, 1994), 90. See also Donald

Symons, *The Evolution of Human Sexuality* (New York and Oxford: Oxford University Press, 1979), 142, 161–62.

2 See Susan Brownmiller, *Against Our Will: Men, Women, and Rape* (New York: Simon and Schuster, 1975); Elisabeth Schüssler Fiorenza and M. Shawn Copeland, eds., *Violence Against Women*, Concilium 1994/1 (Maryknoll NY: Orbis Books, 1994); and Lori L. Heise, et al., *Violence Against Women: The Hidden Health Burden*, World Bank Discussion Papers No. 255 (Washington DC, The World Bank, 1994).

3 See Susan A. Ross, "Evil and Hope: Foundational Moral Perspectives," in Catholic Theological Society of America *Proceedings* 50 (1995), 46–63.

4 Gerda Lerner, *The Creation of Feminist Consciousness* (Oxford, New York, Toronto: Oxford University Press, 1993).

5 SEX, GENDER, AND EARLY CHRISTIANITY

1 Conversations with my Boston College colleague, Pheme Perkins, have been invaluable in the development of this chapter. Carolyn Osiek also supplied me with a good deal of bibliographical advice.

2 As Richard Horsley and Max Myers complain, "Despite the highly sophisticated recent discussions of hermeneutics, when it comes to the relation of the Bible to ethics, both biblical scholars and ethicists often still seem stuck at the elementary stage of 'what does the Bible say about' [or fail to say to us about] a certain issue" ("Idols, Demons, and the Hermeneutics of Suspicion: Biblical Traditions Informing Ethics," in David J. Lull ed., SBL Seminar Papers 1989 [Atlanta: Scholars Press, 1989] 634). These issues typically include homosexuality, adultery, and divorce, debates about which often hinge on narrowly disputed meanings of ancient terms such as *pornoi, porneia, malakos, arsenokoites*, etc. See Victor Paul Furnish, *The Moral Teaching of Paul: Selected Issues*, rev. edn (Nashville: Abingdon Press, 1985); and Robin Scroggs, *The New Testament and Homosexuality: Contextual Background for Contemporary Debate* (Philadelphia: Fortress Press, 1983). Scroggs, for instance, includes a lengthy discussion of *malakos, malakia, malthakos* (62–65). On homosexuality, see also Richard B. Hays, "Relations Natural and Unnatural: A Response to John"; and "Awaiting the Redemption of our Bodies," *Sojourners* 20/6 (1991) 17–21.

3 According to J. L. Houlden, the NT places ethics in the context of a relationship with God which is both present in its qualitative newness and anticipatory in its expectation of a final divine realization and completion. The fundamental faith of the first

Christians demands ever to be applied in a "fresh setting." (J. L. Houlden, *Ethics and the New Testament* [New York: Oxford University Press, 1977], 116–17). Another way to capture this insight is to say that love of neighbor is grounded in love of God. See Edward Collins Vacek, S.J., *Love Human and Divine: The Heart of Christian Ethics* (Washington, DC: Georgetown University Press, 1994).

4 See James D. G. Dunn, *Unity and Diversity in the New Testament: An Inquiry into the Character of Earliest Christianity* (Philadelphia: Westminster Press, 1977); Raymond E. Brown, *An Introduction to New Testament Christology* (New York/Mahwah: Paulist Press, 1994); and, for a developed argument concerning the Jewish character of Matthew's community, persistently misconstrued under "false notions of a unitary and cohesive Christian development in the first two centuries," see Anthony J. Saldarini, *Matthew's Jewish-Christian Community* (Chicago and London: The University of Chicago Press, 1994), 20.

5 Elisabeth Schüssler Fiorenza, *In Memory of Her: A Feminist Theological Reconstruction of Christian Origins* (New York: Crossroad, 1983) 130.

6 Social history is of special interest for ethics, because it can give us a broader perspective in which to understand how specific NT moral attitudes and norms functioned against their own cultures, and thus to understand the sorts of moral relationships they might offer us as models today. In interpreting the Bible for ethics, texts as literary units, the social settings assumed or projected by those texts, the layered revisions of biblical accounts in response to social factors, and the experience of the church today are all important pieces of the hermeneutical process. Yet no one is the supreme arbiter of biblical "meaning" – all alternately can supply a corrective function *vis-à-vis* the regnant consensus. Sandra M. Schneiders, I. H. M., says that the power of the Bible to mediate the encounter with God depends on the world behind the text (its historical setting), the world of the text (its literary structure and content), and the world before the text (appropriation) (*The Revelatory Text* [San Francisco: HarperCollins, 1992]).

7 See E. P. Sanders, *Jesus and Judaism* (Philadelphia: FortressPress, 1985); John P. Meier, *A Marginal Jew: Rethinking the Historical Jesus, Volume Two, Mentor, Message, and Miracle* (New York: Doubleday, 1994), 350, 452; and *Jesus in Contemporary Scholarship* (Valley Forge PA: Trinity Press International, 1994), especially chapters 3 and 4.

8 E. P. Sanders, *The Historical Figure of Jesus* (New York and London: Penguin Books, 1993), 204.

9 For a much more extensive development of these claims, see Lisa Sowle Cahill, *Love Your Enemies: Discipleship, Pacifism, and Just War Theory* (Minneapolis MN: Fortress Press, 1994), 15–38 and 239–46.

10 *In Memory of Her*, 132. See Elisabeth Schüssler Fiorenza, *Jesus: Miriam's Child, Sophia's Prophet* (New York: Crossroad, 1994) for a full development of these themes. See also Marcus J. Borg, *Meeting Jesus Again for the First Time: The Historical Jesus and the Heart of Contemporary Faith* (San Francisco: HarperSanFrancisco, 1994), 113–14; Borg, *Jesus*, 149–50; and Elizabeth Johnson, *She Who Is: The Mystery of God in Feminist Discourse* (New York: Crossroad, 1992), 86–93, 156–58. Borg explicitly credits both Schüssler Fiorenza and Johnson.

11 Just why tax collectors were so repulsive to Jews is a matter of dispute. Although they have in the past been regarded as Jewish collaborators with Rome, the imperial power, it could be simply that they were local customs officers who were routinely dishonest, making good use of their opportunities for extortion. See Sanders, *Historical Figure*, 227–29.

12 Meier, *Mentor, Message*, 452; James D. G. Dunn, *Jesus' Call to Discipleship* (Cambridge University Press, 1992) 11, 16.

13 Pheme Perkins, "Canon, Paradigms and Progress? Reflections on the Essays by Rendtorff, Sugirtharajah and Clines," *Biblical Interpretation* 1/1 (1993) 95.

14 Paul Ricoeur, *Oneself as Another*, trans. Kathleen Blamey (Chicago and London: University of Chicago Press, 1992) 168. Ricoeur's poetic philosophical translation of the love commandment identifies solicitude (180), structured by a norm of reciprocity (219), as the key to ethics. Solicitude is "the primordial relation of the self to the self's other on the ethical level" (203). Acknowledging his debt to Aristotle, Ricoeur defines ethics as "*aiming at the good life with and for others, in just institutions*" (172), based in praxis and its "bond of common mores" (194). The notion of "humanity" is "the plural expression of the requirement of universality," and eliminates the "otherness which is dramatized in the dissymmetrical relation of the power one will holds over another, opposed by the Golden Rule" (223).

15 See Borg, *Jesus*; Halvor Moxnes, *The Economy of the Kingdom: Social Conflict and Economic Relations in Luke's Gospel* (Philadelphia: Fortress Press, 1988); Richard A. Horsley, *The Liberation of Christmas: The Infancy Narratives in Social Context* (New York: Crossroad, 1989) and *Sociology and the Jesus Movement* (New York: Crossroad, 1989); Ched Myers, *Binding the Strong Man: A Political Reading of Mark's Story of Jesus* (Maryknoll NY: Orbis, 1988); Michael H. Crosby, *House of*

Disciples: Church, Economics, and Justice in Matthew (Maryknoll NY: Orbis, 1988); and John Dominic Crossan, *Jesus: A Revolutionary Biography* (San Francisco: HarperSanFrancisco, 1994).

16 Sally B. Purvis, *The Power of the Cross: Foundations for a Christian Feminist Ethic of Community* (Nashville: Abingdon, 1993), 77–78.

17 In addition to Borg's *Jesus* and *Jesus Again*, see, for instance, Moxnes, *Economy of the Kingdom*, 28–30. On this theme as well as those of reciprocity and redistribution, also note A. Horsley, *Jesus and the Spiral of Violence*, 152–53, *Liberation of Christmas*, 68–70, and *Sociology and the Jesus Movement*, 88–92; Myers, *Binding the Strong Man*, 47–53; Crosby, *House of Disciples*, 102–04; and Crossan, *Jesus: A Revolutionary Biography*, 95–101.

18 Moxnes, *Economy of the Kingdom*, 94.

19 Ibid., 156.

20 Horsley, *Liberation of Christmas*, 92, 122–23, 125.

21 For a review of recent work on the NT and ethics which arrives at a similar conclusion, see William C. Spohn, S.J., "Jesus and Ethics," *Theological Studies* 56 (1995) 92–107. Spohn calls the entire story of Jesus the "concrete universal" of Christian ethics, and concludes that we expand the patterns of that story by analogy to new situations (102).

22 Seán Freyne, "The Ethic of Jesus," in Seán Freyne, ed., *Ethics and the Christian* (Dublin: The Columba Press, 1991), 53.

23 Richard Horsley and Max Myers, "Idols, Demons, and the Hermeneutics of Suspicion: Biblical Traditions Informing Ethics," in David J. Lull ed., *SBL Seminar Papers 1989*, (Atlanta: Scholars Press, 1984) 647.

24 Ibid., 639–40 and 642, respectively.

25 See David Jobling, "Globalization in Biblical Studies/Biblical Studies in Globalization," *Biblical Interpretation* 1/1 (1993) 96–110.

26 Borg, *Jesus*, p. 108. See also Marcus J. Borg, *Conflict, Holiness and Politics in the Teachings of Jesus* (New York and Toronto: Edwin Mellen, 1984).

27 Mary Douglas, *Purity and Danger: An Analysis of Concepts of Pollution and Taboo* (London and Henley: Routledge and Kegan Paul, 1966), 115.

28 Mary Douglas, *Natural Symbols: Explorations in Cosmology*, rev. edn (London: Barrie and Jenkins, 1973; originally published in 1971), 12.

29 *Purity and Danger*, 124.

30 *Natural Symbols*, 77–92.

31 *Natural Symbols*, 98; see also 93.

32 Ibid., 97.

33 Ibid., 183; see also 97–98.

34 Ibid., 101.

35 Ibid., 102.

36 Ibid., 99.

37 Charles Taylor, *The Ethics of Authenticity* (Cambridge MA and London: Harvard University Press, 1991).

38 Daniel L. Smith, *Religion of the Landless: The Social Context of the Babylonian Exile* (New York: Meyer Stone Books, 1989).

39 Jacob Neusner, *Purity in Rabbinic Judaism: A Systematic Account, The Sources, Media, Effects, and Removal of Uncleanness* (Atlanta: Scholars Press, 1994), 48–49; Saldarini, *Matthew's ... Community*, 135; Judith Plaskow, "Embodiment and Ambivalence: A Jewish Feminist Perspective," in Lisa Sowle Cahill and Margaret Farley, eds., *Embodiment, Medicine, and Morality* (Dordrecht and New York: Kluwer Publishers, 1995), 23–36.

40 David P. Wright, "Unclean and Clean," *Anchor Bible Dictionary*, vol. 6 (New York: Doubleday, 1992), 740.

41 Sanders, *Historical Figure*, 36.

42 Borg, *Jesus*, p. 109. See also Jerome Neyrey, ed., *The Social World of Luke-Acts* (Peabody MA: Hendrickson, 1991), 271–304; and L. William Countryman, *Dirt, Greed, and Sex: Sexual Ethics in the New Testament and their Implications for Today* (Philadelphia: Fortress, 1988), 45–65.

43 Martin Goodman, *The Ruling Class of Judaea: The Origins of the Jewish Revolt against Rome A.D. 66–70* (Cambridge University Press, 1987), p. 119; Sanders, *Historical Figure*, 41.

44 As discussed above, not all Christian interpreters would endorse the idea of an abrupt rupture between Judaism and early Christianity, or see residual Jewish influence in wholly negative terms. Although Mark's community challenged the validity of purity laws (Mk. 7:1–23), Matthew's sees Jesus as fulfilling them, though they remain in a subordinate relation to the commandments. See Saldarini, *Matthew's ... Community*, 19, 134, 162. The function of purity laws in demarcating class is particularly emphasized by those interpreting Mark: J. Neyrey, "The Idea of Purity in Mark's Gospel," *Semeia* 35 (1986), 91–127; Myers, *Binding the Strong Man*, 69–80, 152–54; Fernando Belo, *A Materialist Reading of the Gospel of Mark* (Maryknoll NY: Orbis, 1981).

45 John Dominic Crossan, *Jesus; A Revolutionary Biography* (New York: HarperCollins Publishers, 1992), 68.

46 Ibid., 69.

47 Crossan, *Jesus*, 82.

48 One of the first to reference Douglas was Wayne A. Meeks, *The*

First Urban Christians: The Social World of the Apostle Paul (New Haven and London: Yale University Press, 1983), 97, 141.

49 Countryman, *Dirt, Greed, and Sex*; and Jerome H. Neyrey, *Paul in Other Words: A Cultural Reading of His Letters* (Louisville KY: Westminster/John Knox Press, 1992).

50 Jerome H. Neyrey, S.J., "Body Language in 1 Corinthians: The Use of Anthropological Models for Understanding Paul and His Opponents," *Semeia* 35 (1986) 163.

51 Countryman, *Dirt, Greed and Sex*, 142. Countryman retains the language of property, but sees each individual as owning her or his own sexual property. He describes Jesus as seeing "sexual access" as a "fundamental good," and "an important possession," of which his followers are forbidden to "rob others" (189).

52 Ibid., 177.

53 Ibid., 241.

54 Ibid., 243–44.

55 Neyrey, "Body Language," 144–48.

56 See Gerd Theissen, *The Social Setting of Pauline Christianity: Essays on Corinth* trans. John H. Schutz (Philadelphia: Fortress Press, 1982) 123–32.

57 Ross Shepard Kraemer, *Her Share of the Blessings: Women's Religions Among Pagans, Jews, and Christians in the Greco-Roman World* (Oxford, New York, Toronto: Oxford University Press, 1992) 156. See also 13–21 for Kraemer's discussion of Douglas.

58 Kraemer, *Her Share*, 199–200, 206.

59 Ibid., 206.

60 *Dirt, Greed, and Sex*, 253. Robin Scroggs is not far away when he reads New Testament condemnations of homosexuality as repudiating exploitative sexual control, especially pederasty, and recommends an ideal of caring, mutual, consensual sex (*New Testament and Homosexuality*, 126).

61 Caroline Walker Bynum, *Holy Feast and Holy Fast: The Religious Significance of Food to Medieval Women* (Berkeley, Los Angeles, London: University of California Press, 1987); and *Fragmentation and Redemption: Essays on Gender and the Human Body in Medieval Religion* (New York: Zone Books, 1991).

62 *Natural Symbols*, 190.

63 How meaningful is sexual freedom if its primary effect is to dissolve men's responsibility for mates and offspring? How meaningful is a right to choose abortion, if women do not have the social means to bear, support, and educate their children? How valuable is a right to divorce when displaced homemakers are left without earning potential or consistent child support? How

helpful is access to new birth technologies and donor gametes, if women are pressured to see pregnancy as essential to a meaningful life, and to yield their bodies to the escalating machinations of a high-profit "therapeutic" imperative?

64 See Sandra M. Schneiders, *The Revelatory Text: Interpreting the New Testament as Sacred Scripture* (New York: HarperCollins, 1991), 182–83.

65 A resource is Joseph Blenkinsopp, "The Family in Israel," to appear in *The Family in Ancient Israel*, ed. Leo G. Purdue (Louisville KY: Westminster/John Knox Press, forthcoming), an early version of which was kindly provided to me by the author. The final study may incorporate changes not reflected in my remarks, however.

66 See Phyllis Trible, *God and the Rhetoric of Sexuality* (Philadelphia: Fortress Press, 1978); and *Texts of Terror: Literary-Feminist Readings of Biblical Narratives* (Philadelphia: Fortress, 1984). See also, J. Cheryl Exum, *Fragmented Women: (Sub)Versions of Biblical Narratives* (Valley Forge PA: Trinity Press International, 1993), 1–9.

67 See Kraemer, *Her Share*, 93–127; Carol Meyers, *Discovering Eve: Ancient Israelite Women in Context* (New York and Oxford: Oxford University Press, 1988); Judith Romney Wegner, *Chattel or Person? The Status of Women in the Mishnah* (New York: Oxford University Press, 1988); and Cheryl Anne Brown, *No Longer Be Silent: First Century Jewish Portraits of Biblical Women* (Louisville: Westminster/John Knox, 1992).

68 For an overview, see Carolyn Osiek, "The New Testament and the Family," in Lisa Sowle Cahill and Dietmar Mieth, eds., *The Family, Concilium* 1995/4 (Maryknoll NY: Orbis, 1995), 1–9.

69 W. K. Lacey, *The Family in Classical Greece* (Ithaca NY: Cornell University Press, 1968), 21.

70 Ibid., 153.

71 Elaine Fantham, H. P. Foley, N. B. Kampen, and S. B. Pomeroy *Women in the Classical World: Image and Text* (New York and Oxford: Oxford University Press, 1994), 115–18.

72 David Cohen, *Law, Sexuality, and Society: The Enforcement of Morals in Classical Athens* (Cambridge University Press, 1991) 140–41.

73 Lacey, *Family in Classical Greece*, 228.

74 Cohen, *Law, Sexuality, and Society*, 149.

75 Ibid., 150–52. On women's religious activity, see also Fantham, et al., *Women in the Classical World*, 83–97; and Kraemer, *Her Share of the Blessings*, 22–49, 79–92.

76 Ibid., 173.

77 Ibid., 193.

78 Eva Cantarella, *Bisexuality in the Ancient World*, trans. Cormac O Cuilleanain (New Haven and London: Yale University Press, 1992) 213.

79 Elaine Fantham et al., *Women in the Classical World*, 140–80; and Sarah B. Pomeroy, *Women in Hellenistic Egypt from Alexander to Cleopatra* (New York: 1984).

80 Peter Garnsey and Richard Saller, *The Roman Empire: Economy, Society and Culture* (Berkeley and Los Angeles: University of california Press, 1987) 147. See also Richard Saller, *Patriarchy, Property and Death in the Roman Family* (forthcoming) chapters 5 and 6.

81 Garnsey and Saller, *The Roman Empire*, 130–31.

82 Ibid., 129.

83 Suzanne Dixon maintains that the Roman ideal of motherhood did not focus on tender nurturance, but on discharge of social obligations, which continued after divorce, and could include, for instance, remembering children in one's will (*The Roman Mother* [Norman OK: Oklahoma University Press, 1988], 9).

84 Keith R. Bradley, *Discovering the Roman Family: Studies in Roman Social History* (New York and Oxford: Oxford University Press, 1991), 190–91.

85 Ibid., 129–30.

86 Ibid., 133.

87 Ibid., 170.

88 Susan Treggiari (*Roman Marriages; Iusti Coniuges from the Time of Cicero to the Time of Ulpian* [New York: Oxford University Press, 1991], 261) makes the point that it was the woman's faithfulness to the man that was especially upheld in the Roman ideology of the eternal marital bond. See Fanthan et al., *Women in the Classical World*, 314–26, for evidence of the idealization of marital affection and of romantic love outside of marriage in Roman writings and art around the time of Christ.

89 Pheme Perkins, "Paul and the Moral Philosophers," unpublished paper, delivered at Lynchburg College (Lynchburg VA, April 19, 1994) 9–10, 13–14.

90 Dixon, *Roman Mother*, 21.

91 Jesus is depicted as approving Mary's choice to listen to his teaching rather than perform household duties, but here, as in the Gospel of Luke generally, women's discipleship roles are more passive than active. See Loveday Alexander, "Sisters in Adversity: Retelling Martha's Story," in George J. Brooke, ed., *Women and the Biblical Tradition* (Lewiston/Queenston/Lampeter: Edwin Mellen, 1992), 167–86.

92 See Andrew D. Clarke, *Secular and Christian Leadership in Corinth: A*

Socio-Historical and Exegetical Study of 1 Corinthians 1–6 (Leiden, New York, Koln: E. J. Brill, 1993), 82–85, 88.

93 Peter Brown, *The Body and Society: Men, Women and Sexual Renunciation in Early Christianity* (New York: Columbia University Press, 1988), 31.

94 Wayne Meeks, *The Origins of Christian Morality: The First Two Centuries* (New Haven and London: Yale University Press, 1993), 131.

95 Both of the Matthean sayings make an exception for *porneia*, the precise original meaning of which is unclear. Often rendered "fornication" or "adultery," it may have referred to marriage within degrees of kinship permitted in gentile society but forbidden to Jews.

96 See Raymond F. Collins, *Divorce in the New Testament* (Collegeville MN: The Liturgical Press, 1992) 27–39; Antoinette Wire, "1 Corinthians," in Elisabeth Schüssler Fiorenza, *Searching the Scriptures, Volume Two: A Feminist Commentary* (New York: Crossroad, 1995)166–71; Mary Rose D'Angelo, "Remarriage and the Divorce Sayings Attributed to Jesus," in William P. Roberts, *Divorce and Remarriage: Religious and Psychological Perspectives* (Kansas City: Sheed and Ward, 1990), 99. See also Pheme Perkins, "Marriage in the New Testament and its World," in William P. Roberts, ed., *Commitment to Partnership: Explorations of the Theology of Marriage* (New York/Mahwah: Paulist, 1987) 17–25, for a discussion of Paul's interest in moderating asceticism.

97 Perkins, "Marriage in the NT," 15.

98 Joseph A. Fitzmeyer, S.J.; *Paul and His Theology: A Brief Sketch*, 2nd ed. (Englewood Cliffs NJ: Prentice Hall, 1989) 104.

99 As Luke Timothy Johnson also concludes, it is fair to say that "early Christianity knew about homosexuality as it was practiced in Greco-Roman culture, shared Judaism's association of it with the 'abominations' of idolatry, and regarded it as incompatible with life in the Kingdom of God" ("Debate and Discernment: Scripture and the Spirit," *Commonweal* 121/2 [1994] 12).

100 Scroggs says, "What the New Testament was against was the image of homosexuality as pederasty and primarily here its more sordid and dehumanizing dimensions" (*New Testament and Homosexuality*, 126).

101 James M. Gustafson, *Ethics from a Theocentric Perspective, Volume Two: Ethics and Theology* (Chicago and London: University of Chicago Press, 1984) 155–56.

102 See Sally B. Purvis, "Doing Violence: Homosexuals, Hetero-

sexuals, and Contemporary Christian Ethics," *Prism* 7/1 (1992) 54.

103 *In Memory of Her*, 33. The household codes have been the object of much critical attention from Schüssler Fiorenza and others because they are explicit directives for the submission of women. However, violence toward women ("harlots"), along with approbation of the lovely bride and birthing mother, is more in evidence in the female metaphors of the Book of Revelation (17:5, 16; 21:2; 12:1–6). For advocacy of the "household codes" on submission as some sort of reciprocal "headship," see Ben Witherington III, *Women in the Earliest Churches* (Cambridge University Press, 1988), 55–61.

104 Meeks, *Origins*, 137.

105 See David L. Balch, "Neopythagorean Moralists and the New Testament Household Codes," in Wolfgang Haase and Hildegard Temporini, *Rise and Decline of the Roman World*, Part II: *Principate*, vol. 26.1 (Berlin and New York: Walter De Gruyter, 1992), 399–400.

106 David L. Balch, "Household Codes," in David E. Aune, ed., *Greco-Roman Literature and the New Testament: Selected Forms and Genres* (Atlanta: Scholars Press, 1988). Balch refers to Franz Laub, *Die Begegnung des fruhen Christentums mit der Antiken Sklaverei* (Stuttgart; Katholisches Bibelwerk, 1982). See also Marlis Gielen, *Tradition und Theologie neutestamentlicher Haustafelethik: Ein Beitrag zur Frage einer christlichen Auseinandersetzung mit gesellschaftlichen Normen* (Bonn: Anton Hain, 1990).

107 David L. Balch, *Let Wives Be Submissive: The Domestic Code in 1 Peter* (Atlanta: Scholars Press, 1981), 82–86; and "Neopythagorean Moralists," 395.

108 Fitzmeyer, *Paul*, 91, 93.

109 See ibid., 100–3.

110 Wayne A. Meeks, *The Moral World of the First Christians*, 126; *The First Urban Christians: The Social World of the Apostle Paul* (New Haven and London: Yale University Press, 1983), 88, 129.

6   SEX, MARRIAGE, AND FAMILY IN CHRISTIAN TRADITION

1   Georges Duby, *Love and Marriage in the Middle Ages*, trans. Jane Dunnett (University of Chicago Press, 1988) 3–4.

2   That is to say, official Roman Catholic insistence on strict observance has been sharpest, and ecclesiastical sanctions against dissenters most aggressive.

3   See Donald J. Goergen, O.P., "Celibacy," in Joseph A.

Komonchak, Mary Collins, and Dermott A. Lane, *The New Dictionary of Theology* (Wilmington DL: Michael Glazier, Inc., 1987), 174–76; Eduard Schillebeeckx, O.P., trans., C. A. L. Jarrott, *Celibacy* (New York: Sheed and Ward, 1968), 19–50; and John T. Noonan, Jr., "Celibacy in the Fathers of the Church: The Problematic and Some Problems," in George H. Frein, ed., *Celibacy: The Necessary Option* (New York: Herder and Herder, 1968), 420. Schillebeeckx remarks that the law of continence was "a dead letter" for married clergy before the twelfth century, because the practice of living "like brother and sister" was humanly abnormal and in fact regularly resulted in the births of additional children (41–42).

4 Schillebeeckx, *Celibacy*, 116–17.

5 Donald Goergen, *The Sexual Celibate* (New York: Seabury, 1974), v. See also, Mary Anne Huddleston, I. H. M., ed., *Celibate Loving: Encounter in Three Dimensions* (New York and Ramsey NJ: Paulist Press, 1984).

6 See Karl Rahner, S.J., "The Theology of Renunciation," *Theological Investigations III*; essays by Jerome Murphy-O'Connor, O.P. ("Celibacy and Community") and David M. Knight ("Will the New Church Need Celibates?") in Huddleston, *Celibate Loving*, 198–225; and especially, William C. Spohn, S.J., "St. Paul on Apostolic Celibacy and the Body of Christ," *Studies in the Spirituality of Jesuits* 17/1 (1985).

7 Peter Brown, *Body and Society: Men, Women, and Sexual Renunciation in Early Christianity* (New York: Columbia University Press, 1988), 149–50.

8 Jo Ann McNamara, *A New Song: Celibate Women in the First Three Christian Centuries* (New York: The Haworth Press, 1983).

9 Brown, *Body and Society*, 148–50.

10 Ibid., 170.

11 Ibid., 78–79, 153. See also McNamara, *A New Song*, 110–11.

12 Ibid., 138.

13 McNamara, *A New Song*, 94–98. (Citing *Stromata* 4.8.)

14 Brown, *Body and Society*, 205. (Brown cites Eusebius, *Demonstratio Evangelica* 1.8.)

15 See also Gerard Sloyan, "Biblical and Patristic Motives for Celibacy of Church Ministers," in William Bassett and Peter Huizing eds., *Celibacy in the Church*, *Concilium* 78 (NY: Herder & Herder, 1972), 29.

16 Brown, *Body and Society*, 144.

17 Ibid., 307.

18 Ibid., 311. (Citing, *Hom in Matt.* 47:4.)

19 Jo Ann McNamara, "Sexual Equality and the Cult of Virginity in Early Christian Thought," *Feminist Studies* 3/3–4 (1976) 149. (Citing *De Abraham*, 1, 35.)

20 Ibid., 150–51. (Citing *De Virginibus*, 1, 56.)

21 Brown, *Body and Society*, 344. (Citing, Ambrose, *de Virginibus* 1.11.65–66.)

22 Ibid., 385.

23 Peter Brown, *Augustine of Hippo: A Biography* (New York: Dorset Press, 1967), 62. Such liaisons were common and socially acceptable for young men who could not yet afford to marry.

24 *Confessions*, VI.11, 13. (Hal M. Helms, trans., *The Confessions of St. Augustine: A Modern English Version* [Paraclete Press, 1986]).

25 Ibid., VI.15.

26 Margaret R. Miles, "The Erotic Text: Augustine's Confessions," *Continuum* 2/1 (1992) 134.

27 Lack of control and need for external constraint are common themes in Augustine's views of sin and ethics generally. See Brown, *Augustine*, 238.

28 Augustine, *City of God*, trans. Henry Bettenson, ed. David Knowles (New York: Penguin Books, 1972), XIV.19, 21, 23–24.

29 *Confessions*, III.1.

30 Ibid., VI.15.

31 Ibid., VI.12.

32 Ibid., IX.6.

33 Miles, "Erotic Text," 145.

34 *Confessions*, II.3.

35 Ibid, III.4.

36 Ibid., IX.9.

37 Ibid., VIII.11.

38 Ibid., IV.4.

39 Ibid., IX.4.

40 Miles, "Erotic Text," 143.

41 *ST*, II–II. 152, 155.

42 *ST*, II–II.152.4; suppl. 49.1.

43 *ST*, suppl., 42.4.

44 *ST*, II–II.152.4.

45 Ibid., 152.4.

46 James A. Brundage informs us that "Bishop Arnulf of Lisieux (d. 1184) reported to Pope Alexander III (1159–81), for example, that he had banished no less than seventeen concubines from the chambers of his cathedral canons in a single day" (*Law, Sex and Christian Society in Medieval Europe* [Chicago and London: University of Chicago Press, 1987] 314–15).

47 Schillebeeckx, *Celibacy*, 60–61.

48 Angela M. Lucas, *Women in the Middle Ages: Religion, Marriage and Letters* (New York: St. Martin's Press, 1983) 30–42. See also Brundage, *Law, Sex, and Christian Society*, 151.

49 Ibid., 47–50.

50 McNamara, "Sexual Equality," 154. (Citing Palladius, *The Lausiac History*, 132).

51 Dyan Elliott, *Spiritual Marriage: Sexual Abstinence in Medieval Wedlock* (Princeton University Press, 1993).

52 Philip S. Keane, S.S., *Sexual Morality: A Catholic Perspective* (New York, Ramsey, Toronto: Paulist Press, 1977), 151.

53 Spohn, "St. Paul on Apostolic Celibacy," 21.

54 Consult Ladislas Orsy, S.J., "Annulment," in Komonchak et al., eds., *Dictionary of Theology*, 19–21; and "Questions Concerning Matrimonial Tribunals and the Annulment Process," in William P. Roberts, *Divorce and Remarriage: Religious and Psychological Perspectives* (Kansas City: Sheed andWard, 1991), 138–55.

55 Paula Ripple, "Remarriage: Shaping the Pastoral Questions That Facilitate Life," in Roberts, *Divorce and Remarriage*, 6. See Gerald D. Colman, S.S., *Divorce and Remarriage in the Catholic Church* (New York and Mahwah: Paulist, 1988), which discusses the "internal forum" solution, by which a couple unable to obtain a church annulment may view themselves in conscience as free to remarry and receive the sacraments.

56 Eduard Schillebeeckx, O.P., trans. N. D. Smith, *Marriage: Human Reality and Saving Mystery* (New York: Sheed and Ward, 1966), 137.

57 Theodore Mackin, S.J., *Divorce and Remarriage* (New York/Ramsey NJ: Paulist Press, 1984), 172–74.

58 Ibid., 255, 275–76, 280. See also Michael G. Lawler, *Secular Marriage, Christian Sacrament* (Mystic CT: Twenty-Third Publications, 1985).

59 Brundage, *Law, Sex and Christian Society*, 124–25.

60 Ibid., 128–29.

61 Ibid., 151, 148, n. 102, respectively.

62 Charles J. Reid, Jr., "History of the Family," in Lisa Sowle Cahill and Dietmar Mieth, eds., *The Family* (Maryknoll NY: Orbis, 1995), *Concilium* 1995/4, 10–17. Reid offers an overview of the medieval history of the Christian family, emphasizing effects on barbarian customs.

63 Ibid., 134–35.

64 "The Good of Marriage", in Roy J. Deferrari, ed., *The Fathers of the Church*, Vol. 15, *St. Augustine: Treatises on Marriage and Other Subjects* (New York: Fathers of the Church, Inc., 1955), ch. 1. In *The*

City of God, Augustine says that to multiply the human race is the purpose for which God instituted marriage from the beginning (XIV.22).

65 "Good of Marriage," ch. 3.
66 Ibid., ch. 6–7.
67 See Lawler, *Secular Marriage*, 44–46.
68 Ibid., ch. 15, 24.
69 For a detailed discussion of and substantial quotations from Augustine's works on marriage and divorce, see Mackin, *Divorce and Remarriage*, 194–221.
70 Mackin, *Divorce and Remarriage*, 170.
71 Schillebeeckx, *Marriage*, 141, 284.
72 David Herlihy, *Medieval Households* (Cambridge MA and London: Harvard University Press, 1985), 100.
73 Lucas, *Women in the Middle Ages*, 85.
74 Ibid., 89–90.
75 Duby, *Love and Marriage*, 62–63.
76 Herlihy, *Medieval Households*, 81; Schillebeeckx, *Marriage*, 294–95; Theodore Mackin, S.J., *The Marital Sacrament*, (New York/ Mahwah NJ: Paulist, 1982), 291.
77 Phillipe Ariés, "The Indissoluble Marriage," in Phillippe Ariés and André Béjin, eds., *Western Sexuality: Practice and Precept in Past and Present Times* (Oxford and New York: Basil Blackwell, 1985) 153.
78 Ibid., 108.
79 Herlihy, *Medieval Households*, 136; Duby, *Love and Marriage*, 124.
80 In a late fourteenth-century romance which enjoyed wide popular circulation, an emperor obtains a papal dispensation to marry his own beautiful daughter (who voices disgust and dismay at the prospect). "It must have been thought in some quarters that a king could be permitted to do exactly what he liked" (Lucas, *Women in the Middle Ages*, 93).
81 The church's equalizing of sexual morality across social classes is a large part of Herlihy's thesis (*Medieval Households*, 61); but certainly people with money were better able to manipulate the system, as they still are in the case of annulments. A parallel situation exists with the sexes. The more rigorous laws about adultery and divorce were applied with increasing stringency to men as well as women, but men remained the more equal among equals in sex and marriage. At the root of the problem is the gender inequity in the analogy of Ephs. 5:25. See Margaret A. Farley, R.S.M., "Divorce and Remarriage: A Moral Perspective," in Roberts, *Divorce*, 109.

82 Schillebeeckx, *Marriage*, 297, 301; Peter Huizing, S.J., "Canonical Implications of the Conception of Marriage in the Conciliar Constitution *Gaudium et Spes*," in William P. Roberts ed., *Commitment to Partnership: Explorations of the Theology of Marriage* (New York/ Mahwah NJ: Paulist, 1987), 122–23, 125.

83 Ibid., 303.

84 Martos, "Marriage," 54–55.

85 *ST*, 1.92.

86 *ST*, ii.153; Suppl. 49, 65, 67.

87 *ST*, Suppl. 49. especially 3; 67.1; *ST*, ii–ii.153.2; *Summa Contra Gentiles*, 3/ii.123, 126.

88 *SCG*,. 3/ii.123–124.

89 *ST*, ii–ii.26.11–12; SCG 3/ii.123.

90 Walter Kasper, *Theology of Christian Marriage* (New York: Crossroad, 1981), 30. The residual patriarchal bias of the wording is also representative of much theological idealization of love, especially in magisterial writings.

91 Herbert Doms, *The Meaning of Marriage* (New York: Sheed and Ward, 1939): originally *Vom Sinn und Zweck der Ehe* (Breslau: Ostdeutsche Verlagsanstalt, 1935); and Dietrich von Hildebrand, *Marriage* (New York: Longmans, 1942); originally *Die Ehe* (Munich: Kosel-Pustet, 1929). For a history, see Theodore Mackin, S.J., *What Is Marriage?* (New York/Ramsey: Paulist, 1982), 225–231.

92 John C. Ford, S.J., "Marriage: Its Meaning and Purposes," *Theological Studies* 3 (1942) 348.

93 Bernard Cooke, "Indissolubility: Guiding Ideal, or Existential Reality?" in Roberts, *Commitment to Partnership*, 64–75; Huizing, "Canonical Implications," 123, 126. In 1977, the International Theological Commission, sponsored by the Congregation for the Doctrine of the Faith, met to study marriage, and focused much of its attention on indissolubility, which it reaffirmed. For its conclusions and a set of supportive theological essays mostly by members of the Commission, see Richard Malone and John R. Connery, S.J., *Contemporary Perspectives on Christian Marriage: Propositions and Papers from the International Theological Commission* (Chicago: Loyola University Press, 1984).

94 Ford, "Marriage," 345, 360.

95 The 1983 Code of Canon Law provides that:

The matrimonial covenant, by which a man and a woman establish between themselves a partnership of the whole of life, is by its nature ordered toward the good of the spouses and the procreation and education of offspring; this covenant between baptized persons has been raised by Christ the Lord to the dignity of a sacrament.

For this reason a matrimonial contract cannot validly exist between baptized persons unless it is also a sacrament by that fact.

The essential properties of marriage are unity and indissolubility, which in Christian marriage obtain a special firmness in virtue of the sacrament.

Marriage is brought about by the consent of the parties . . .

Matrimonial consent is an act of the will by which a man and a woman, through an irrevocable covenant, mutually give and accept each other in order to establish marriage. (Cans. 1055–1057)

96 Philippe Ariés, "Love in Married Life," in *Western Sexuality*, 133–34.

97 Jack Dominian, "The Consequences of Marital Breakdown," in Roberts, *Divorce and Remarriage*, 128–37; Sylvia Ann Hewlitt, *When the Bough Breaks: The Cost of Neglecting Our Children* (New York: HarperCollins, 1991), 110–17, 135–47; Pamela D. Couture, *Blessed Are the Poor? Women's Poverty, Family Policy, and Practical Theology* (Nashville: Abingdon, 1991).

98 Explains Augustine, "the genital organs have become as it were the private property of lust, which has brought them so completely under its sway that they have no power of movement if this passion fails. If it has not arisen spontaneously or in response to a stimulus. It is this that arouses shame; it is this that makes us shun the eyes of beholders in embarrassment" (*City of God*, XIV.19).

99 Mary D. Pellauer, "The Moral Significance of Female Orgasm: Toward Sexual Ethics That Celebrates Women's Sexuality," in James B. Nelson and Sandra P. Longfellow, eds., *Sexuality and the Sacred: Sources for Theological Reflection* (Louisville KY: Westminster/ John Knox Press), 149–68.

100 On distrust of sexual pleasure as in competition with the "personal aspect" that should center sacramentality, see Wilhelm Ernst, "Marriage as Institution and the Contemporary Challenge to It," in Malone and Connery, *Contemporary Perspectives on Christian Marriage*, 53–55.

101 For a fine historical analysis of procreation and birth control in Christianity, see John T. Noonan, Jr., *Contraception: A History of Its Treatment by the Catholic Theologians and Canonists* (enlarged edn.: Cambridge: Harvard University Press, 1986; original edn., 1965).

102 See Susan A. Ross, "The Bride of Christ and the Body Politic: Body and Gender in Pre-Vatican II Marriage Theology," *Journal of Religion* 71 (1991) 345–61.

103 The primacy of procreation was repeated in several subsequent documents prior to Vatican II, including "The Order of the Purposes of Matrimony," Holy Roman Rota, January 22, 1944; Address of Pope Pius XII to the Italian Medical–biological Union

of St. Luke, November 12, 1944; Address of Pope Pius XII to
Delegates at the Fourth International Congress of Catholic
Doctors, September 29, 1949; Address of Pope Pius XII to Midwives, October 29, 1951. Excerpts from all these, as well as *Castii
connubii*, are included in Odile M. Liebard, *Official Catholic Teachings: Love and Sexuality* (Wilmington NC: McGrath Publishing
Company, 1978).

104 For a detailed analysis of developments in Catholic sexual
theology during this period, including the debate over contraception, see my "Catholic Sexual Ethics and the Dignity of the
Person: A Double Message?," *Theological Studies* 50/1 (1989)
120–50.

105 The idea that sex could be viewed as a "language" had already
been offered by Paul Ricoeur, "Wonder, Eroticism and Enigma,"
Cross Currents 14 (1964) 133–41; and André Guindon, *The Sexual
Language: An Essay in Moral Theology* (Ottawa: University of Ottawa,
1976). However, Ricoeur and Guindon use the metaphor to
reconsider sexual meaning, and Guindon in particular suggests
that a linguistic understanding of sex implies changes in moral
norms; the pope keeps it firmly attached to the ban on contraception. The "Theology of the Body" is the theme of the Pope's
Wednesday afternoon general audience talks in 1979–81. The
series is published in three volumes by the Daughters of St. Paul
(Boston). They are *Original Unity of Man and Woman: Catechesis on the
Book of Genesis* (1981); *Blessed are the Pure of Heart: Catechesis on the
Sermon on the Mount and Writings of St. Paul* (1983); *Reflections on
Humanae Vitae: Conjugal Morality and Spirituality* (1984). An apology
for the tradition which the pope represents is Rev. Ronald Lawler,
O.F.M. Cap., Joseph Boyle, Jr. and William E. May, *Catholic
Sexual Ethics: A Summary, Explanation, & Defense* (Huntington, Ind.:
Our Sunday Visitor, 1985).

106 *Original Unity of Man and Woman*, 109–10.

107 Ibid. 111.

108 The ban on contraception is affirmed vehemently in *Familiaris
Consortio*, no. 32; and in *Reflections on Humanae Vitae*.

109 The pope has claimed that "lack of direct personal experience" is
"no handicap" at all to celibate authors, who can rely on
experience which is "second-hand, derived from their pastoral
work". See Karol Wojtyla, *Love and Responsibility* (New York:
Farrar, Straus, Giroux, 1981), 15, originally in Polish (Krakow:
Wydawnicto, Znak, 1960).

110 Rosemary Radford Reuther, "Birth Control and the Ideals of
Marital Sexuality," in *Contraception and Holiness: The Catholic Predica-*

ment, ed. Thomas D. Roberts, S.J. (New York: Herder and Herder, 1964), 87.

111 The term "self-mastery" appears as a separate index entry in Janet E. Smith, ed., *Why Humanae Vitae Was Right: A Reader* (San Francisco: Ignatius Press, 1993). The reader is referred to two essays by Smith and one by John Crosby.

112 See, for instance, the general audience talk of March 12, 1980, "Mystery of Woman Revealed in Motherhood," *Original Unity of Man and Woman*, 153–161; *Familiaris Consortio*, no. 23; and *Mulieris Dignitatem* (September 30, 1988), *Origins* 18/17 (October 6, 1988) nos. 17–19, especially 18.

113 *Familiaris Consortio*, no. 24; *Mulieris Dignitatem*, no. 14; and John Paul's June 1995 "Letter to Women" in preparation for the September 1995 Fourth World Conference on Women In Beijing. In this letter, he recognizes for the first time that working women make vital contributions to culture, apologizes for church culpability for discrimination against women, and commends women's fight "for basic social, economic, and political rights" (.6). Yet he also holds up Mary in her maternal role as "the highest expression of the 'feminine genius,'" and insists that men's and women's roles are different and complementary (.10). This allows the pope to reaffirm the exclusion of women from the ministerial priesthood (.11).

114 See *Mulieris Dignitatem*, no. 10, on Gen. 3:16 as a consequence of sin; and no. 16 on Mary Magdalene as the first witness to the resurrection and " 'apostle to the apostles.' "

115 Paul M. Quay, S.J., "Contraception and Conjugal Love," 40.

116 Ibid. p. 35.

117 It appears in *Why Humanae Vitae Was Right*, 19–43. It is presented as a "superb defense" of church teaching, and especially of the "human and spiritual meaning" of sexuality and marriage.

118 Janet E. Smith, "Paul VI as Prophet," in *Why Humanae Vitae Was Right*, 521–23.

119 Editorial, "It Still Doesn't Scan," *Commonweal* 121/13 (1994) 4. The editors were responding to, and in large part in agreement with, a defense of Natural Family Planning which appeared in the same issue: Paul Murray, "The Power of 'Humanae Vitae'," ibid., 14–18.

120 As one presentation of Catholic teaching states it, "Marriage is one of the most profound and important aspects of human social existence." "Since marriage is an institution for the procreation and education of children, marital consent involves a commitment to this worthy enterprise" (Rev. Ronald Lawler, O.F.M., Cap.,

Joseph Boyle, Jr., and William E. May, *Catholic Sexual Ethics: A Summary, Explanation, & Defense* [Huntington IN: Our Sunday Visitor, Inc., 1985] 134, 137).

121 For a historical survey of the function of the concept "domestic church," see Norbert Mette, "The Family in the Official Teaching of the Church," and Michael Fahey, S.J., "The Christian Family as Domestic Church at Vatican II," in Lisa Sowle Cahill and Dietmar Mieth, eds., *The Family, Concilium* 1995/4 (Maryknoll NY: Orbis, 1995).

122 For a largely sympathetic but also critical discussion of the Catholic ideology of the family, see Margaret Farley, "The Church and the Family," *Horizons* 10 (1983) 49–71; Mitch and Kathy Finley, *Christian Families in the Real World: Reflections on a Spirituality for the Domestic Church* (Chicago: The Thomas More Press, 1984); James and Kathleen McGinniss, "Family as Domestic Church," in John Coleman, S.J., ed., *One Hundred Years of Catholic Social Thought* (Maryknoll NY: Orbis, 1991), 120–34; Toinette M. Eugene, "African American Family Life: An Agenda for Ministry Within the Catholic Church," *New Theology Review* 5 (1992) 33–47; and the articles in Cahill and Mieth, *The Family*.

123 Egalitarian themes and messages are now astoundingly common, if compared to the official rhetoric of less than a generation ago. But the social mission of Christianity, to create ecclesial and human solidarity with "the poor," will never be fulfilled in Catholic teaching as long as it is tainted by the residue of sexism. The same year, 1994, that saw the promulgation of John Paul II's new letter on the family also saw the publication of an encyclical insisting on women's inability to represent Christ in priestly ministry; and the much-delayed publication of the English version of the *Universal Catechism*, which had to undergo a second translation from the French in order to extirpate gender-inclusive language.

124 US Bishops' Committee on Women in Society and in the Church and Committee on Marriage and Family Life, *When I Call for Help: A Pastoral Response to Domestic Violence*, in *Origins* 22 (November, 1992), 353, 355–58.

125 US National Conference of Catholic Bishops, *Putting Children and Families First: A Challenge for Our Church, Nation and World*, *Origins* 21 (1991) 393, 395–404; US National Conference of Catholic Bishops, *Follow the Way of Love: Pastoral Message to Families*, *Origins* 23 (1993) 433, 435–448; Australian Catholic Bishops Conference, "Families: Our Hidden Treasure," *Catholic International* 5 (1994) 315–28.

126 Peruvian Bishops' Conference, "The Family: Heart of the Civilization of Love," *Catholic International* 5 (1994) 270–72.

127 Gilbert Meilaender, "A Christian View of the Family," in David Blankenhorn, Steven Bayme, and Jean Bethke Elshtain, eds., *Rebuilding the Nest: A New Commitment to the American Family* (Milwaukee: Family Services America, 1990), 145.

128 James and Kathleen McGinnis, "Family as Domestic Church," in John Coleman, S.J., *One Hundred Years of Catholic Social Thought* (Maryknoll, NY: Orbis, 1991) 125. See also William P. Roberts, "The Family as Domestic Church: Contemporary Implications," in Roberts, ed., *Christian Marriage and Family: Contemporary Theology and Pastoral Perspectives* (Collegeville MN: Liturgical Press, forthcoming 1996). Roberts maintains that "the domestic church of the family serves the cause of justice." As examples, he mentions that family members learn equity in their own relationships; they contribute time and money to the poor; they lobby to change sinful social structures.

129 Alan Cowell, "How Vatican Views Cairo: Damage Control Seen in the Talks' Details," *New York Times*, September 18, 1994, 25.

130 John Thavis, "U.N. Conference Struggles With Abortion Issue," *Arlington Catholic Herald*, September 15, 1994, 12. The second Vatican delegate is an Australian, Msgr. Peter Elliott.

131 Thavis, "U.N. Conference," 1.

132 Barbara Crossette, "A Third-World Effort on Family Planning," *New York Times*, September 7, 1994, A8. The countries are Bangladesh, Colombia, Egypt, Indonesia, Kenya, Mexico, Morocco, Thailand, Tunisia, and Zimbabwe.

133 Renato Martino, "Population and Development: The Issues, the Context," *Origins* 24/25 (September 22, 1994) 261.

134 As quoted by David S. Toolan, "Hijacked in Cairo," *America* 171/9 (1994) 4. Toolan was present at the conference, and his assessment seems right on target:

> Somehow the deeper symbolism of the event was missed – that this was another threshold in the historic march to give women, especially poor women, a decent share in the world's goods, a say in shaping their own destiny. From the outset, the Vatican had put the worst possible interpretation on the drafters (and their motives). And then, rallying conservative Islamic patriarchalists to its side, it had committed the mistake of positioning itself, at least in the eyes of the Western press, as hostile to the cause of women. In a strange way, a penchant for the perfect text became the enemy of the good, and any chance of strengthening the Program of Action in the area of development vanished into the smoggy Cairo air. (3)

7 THE NEW BIRTH TECHNOLOGIES AND PUBLIC MORAL ARGUMENT

1 Committee of Inquiry into Human Fertilisation and Embryology, *Report of the Committee of Inquiry into Human Fertilisation and Embryology* (London: Her Majesty's Stationery Office, London, 1984); Congregation for the Doctrine of the Faith, *Instruction on Respect for Human Life in Its Origin and on the Dignity of Procreation – Replies to Certain Questions of the Day*, Origins 16 (1987) 697–711; United States Congress, Office of Technology Assessment, *Infertility: Medical and Social Choices*, OTA-BA-358, 1988 (Washington, DC: U.S. Government Printing Office, 1988. References to page or section will hereafter be given in the text.

2 Jeffrey Stout, *Ethics After Babel: The Languages of Morals and Their Discontents* (Boston: Beacon Press, 1988), 302.

3 The quotation in the text is from John XXIII's *Mater et Magistra* (1961).

4 "Heterologous artificial fertilization violates the rights of the child; it deprives him of his filial relationship with his parental origins and can hinder the maturing of his personal identity. Furthermore, it offends the common vocation of the spouses who are called to fatherhood and motherhood: it objectively deprives conjugal fruitfulness of its unity and integrity; it brings about and manifests a rupture between genetic parenthood, gestational parenthood, and responsibility for upbringing. Such damage to the personal relationships within the family has repercussions on civil society: what threatens the unity and stability of the family is a source of dissension, disorder and injustice in the whole of social life" (II.A.2.).

5 Ibid. no. 4.

6 Louis Janssens, "Artificial Insemination: Ethical Considerations," *Louvain Studies* 8 (1980) 3–29, especially 28.

7 Jean-François Lyotard, *The Postmodern Condition: A Report on Knowledge*, trans. Geoff Bennington and Brian Massumi (University of Manchester Press, 1984) xxiii, xxiv.

8 Stout, *Ethics After Babel*, 282.

9 Richard Bernstein, *Beyond Objectivism and Relativism: Science, Hermeneutics and Praxis* (Philadelphia: University of Pennsylvania Press, 1985) 18.

10 See Protestants Martin E. Marty, *The Public Church: Mainline, Evangelical, Catholic* (New York: Crossroad, 1981); Kent Greenawalt, *Religious Convictions and Political Choice* (New York: Oxford University Press); Ronald F. Thiemann, *Constructing a Public*

Theology: The Church in a Pluralistic Culture (Louisville KY: Westminster/John Knox Press, 1991); Max L. Stackhouse, *Public Theology and Political Economy: Christian Stewardship in Modern Society* (Grand Rapids: Wm. B. Eerdmans Publishing Co., 1987).

11 J. Bryan Hehir, "Policy Arguments in a Public Church; Catholic Social Ethics and Bioethics," *Journal of Medicine and Philosophy* 17 (1992) 355.

12 Ibid., 349.

13 Edward Collins Vacek, S. J., "Catholic 'Natural Law' and Reproductive Ethics," *Journal of Medicine and Philosophy* 17 (1992) 339.

14 Ibid., 342–43.

15 David Hollenbach, "After word: a community of freedom," in R. Bruce Douglass and David Hollenbach, eds., *Catholicism and Liberalism: Contributions to American Public Philosophy* (Cambridge and Melbourne: Cambridge University Press, 1994) 324.

16 "Ethics Committee of the American Fertility Society," Ethical Considerations of the New Reproductive Technologies, *Fertility and Sterility*, supplement 2, 53/6 (June, 1990) 1S.

17 See Walter M. Abbot, S. J., ed., *The Documents of Vatican II* (New York: America Press, 1966).

18 "Appendix A," in AFS, "Ethical Considerations," 87S.

19 R. Bruce Douglass, "Introduction," in Douglass and Hollenbach, *Catholicism and Liberalism*, 12–13.

20 "Guidelines for Gamete Donation: 1993," *Fertility and Sterility*, supplement 1, 59/2 (February 1993) 8S.

21 Mark V. Sauer, M.D., and Richard J. Paulson, M.D., "Understanding the Current Status of Oocyte Donation in the United States: What's really Going On Out There?," *Fertility and Sterility* 58/1 (July, 1992) 17.

22 See Margaret Carlson, "Old Enough to Be Your Mother," *Time* (January 10, 1994) 41.

23 Mark Sauer, as quoted in Susan Chira, "Of a Certain Age, and in a Family Way," *New York Times*, Sunday, January 2, 1994, 5. See also Mark V. Sauer, et al., "Reversing the Natural Decline in Human Fertility: An Extended Clinical Trial of Oocyte Donation to Women of Advanced Reproductive Age," *Journal of the American Medical Association* 268/10 (September 9, 1992), 1275–79. An editorial in the same issue identifies oocyte donation as "the most appropriate treatment" for women over 40, and calls its development "truly exciting" (Martin M. Quigley, M.D., "The New Frontier of Reproductive Age," 1321]. Quigley's title speaks volumes about the individualist, conquest-oriented, and entrepreneurial attitudes toward women's bodies of which many feminists

have been critical. See, for instance, Emily Martin, *The Woman in the Body: A Cultural Analysis of Reproduction* (Boston: Beacon Press, 1989).

24 Gina Kolata, "Reproductive Revolution is Jolting Old Views," *New York Times*, January 11, 1994, C12. Germain Greer is reported to have remarked, "The problem is that nobody seems to know what is pathological behavior anymore ... These women are going to have a terrible time when they finally meet the Grim Reaper. They're really out of touch with reality, and most women are not" (in Chira, "Of a Certain Age," 5).

25 Ethics Committee of the American Fertility Society, "Ethical Considerations of the New Reproductive Technologies, *Fertility and Sterility*, supplement 2, 53/6 (June, 1990) 24S.

26 Charles Taylor, *The Ethics of Authenticity* (Cambridge, MA and London: Harvard University Press, 1993) 102.

27 Maura A. Ryan, "The Argument for Unlimited Procreative Liberty: A Feminist Critique," *Hastings Center Report* 20/4 (1990) 6–12.

28 Ibid., 10.

29 Sidney Callahan, "The Ethical Challenge of the New Reproductive Technology," in John F. Monagle and David C. Thomasma, eds., *Medical Ethics: A Guide for Health Professionals* (Rockville MD: Aspen Publications, 1988) 34.

30 Ibid., 28.

31 Paul Lauritzen, "What Price Parenthood?," *Hastings Center Report* (March/April, 1990) 41. The article contemplated a possible choice for donor insemination. A subsequent book envisioning such a choice as morally defensible is *Pursuing Parenthood: Ethical Issues in Assisted Reproduction* (Bloomington and Indianapolis: Indiana University Press, 1993). Lauritzen does not believe that the union in one relationship of genetic and social parenthood is part of the core or normative ideal of parenthood (81). I would argue that this union is not "core" in the sense of an indispensable minimum; hence adoptive relationships. But I would argue that it is part of the ideal which social policy should encourage. Social policies which portray the parental relationship as essentially a matter of autonomous control and contractual choice do a disservice not only to this ideal, but to clients whose choices are in fact not quite so self-determined as the political and clinical rhetoric would make them seem.

32 Cindy Loose, "A Holiday Comes to Life: Mom's Celebration Was 4 years in Making," *Washington Post*, May 9, 1993, A1, A22–23.

33 Sarah Franklin, "'Deconstructing Desperateness': The Social

Construction of Infertility in Popular Representations of New Reproductive Technologies," in Maureen McNeil , Ian Varcoe, and Steven Yearly, eds., *The New Reproductive Technologies* (London: Macmillan, 1990), 200–29.

34 Ibid., 203–04.

35 Kirsten Kozolanka, "Giving Up: The Choice That Isn't," in Renate Klein, ed., *Infertility: Women Speak Out About Their Experiences of Reproductive Medicine*, (London: Pandora, 1989), 128; as quoted in Janice G. Raymond, *Women as Wombs: Reproductive Technologies and the Battle Over Women's Freedom* (New York: HarperCollins, 1993), 87.

36 Gena Corea, *The Mother Machine: Reproductive Technologies from Artificial Insemination to Artificial Wombs* (New York: Harper & Row, 1985), 62, 64, 65.

37 Raymond, *Women as Wombs*, xxxi.

38 "Increasingly, more and more control is taken away from an individual's body and concentrated in the hands of 'experts' – the rapidly – and internationally – growing brigade of 'technodocs': doctors, scientists, pharmaceutical representatives (most of them male, white, and of Euro-American origin) who fiercely compete with one another on this 'new frontier' of scientific discovery and monetary profits" (Renate Duelli Klein, "What 'new' about the 'new' reproductive technologies?," in Gena Corea, Renate Duelli Klein, and Jalna Hanmer eds., *Man-Made Women: How New Reproductive Technologies Affect Women* [Bloomington and Indianapolis: Indiana University Press, 1987], 65).

39 Elizabeth Bartholet, *Family Bonds: Adoption and the Politics of Parenting* (Boston and New York: Houghton Mifflin, 1993), 30.

40 Bartholet cites an organization which has been critical of international adoption, Defense for Children International, as acknowledging that abuses are numerically rare. Trafficking cases undoubtedly "constitute only a tiny proportion of the displacements of children for adoption purposes" (Marie-Françoise Lucker-Bubel, *Inter-Country Adoption and Trafficking in Children: An Initial Assessment* [Geneva: Defense for Children International, 1990], 2, as cited in Bartholet, *Family Bonds*, 248).

41 Ibid., 156.

42 Janice G. Raymond argues against reproductive technologies, seeing "trafficking" in women's reproductive body parts as of a piece with the market in children and with the sexual prostitution or enslavement of women (*Women as Wombs: Reproductive Technologies and the Battle over Women's Freedom* [New York: HarperCollins, 1993]). While not totally discounting adoption, Paul Lauritzen

argues that donor therapies are preferable because the institution of adoption is on the whole exploitative (*Pursuing Parenthood: Ethical Issues in Assisted Reproduction* [Bloomington and Indianapolis: Indiana University Press, 1993]).

43 Nelson, "Genetic Narratives," 75.

Index

317

New Studies in Christian Ethics

DATE DUE		